The following officers were then elected for the present year.

Officers for 1894.

Honorary President.
Hon. John Beverley Robinson.
President
Revd. E. W. Bland. (Hamilton)

Vice President.
Walter Read.

Commodore.
Dr. A.Y. Scott.

Vice. Commodores.
E. Fearman. R. Millichamp. W. B. McMurrich. Q.C.

Secretary. Treasurer.
Dr. E. Herbert Adams.

Asst. Secretary Treasurer.
W. F. Adams.

SUMMERTIMES

SummerTimes

In celebration of 100 years of the Muskoka Lakes Association

Stoddart

A BOSTON MILLS PRESS BOOK

CANADIAN CATALOGUING IN PUBLICATION DATA

Main entry under title:
Summertimes: In celebration of 100 years of the Muskoka Lakes Association

Includes bibliographical references.
ISBN 1-55046-081-1

1. Muskoka (Ont.) – History.
2. Muskoka (Ont.) – Description and travel.   I. Muskoka Lakes Association.

FC3095.M88S 1994   973'16   C94-930628-2

Design by Lyn Gaby
Typography by Stuart Inglis
Printed in Singapore

First Published in 1994 by
Stoddart Publishing Co. Limited
34 Lesmill Road
Toronto, Canada
M3B 2T6
(416) 445-3333

A BOSTON MILLS PRESS BOOK
The Boston Mills Press
132 Main St.
Erin, Ontario
N0B 1T0

The publisher gratefully acknowledges the support of the Canada Council, Ontario Ministry
of Culture and Communications, Ontario Arts Council and Ontario Publishing Centre in the
development of writing and publishing in Canada.

Endpapers: Minutes from the first two Muskoka Lakes Association meetings.

Frontispiece photo by Beverley Bailey

Contents

6

ACKNOWLEDGMENTS

WHEN THE BOARD OF DIRECTORS of the Muskoka Lakes Association decided that a permanent record of the MLA Centennial should be created, naturally a book came to mind. Usually the organizations, clubs, and schools that produce such books do so introspectively, and only for a narrow audience. We have decided to take a broader approach. *Summertimes* is intended to be of interest to all who enjoy Muskoka, not just MLA members.

We would like to thank the Board and members of the Association for their encouragement and advice on this project, as well as all those members of the Muskoka community who created its contents.

Specifically, we acknowledge the support of John Denison of Boston Mills Press, whose firm has underwritten the production of this book; Gil Scott, for co-ordinating the efforts of the many fine Muskoka artists whose works grace the pages of this book; Richard Tatley, Bill Gray, Lindsay Hill, Brendan O'Brien, Graham Smith, Paul Gockel, Elizabeth Mason, and Robert Wilson, all of whom helped with the photographic selection; Maryan Gibson, who took on the difficult task of editing the diverse chapters and lived to read about it; Mike Wallace for overseeing production; and Lyn Gaby, MLA board member and yearbook editor extraordinaire, who along with Stuart Inglis, created the "look" of *SummerTimes*.

Enjoy!

Robert G. Purves
Honorary Commodore
Chairman Centennial Committee

8

FOREWORD

THE MUSKOKA LAKES ASSOCIATION Board of Directors is proud and pleased to bring you this book in celebration of the Muskoka Lakes Association's 100th anniversary.

Looking back to the organization's inception in February of 1894 is a very interesting exercise, and worthy of note on two accounts: one, that the mission statement

to unite together all those interested in the three lakes, Muskoka, Rosseau and Joseph, and their vicinities, for the purposes of protecting and promoting the interests of property owners, cottagers and tourists; preserving the healthful, sanitary condition and scenic beauty of the vicinity and encouarging aquatic and other sports

has remained unchanged, and two, that present generations of some of the families who served in the early years are still contributing today.

Muskokans are a unique people in that they are very proud and fiercely protective of the beautiful area where they have chosen to live and to relax. Preserving Muskoka for everyone is what the Association is all about.

It is therefore fitting that we bring you this book, which will take you back to uncharted times and bring you forward to the present. In these pages you will find the very essence of Muskoka, then and now, and you will see that, although there have been many changes, the spirit remains true.

Joan M. Booth
President
January 1994

DEEP WATER, OIL, JANE GORDON.

10

1
ENDURING LAND OF ROCK

Natural History of Muskoka

BY RON REID

A BILLION YEARS AGO, Muskoka was rock. Not the smooth rounded rock of rolling hills and gentle lakes we know today, but the huge jagged upthrust stone of mountains, as grand as the Canadian Rockies.

Where did the mountains come from? Of that, no one can be sure, but there is enough geological evidence to let us piece together their likely history. We know that to the north lay the ancient stable rocks of a continent called Laurentia, and to the east and south, sediments and volcanic outpourings on the bed of a sea more vast than the Atlantic. As the enormous continental plates ground together on the earth's surface over a period of 10 million years, they wrinkled and split, forced upward by the pressure of their meeting. Far beneath the surface, a massive dome of granite was also pushed upward, adding to the mountain-building process.

For the past billion years, these mountains have eroded grain by grain, dissolved by rain, cracked by frost, attacked by lichens, scraped and chipped by recurring glaciers. A great dome of rock still rises under the highlands of Algonquin Park. But today, all of central Ontario stands on the roots of these ancient mountains.

From the outside, a mountain may appear impassive, unchanging—as solid as a rock. But inside the mountain, change is occurring slowly, imperceptibly. Its agents are heat and pressure—heat from the molten core of the earth below, pressure from the weight of mountain above and the inexorable movement of the continental plates. The results are a whole new class of rocks, known as metamorphic, which characterize Muskoka today.

The most common by far of these metamorphic rocks is gneiss, the familiar striped bedrock that shows in nearly every rock-cut in Muskoka. At first you might think that the bands come from the pattern of long-ago sediments, laid down on a lake bed and gradually cemented into rock. In a few places in Muskoka, that is the case. For example, a narrow band of rock west of Highway 69 near the Moon River has a trace of marble, which is the metamorphic transformation of a strip of sedimentary limestone.

But in most of Muskoka, the distinctive bands of gneiss have quite a different origin. Most are metamorphosed granite, a crystalline stone created as liquid rock cooled slowly underground. As this granite was slowly transformed by heat and pressure, its crystals of feldspar and quartz—the lighter colours—separated into bands from the darker hornblendes and other minerals.

Even a quick look at the gneissic bedrock of Muskoka tells you that its fate was not to lie quiet and undisturbed. Everywhere the bands are bent and folded and distorted, as the rock responded to the overwhelming pressures beneath the earth's surface. A particularly good example of this warping can be seen in the Birkendale rock-cut along Highway 35 south of Dwight, where the dark bands are very distinct and very convoluted. Just to the west of Mactier and also to the west of Sparrow Lake, the bedrock ridges are curved in a broad oval pattern.

Not surprisingly, in many places the warping bedrock split, and liquid rock from below flowed into the resulting fissures, slowly cooling to form the "dikes" that cut across the grain of the bedrock on the surface today. These dikes are usually lighter in colour and often more resistant to erosion, making them protrude somewhat from the surrounding gneiss.

Another form of intrusion is found on small sites along the Brackenrig Road and just east of Port Cunnington. These pluglike intrusions consist of soft *ultramafic* rocks, which contain a range of minerals, including iron and magnesium. Their surface is deeply weathered, most of which probably occurred during the warm wet period of the dinosaurs, about 65 million years ago. This soft colourful rock is popular with local cottagers for their laneways, and both deposits are actively worked.

There is more to Muskoka's geological history, however, than the long slow erosion of ancient mountains. About 500 million years ago, in the Ordovician period, southern and central Ontario was covered by a warm tropical sea, somewhat like the Gulf of Mexico. Coral reefs and seabed sediments built up a thick layer of limestone, which persists as the foundation of southern Ontario today. In Muskoka, that limestone has almost totally worn away. Two tiny exceptions remain—the interior of Quarry Island

Echo Rock, Lake Joseph, Muskoka Lakes

in Severn Sound and a small "outlier" of limestone near the road to Honey Harbour.

One intriguing bit of evidence that limestone was once more widespread comes from Skeleton Lake. This lake is a geological celebrity for two reasons. First, the deep rounded bowl of the lake is Muskoka's only known meteor crater; the distinctive rocks along its north shore and on Opal Island were created by the splash from the meteor's stupendous impact. Second, along the southern edge of the lake are pebbles and small boulders of limestone, apparently dragged from the lake bed by the passage of the glaciers. It is possible, even likely, that a remnant of the limestone mantle yet lies sheltered on the floor of the lake. The only way to tell for certain would be to drill the lake bed.

While Muskoka's limestone remnants are a product of a warmer age, its soils are the result of a much colder period. We have no way of knowing how many times over the past billion years the climate turned colder and the venerable rocks of Muskoka felt the weight of the glaciers. We do know that four times in the past 100,000 years, a thick mattress of ice, two kilometres or more in depth, ground its way southward across the region.

Each time the glacier advanced, it incorporated loose rocks and sand into its base and rasped the unyielding bedrock with its rough caress. Although the powerful glaciers could not alter the basic pattern of Muskoka's Precambrian stone, bedrock surfaces across the district show the southward-pointing scratches left by the glacier's passing, as well as "chatter marks" caused by ice-bound boulders skipping along. Where bedrock faults such as the Severn River valley lay across the path of the glacier, the ice often broke away the northern lip, smoothly scouring the southern bank as it emerged, in a formation known as "pluck and scour."

In time, the glaciers retreated—not by drawing back, but by melting away along their advancing front. Where the melting was rapid, as in most of Muskoka, an uneven carpet of silt and stones, known as "till," was left behind. Where the vast quantities of water and sediments pouring off the glacier produced rivers, the currents left well-sorted sands and gravels. These glacial spillways followed the route of many of Muskoka's present rivers—the Big East, the North and South Muskoka, and the Black. Spillways also cut across country, through Skeleton Lake to the Milford Bay area, and south from Purbrook to Barkway and Cooper's Falls. The major drainage from the Muskoka Lakes area

was also to the south; Highway 11 follows the sandy course of an old spillway.

As the glaciers melted, the water levels in the Great Lakes were much higher than we see now. Lake Algonquin, as the glacial lake in this area is known, rose to cover the western two-thirds of Muskoka, and its waves washed and rearranged many of the glacial deposits. The lake had a variable and complex shoreline and many islands, but it extended well east of where Bracebridge and Port Sydney stand today, with a long arm extending through Peninsula Lake to take in most of Lake of Bays. Gravenhurst and all of the Muskoka lakes were under water.

In the 10,000 years since Lake Algonquin's largest extent, the Great Lakes have more than once fallen well below their current level and risen again over a part of Muskoka. Where major rivers met these lakes, sandy deltas have built up at the mouth of the Big East in Lake Vernon, the Oxtongue in Lake of Bays, and the Muskoka at Alport Bay. In quieter bays, pockets of finer sand and clays were laid down, creating a base for the scattered better farmlands of Muskoka. As a generation of later settlers discovered, these deep rich soils are a scarce commodity in Muskoka, and the thin stony tills on which grow such good timber are of little use to farmers.

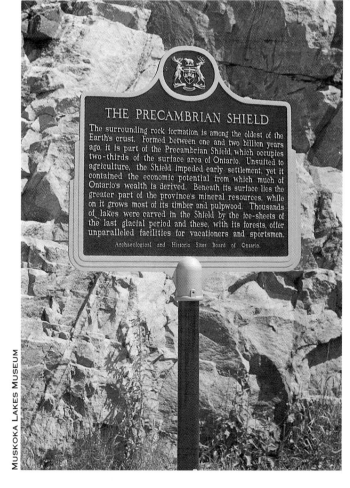

ECHO ROCK, AT THE NORTH END OF LAKE JOSEPH, WAS A FAVOURITE DESTINATION OF GUESTS STAYING AT THE NEARBY SUMMIT HOUSE HOTEL. AS YOU CAN SEE, GRAFFITI ON ROCKS IS NOTHING NEW.

MUSKOKA LAKES MUSEUM

13

The mythical prospect of abundant good farmland throughout Muskoka persisted long after the first generation of farmers took advantage of free land grants to open up the bush. As late as 1886, Barlow Cumberland wrote:

Having crossed the [Severn] river upon a lofty bridge, the line passes the height of land separating the Lakes of Muskoka from Lake Couchiching. False impressions of the free grant district are frequently taken from the appearance of the country seen along this part of the trip; but, as on the south side there are tracts of fine farming land, so, to the north, this ridge being passed over, lies the wide arable country which is being so rapidly peopled by thrifty settlers.

– *The Northern Lakes of Canada,* 1886. Barlow Cumberland, editor.

And so, the enduring rock of the Precambrian shield forms the character of Muskoka today. The softer limestone has come and gone; the glaciers have ploughed their mighty course across the landscape. Traces remain of both, but it is the old rock, binding the lakes and controlling the course of the rivers, that acts as the foundation for Muskoka's ecology and beauty.

But if the rock is the foundation, it is water that brings this rugged landscape to life. Trickling down from the highlands of the Algonquin dome, held back by spongy swamps, innumerable beaver ponds, and lakes large and small, that water slowly descends some 340 metres to Georgian Bay. The influence of the ancient mountains is felt yet in Muskoka's abundant water, for the rising elevation brings a third more precipitation here than in the Ottawa valley to the east. This effect is especially noticeable in early winter, when the western winds, laden with moisture from the open waters of Georgian Bay, drop more snow on Muskoka than almost anywhere else in southern Ontario.

The complex interplay between rock and water shows itself in other ways as well. The endless erosion of the rock, following the trend of ancient folds, has created an interesting pattern of lakes and rivers between parallel ridges. The pattern is particularly striking in the wild country to the west of Gravenhurst. Pine Lake, Loon Lake, Muldrew, Nine Mile, Turtle, and many others are all long, narrow, and parallel, hemmed in by the rhythm of the rocks.

And just as the Precambrian rocks are poor in nutrients and slightly acidic, so too are the waters of Muskoka. Dead vegetation decays slowly in the cool acidic waters, allowing thick beds of organic peat to build up over the centuries, often completely filling in former ponds. In some wetlands, such as the conifer swamp along Brandy Creek, the layers of peat are up to 36 metres deep. In turn, the natural tannins in the wood and bark slowly leach from these peaty bogs and swamps, giving Muskoka lakes and rivers their characteristic rust-brown stain.

This relationship between water and rock—and the rock fragments that are the basis of soil—also set the stage for the vegetation of Muskoka. The trees and plants of the southern shield grow where they do, not by mere coincidence, but rather in response to quite specific site conditions. Some plants are very specialized; others are more tolerant, better able to adapt to a broader range of conditions. But to a large extent, all are quite predictable; if you know the plant "communities" growing on a particular corner of the landscape, you can tell a great deal about the land form and moisture in the ground below.

On the hills of eastern Muskoka, for example, where deep tills and sands are common, hardwood forests of maple and beech cover almost all the uplands. This is classic sugar-maple country; in fact, sugar maple is so good at replacing itself in the shady leaf-covered forest floor that other trees often play a minor part. Where a fallen tree creates an opening for sunlight, white ash or black cherry have a chance to stretch upward. On cooler moister sites, such as north-facing slopes, hemlock and yellow birch have an opportunity to become part of the canopy.

All forests are arenas of cutthroat competition—plants must outcompete, adapt, or die. Beneath the dense shade of the maples, a number of shrubs and ferns have successfully adapted to life with little summer sunlight. The hobblebush, with its large paired leaves and sprawling stems, is one such example; the marginal shield fern, with its stately leathery fronds, is another. Many woodland flowers adapt by completing their life cycle early, before the trees leaf out. Called spring ephemerals, they include such favourites as trilliums, spring beauty, trout lily, and hepatica.

But the upland forest of Muskoka is far from uniform, responding as it must to the imperatives of rock and water, as well as to its own recent history. Where the rock rises closer to the surface, causing warmer drier soils, white pine begins to play a major role. As the soils become thinner yet, the scattered white pines are joined by red and white oaks, whose roots can withstand extremes of summer heat and drought that maples cannot. In the barrens south of Lake Muskoka, even the pines have difficulty, leaving a rocky landscape dotted with oaks, low juniper bushes, and such hardy perennials as poverty grass.

Where the forest has been disturbed by farming, logging, or fire, a new cast of forest characters takes advantage of the sunny conditions. Typically these stands are dominated by "pioneer" species, such as aspen and white birch. Red maple and a mix of other hardwoods provide a bridge into more mature forest, especially on moister sites. Where there are deeper sands, red and white pine may prevail; on very dry sands there are even scattered stands of jack pine.

Mature forests on richer clay soils are surprisingly rare in Muskoka, since most of these sites have been heavily logged or cleared for farming. Where pockets of rich forest are found, they show an especially rich "understory" (forest undergrowth), with "signature" plants like maidenhair fern, wild leek, Christmas fern, blue cohosh, and Virginia waterleaf.

The wetland communities of Muskoka are equally specialized in their choice of sites. On wet clay soils, soft maple swamps can develop, often together with the shaggy-barked

IN THE OLD DAYS MUSKOKA WAS FAMOUS FOR ITS LUSH FERNS, AND GATHERING THEM TO TAKE HOME WAS ONE OF THE SUMMER'S GREAT PASTIMES. THE LICHEN IN THE PHOTOGRAPH RIGHT IS INTERESTING BECAUSE IT IS ACTUALLY "A DUAL PLANT MADE UP OF A CERTAIN FUNGUS AND A CERTAIN ALGA GROWING IN A INTIMATE SYMBIOTIC ASSOCIATION."

GARY McGUFFIN

GARY McGUFFIN

The flora of the district is, as might be expected from its situation, peculiar to itself, and walks through the woods will bring to the untaught eye many unaccustomed varieties and to the educated botanist, a rare storehouse of pleasure. One of them says: "The vegetation is almost tropical in its undisturbed luxuriance. The beautiful white fringed Orchis — the loveliest of all the Habernarias — and the splendid Cinnamon and Royal Osmund ferns grow to perfection in low and moist situations, while the Polypody and the Shield-fern flourish in the higher grounds. In the district are also found, in exceptional abundance, Club-mosses of various species, and the curious Pitcher plant nestles in its moss setting along the margins of the sequestered pools."
— The Northern Lakes of Canada, 1886

WINTER BERTH, PEN & INK, KENT TAYLOR.

black ash. More typically, however, the peaty wetlands support shrubby or conifer forest communities. The development of these forests follows a sequence you can see in its various stages in many parts of Muskoka.

Development of organic soils, or peat, usually begins around the edges of Muskoka ponds. Floating mats of peat develop open communities of grasses and sedges, often with several kinds of orchids, cotton-grass, and scattered shrubs. These nutrient-poor bogs again attract plants that can adapt to specialized environments—in this case, sundews and pitcher-plants, which trap insects to meet their nutrient needs. On some mats, shrub-bog communities of Labrador tea, leatherleaf, and sweet gale take over; on others, the most visible plant is the large Virginia chain fern, which thrives in acidic conditions.

As the peat mat thickens and becomes drier on the surface, scattered black spruce, tamarack, and cedar trees appear. The moist ground surface is usually carpeted with sphagnum and other mosses, along with wildflowers like clintonia, Canada mayflower, and goldthread, which flourish in the shade. On the oldest and most mature peatlands, such as the extensive wetland south of Novar, almost pure stands of black spruce create a dense canopy, with only a sparse understory of shrubs and flowers.

Because peatlands need conditions with low levels of nutrients and oxygen, they do not develop on the shores of lakes or fast-flowing rivers. Instead, the shallow waters and wet soils in these sites grow shrub thickets of alder or winterberry and mountain holly.

In deeper waters, aquatic vegetation uses three different strategies to survive. "Emergent" plants, such as cattail, pickerelweed and bulrushes, have their roots in the soft bottom but their leaves emerging above the water level. Floating-leaved plants, such as water lilies and pondweeds, have leaves and blossoms that lay flat on the water surface, usually attached to a tuberlike root in the bottom. "Submergent" plants keep their leaves below water, although many extend a small flower stalk into the air to help spread their seeds.

These weedy bays are often extremely important to a lake's fish communities. They provide spawning beds for such species as pike and bass, and nursery areas for the young of many others. They also provide a critical habitat for most of Muskoka's frogs and turtles, especially during the spring when the nightly frog chorus provides auditory evidence that spawning is under way.

The cool nutrient-poor waters of Muskoka are not ideal conditions for aquatic plants, and their distribution and diversity is somewhat limited. There is one exception—the Severn River corridor, which forms the southern boundary of the District of Muskoka. Most of the clear green waters of the Severn arise from the Lake Simcoe watersheds to the

south, an area rich in limestone, and hence in nutrients. In a rare reversal of the norm in Ontario, these nutrient-laden waters flow into the shield through a series of relatively shallow channels and lakes.

The result, in terms of aquatic plants, is spectacular. Sparrow Lake and the Severn River support the greatest diversity of aquatic plants known anywhere in Canada. Near Big Chute grows one kind of water plant—Eaton's quillwort—not found anywhere else in the country. Some bays in Sparrow Lake have 15 different kinds of pondweed alone.

As might be expected, the great diversity of vegetation in Muskoka results in a great diversity of wildlife. Some 174 species of nesting birds have been documented for the district, along with 54 kinds of mammals, 36 reptiles and amphibians, 70 butterflies, and 89 dragonflies and damselflies. The southeastern corner of Georgian Bay supports the best diversity of reptiles and amphibians in the province, and most areas support healthy populations of wild creatures.

But since the coming of European settlement, Muskoka's wildlife has undergone change. Before the advent of guns, the hardwood forests were host to throngs of the now extinct passenger pigeon, and Muskoka waters were graced by the white trumpeter swans. Peregrine falcons no longer swoop from the lakeside cliffs of Muskoka, and bald eagles are only an occasional winter visitor. But other birds have weathered the abuses of mankind; osprey, for example, victims of persistent chemicals in past decades, are making a remarkable comeback.

The mammals we see today are considerably different from those the first Europeans into Muskoka noted. Woodland caribou and elk are long gone, pushed out by over-hunting and habitat changes; wolverines have been pushed to the far margins of Ontario; eastern cougars are extinct; and the other large cats, lynx and bobcat, are much less common. The timber wolf may yet occur in the far north-eastern sections of Muskoka, but it, too, has been largely pushed out by settlement.

On the other side of the equation, some wildlife has revelled in the openings and new edges created by farming and logging. White-tailed deer are much more abundant now than they were in the closed forests prior to settlement; moose, too, have benefitted from the younger forests they use for browse. Coyotes, originally from the Prairies, have found modern Muskoka to their liking and have largely replaced the timber wolf. The beaver population has expanded as well, despite a period of very low numbers early in this century due to overtrapping. The abundance of pioneer forests of aspen and birch created ideal conditions for this ambitious rodent, since aspen and birch are the beaver's favourite foods.

The changes in habitat brought about by human endeavours

BRACEBRIDGE FALLS, PEN & INK, NORA TELFORD.

DRAWN TO THE EDGE

Certain birds and other wildlife live along the boundaries between different habitats because of solid practical advantages—a greater diversity in food sources, perhaps, or quick access to cover to escape predators. But for other species, the attraction is less readily explained.

Consider our own species. Allow a human family their choice in a forested landscape, and most likely they will build their house at the edge of a clearing, or create a small grassy clearing in front of the home. Put the same family on the bald prairie, and they will plant trees near their house, again creating the sense of habitat edge. And if that family is given their choice in Muskoka, with its abundance of water, sure enough they will cluster with others of their kind along the water's edge.

have also created new opportunities for field and edge birds. Field birds like meadowlarks, bobolinks, savannah sparrows and bluebirds have either moved in or greatly increased their numbers. Edge species, which tend to feed or nest along the boundaries between different habitats, have also benefitted. Blue jays, song sparrows, red-tailed hawks, cowbirds, grackles, and many other kinds of common birds feel more at home in a landscape with fields and openings than in solid forest.

But if the mosaic of Muskoka's plants and wildlife has been affected by human activities, so too is it influenced strongly by geography. Muskoka is what ecologists label a "transition zone." As Precambrian shield country with shallow infertile soils and acidic waters, it holds on to much of the ecological character of areas to the north; in effect, acts as the southern edge of the north. But the richer flavour of southern Ontario forests are just to the south, and the moderating effects of Georgian Bay on Muskoka's climate tempt many species to probe just a little farther north. In effect, then, it also acts as the northern edge of the south.

This transition is made stronger still by the east-west differences in Muskoka, from the longer summers and milder winters along Georgian Bay to the cooler climate along the Algonquin dome rising to the east of Huntsville. A flight in a small plane in early May makes the transition clear—you can barely see the ground through the new green leaves around Severn Bridge, but the hills around Dwight still have some snowdrifts, and the lakes are locked in ice.

The effects of wildlife are dramatic. In the spruce forests and northern bogs along the Big East River corridor, you can find spruce grouse, gray jays, black-backed woodpeckers, boreal chickadees, and other species that are common across northern Ontario but only lightly intrude into Muskoka. Other northern species range across most of Muskoka but are scarce farther south, such as black bear, moose, raven, fisher, and lynx.

In a similar way, southern wildlife species like willow flycatcher, yellow-throated vireo, cerulean warbler, and fox snake are found only in the southern parts of Muskoka. Many plants show the same pattern: butternut trees have been found only along the Severn River; white oak are common in the rocky barrens of southern Muskoka but seldom extend north of Lake Muskoka; the range of such southern shrubs as downy arrowwood, buttonbush, and fragrant sumac extends over only part of the district.

There are other influences as well, connections to the east and west that point to unique parts of the Muskoka landscape's long history. Just as the tide of human history leaves its distinctive signs in a city's architecture, the vegetation of an area shows traces of its history. Consider the prairie influences in Muskoka's flora—such grasses as big bluestem, cord grass, and prairie dropseed—which show up along the sun-baked rocks of the Severn River corridor. In all likelihood, they are remnants of a warmer drier period in Ontario's history about 6000 years ago, when prairie plants had a competitive advantage against the forest and moved eastward.

Even more significant in Muskoka is the eastern seaboard connection, reflected in an assemblage of about 20 plant species known as Atlantic coastal-plain flora. Most of these species are fairly widespread in Muskoka and parts of the District of Parry Sound, but then there is a huge gap in their distribution, with their main range restricted to the coastal plain from New Jersey to the Carolinas. How did they get here, and why do they remain?

Ecologist Paul Keddy did a bit of botanical detective work and noted that all the species involved are shoreline plants. Geologists have been able to tell us that at one stage, some 12,000 years ago, the Great Lakes drained south down the Mohawk valley, and not into the St. Lawrence. Thus the connection was made, and these shoreline plants were able to colonize up along the riverbanks to reach Muskoka. Their success in persisting seems to be related to regular water-level fluctuations in many Muskoka lakes—the high water keeps shoreline shrubs from taking over, and dropping water levels allow the long-lived seeds of the coastal-plain flora to germinate.

This quirk of history adds an interesting dimension to Muskoka's plant life. Especially in such central Muskoka lakes as Hardy, Axe, Morrison, Echo, and others, as well as along the Moon River, late-summer sandy shorelines show eye-catching displays of Virginia meadow beauty, slender yellow-eyed grass, golden hedge hyssop, and other Atlantic coastal plain species.

The past century and a half of European occupation has also left its mark on the composition of Muskoka's flora. Twenty-two per cent of the district's more than 1200 wild plant species are non-native, introduced as escapees from gardens or as weeds coming along with farm crops. Many are now widespread—the daisies and chickory of roadsides, the hawkweeds and goat's-beard of grassy openings. This process of introductions has been going on for a long time—the natives called plantain "white man's foot," since its low spreading leaves appeared only where the white settlers had inadvertently helped its spread. The process continues, with the recent invasion of purple loosestrife, a non-native plant that is rapidly elbowing its way into many wetlands.

Other Muskoka wildlife specialties are also tied to specific habitats. Southern Muskoka is the best area in the province for Ontario's only lizard—the five-lined skink. Colonies of skinks, the adults of which have five narrow stripes down their backs, feed on wood roaches found under slabs of rock in the region's oak barrens. The area near Georgian Bay, where the barrens have more scattered pine and shrub junipers, is the core habitat of Ontario's small population of prairie warblers.

Another Muskoka specialty is a forest raptor called the red-shouldered hawk, a species that has declined quickly over much of its range. Red-shouldereds still thrive in Muskoka, nesting in such places as Walker's Point. The reason seems clear—these birds need large areas of mature hardwoods, preferably close to water. As the forests of the south are more and more fragmented into smaller parcels, the woodlands of Muskoka take on added importance as a refuge for this hard-pressed species. Evidence is mounting that many other "interior forest" songbirds are in dire threat as well. For many of the thrushes, warblers, tanagers, and other birds of the deep forest, the tall timber of Muskoka may well become a vital reserve.

Without question, the distinctive ecology of Muskoka has shaped the nature of human endeavour in this region. Muskoka's interconnected mosaic of waterways defined the pattern of transportation during a critical period of the district's development. The thin soils brought up short the rosy plans for a new agricultural frontier. The forests of maple and pine fostered the first, and so far the largest, wave of industrial activity. The abundant groves of hemlock supplied the bark from which tannin is extracted, and supported the leather-tanning factories that shaped the towns of Bracebridge and Huntsville.

But the rocky lakes and forested hills also attracted a unique facet of human culture that has proved perhaps the most lasting of economic activities in Muskoka—cottaging. A century ago, the first cottagers in the area were attracted by the fresh air, the scenery, the abundant fish and wildlife. Today, the attraction is much the same.

The passing of a century does make one difference, however—we can no longer afford to take the natural assets of Muskoka for granted. Overcrowding threatens the scenery, the sense of relaxation, the very quality of the water itself. Overuse threatens the vastness of the unbroken forests, the diversity and abundance of fish and wildlife. It is time to bring the tools of the modern age to bear on the vital task of preserving and restoring Muskoka's grand natural heritage.

The tools are well-known: the powers of municipalities to plan and approve (or reject); the ability of community groups to promote wise stewardship with landowners; the rights of citizens and citizen groups to participate in decisions that affect their environment. What we need most, in the century to come, is a strong common determination to use those tools and others to keep Muskoka intact for future generations. ▷

2
OBAJEWANUNG

The First Peoples

BY WILLIAM M. GRAY

O N THE LAST DAY OF JANUARY 1862, in the village of Obajewanung,* the chief and assembled warriors of the Muskoka† band drafted a petition to the Crown. John Stoughton Dennis, a land surveyor working in the area, met with them in council and recorded their words. They were addressed to His Excellency, the Right Honourable Lord Monck Governor General of British North America:

FATHER

We the Indians known as the Muskoka Band of the Ojibwa Tribe living at our Village of Obajewanung, being in the straits between Lakes Rosseau and Muskoka, desire to convey through you to our Great Mother the Queen [Victoria] the renewal of our dutiful and affectionate loyalty.

We have heard with much sorrow that the Great Spirit has taken away the husband [Prince Albert] of our Great Mother.

We hope that the Great Spirit will take her by the hand at this time and that He will walk by the side of the Great Mother through life.

FATHER

We are in trouble and we come to you to help us out. We believe that your ears are always open to listen to the complaints of your Red Children and that your hand is always ready to lead them in the right path.

FATHER

When you sent Mr. Robinson to Sault Ste. Marie twelve years ago to make the Treaty with your Red Children, they ceded to you all their lands in the north shore of Lakes Huron and Superior with the exception of certain Reserves for the several Bands at different points upon those Lakes, and the land reserved by that Treaty to us was a tract, in the main land, the shore of Lake Huron at Wa-Ja Quising

[Wasaquishing], north of Parry Island and L'Isle au Sable [Sandy Island]. Three miles wide by six miles long: afterwards when you sent Mr. Dennis [J. S. Dennis] and Mr. Keating to point out our land we thought we would rather have Parry Island for our Reserve than the land on the shore which was not very good and we told the Gentlemen this and they gave us the Island instead, and it has therefore belonged to us ever since—at this time we thought we would all go out to Lake Huron and live on our Reserve.

FATHER

Our feelings have changed.

This place is beautiful in our eyes, and we found we could not leave it.

Many winters have passed since we settled here and began to cultivate our gardens.

We have good houses and large gardens where we raise much corn and potatoes.

Our children have grown up here and cannot make up their minds to go to a new place. We are not so fortunate as some of your Red Children who have large farms cleared and plenty of cattle.

We live by hunting and taking furs—and our hunting grounds are all near here. Were we to go to Parry Island we should have to clear new Gardens and our hunting grounds would be far off.

FATHER

We wish that you would take back Parry Island, our Reserve on Lake Huron, and instead of it give us our Reserve of three miles by six miles at this place.

We wish you could send someone to our Council to make Treaty with us and we will surrender Parry Island, and our land here can then be pointed out and surveyed and Reserved to us.

FATHER

We hope you will grant the wish of your Red Children, and do it soon, because the whites are coming in close to us and we are afraid that your Surveyors will soon lay out our lands here into lots.

THIS COLLECTION OF NATIVE ARTIFACTS IS FROM THE MUSKOKA LAKES MUSEUM IN PORT CARLING.

* Port Carling
† Also called Miskoko

8075

78

17/18 February 1862

John S. Dennis

Muskoko Indians.

Petition to His Excellency
Lord Monck to surrender
Parry Island & get a tract
of six miles square in place
of it.

Report to Mr Walcot
25 Feby 1862

779

... to Parry Island, and they will come back
if we can get our Reserve here
This is all we have to say at present.

Signed

Pa ga munga bru Chief   his mark
Nebn e-ghosto   his mark
Me nis nue nie   his mark
To ba que ne ga winisung   his mark
Ga ba im   his mark
Kindebaonse   his mark
Kewage   his mark
Ojibway   his mark
Bay o Sung   his mark
Ajitamoo   his mark
Kenoganee   his mark
Me a be nanse   his mark
Kah ge ganse   his mark
Kah me ya que set   his mark
Kah douse   his mark

Done in Council
at our Village of
Wage waukky
this 31 day of
January 1862
in presence of
J. Stoughton Dennis
P.L.S.

We are all of one mind in this matter, there are only three of our band who moved out to Parry Island, and they will come back if we can get our Reserve here.

This is all we have to say at present.

The petition, found in the records of the Indian Department, is signed with the totems of Chief Bah-ga-me-gah-bow, Mish-e-quods, Me-nis-me-nie, To-ba-qui-ne-ga-winis-ing, Ga-ba-un, Windebaonse, Kewalje, Ojibway, Boy-o-Sung, Ajitamoo, Kenogance, Mea-he-nanse, Kah-ge-ganse, Kah-me-ga-qui-sit, and Kah-douse. Eleven of these names are marked with the reindeer totem and three with what appears to be the otter totem.

This unique document is both powerful and important: in it we hear the authentic voice of the Ojibwa people of Muskoka; we learn of their fears and their desires. We see the names of the last of the Muskoka band who lived in this district. We see a community of people.

Their community was a part of a group known in the nineteenth century as the Sandy Island Ojibwa, and they in turn were considered part of a larger group, the Chippewa of lakes Simcoe and Huron. The nomenclature is admittedly confusing, but it reflects the customary British usage of the day. The Ojibwa nation was referred to as both Mississauga and Chippewa at different times and in different localities in the southern parts of the province. The distinction in this particular case is unimportant as the Ojibwa who lived in the Parry Sound and Muskoka districts recognized William Yellowhead, the chief of the Chippewa of lakes Simcoe and Huron, as their principal chief.

Among the earliest government records of the province of Upper Canada are found many references to a chief who resided in the interior. He was known to the British as Yellowhead. In about 1818 he was succeeded by his son, who was also known as Yellowhead, or William Yellowhead, and he was to remain the acknowledged principal chief of the bands that were later identified with Rama, Snake Island, Beausoleil Island, Colpoy's Bay, and L'Isle aux Sables (Sandy Island)—which included the Muskoka Indians—until his death in 1864.

No chief was ever to command the same authority again as the different bands gradually evolved into independent administrative centres dealing directly with the Indian Department. Broadly speaking, Yellowhead in the first quarter of the nineteenth century was seen as the principal chief of a number of nomadic bands that ranged to Bing Inlet in the north, east into Haliburton, west to Georgian Bay, and south to the settlements fronting Lake Ontario and the lands already surrendered by treaty to the Crown.

PETITION TO THE CROWN, JANUARY 31, 1862.

An important point to keep in mind is that there were many chiefs. The Indian Department had established a policy of officially recognizing no more than two chiefs in each band that had entered into a treaty relationship with the Crown and located on a reserve. One of these chiefs was denoted as principal chief and was expected to speak for his community. In return he received what was in effect a pension, in addition to any annuity payments that were made to the rest of the band members. As a mark of their station both chiefs were presented with a large medal and a flag.

A number of land surrenders had been negotiated with the Chippewa of lakes Simcoe and Huron from the late 1790s. Over the ensuing 40 years vast tracts of land were given up in south and central parts of the province. By 1830 several of the bands were enticed, or at least agreed, to settle and adopt a more sedentary, agriculturally based lifestyle and locate on specified lands. These eventually became known as the Rama, Snake Island, and Beausoleil Island bands. (The Beausoleil band moved from Beausoleil Island to Christian Island in the 1850s, but were referred to as the Beausoleil Indians for many years afterward.) Other members who were associated with and recognized Yellowhead as their overall chief, and who lived on the shores of Georgian Bay and in the interior, did not surrender their traditional hunting grounds. They did not indicate any interest in adopting a more settled lifestyle or converting to Christianity. They were known as the Sandy Island Indians.

The name was, as one might expect, not of their own choosing. A trader by the name of Bourassa, who was an agent of the Hudson's Bay Company, had established a post on Sandy Island in the 1820s. The Ojibwa who traditionally fished from Moose Deer Point in the south to the Magnetawan in the north, and whose hunting grounds extended inland to encompass what we now know as Muskoka and Parry Sound, traded at Sandy Island. It became their rendezvous and the established point of contact with both traders and officials of the Indian Department.

This situation continued until 1850 when the last of the Chippewa of lakes Simcoe and Huron signed an agreement with the Crown and located on reserves. In the 1840s, before it had any legal title or right to do so, the government had awarded some 30 licences to different mining ventures on Lake Superior. There had been an ugly incident at a mining site in Mica Bay when a number of Indians tried to close an operation by force. The government settled this in short order by dispatching troops. In addition, tensions were rising among the different bands because of fur-trade rivalries and disputes over hunting grounds. Indians from the Pic River had reportedly murdered 14 other Indians whom they accused of trespassing.

In August 1849 Alexander Vidal, a surveyor, and Thomas Gummersall Anderson, a longtime employee of the Indian

Department, were ordered to visit the bands and see if members were amenable to a settlement. They subsequently reported that virtually all the bands they contacted were eager to establish a treaty relationship with the Crown.

As a result, William Benjamin Robinson* was commissioned by an order in council on January 11, 1850, to negotiate "for the adjustment on the [native] claims to the lands in the vicinity of lakes Superior and Huron, or of such portions of them as may be needed for mining purposes."

Robinson was a good man for the job. He was a well-known politician and fur trader and had established in the early to mid-nineteenth century two trading posts in the district: one on Georgian Bay at the mouth of the Muskoka River and the other on Yohocucaba Island in Lake Joseph. His instructions allowed him up to £7500 currency in cash and a capital fund of up to £25,000 to provide perpetual annuities to bargain with the Ojibwa and hopefully arrive at a mutually satisfactory settlement. The principal negotiations were held at Sault Ste Marie, and eventually two treaties were signed—one with the bands on Lake Superior on September 7 and one with bands on Lake Huron two days later. The Robinson-Superior Treaty involved the surrender of 16,700 square miles and 1422 people, and the Robinson-Huron Treaty more than 35,000 square miles and 1240 people.

These two treaties resulted in the establishment of three reserves on Lake Superior and 21 on Lake Huron. The chiefs chose the locations of their own reserves, which were generally areas they had been long accustomed to using as fishing stations or summer encampments.

The chiefs of the band we are particularly interested in, Sandy Island, signed a week later in Pentanguishene, on September 15, 1850. They had not travelled to the Soo for the formal council, but had participated in the initial discussions with Vidal and Anderson at Penetanguishene the previous November. The only concern they'd raised that was particularly noted was their desire to receive their annuity payments in cash and not in kind or goods determined by the Indian Department. The Sandy Island chiefs chose three locations for their reserves: Nash-ko-to-zing, Shawanaga, Wasaquising, which is a place on the mainland described as opposite Sandy Island, the present site of Parry Sound.

With the signing, Muskoka was opened for settlement and three reserves were established for the Indians of the district. Controversy surrounded the details of the agreement for decades. The size of the reserves, title to the islands, and fishing rights were all questioned, and as far as some of the bands are concerned, have never been satisfactorily settled.

INDIAN HEAD ROCK, LAKE MUSKOKA NEAR BEAUMARIS.

The two chiefs from the Sandy Island band in attendance at the councils that resulted in the Robinson Treaty were Chief Mah-kah-da-mi-zhu-quod (printed in government records as Muckta Mishaquet) and Chief Megis. Mah-kah-da-mi-zhu-quod was recognized as the principal chief of all the Sandy Island Ojibwa; Megis was recognized as his subordinate and as the chief of a constituent part of the Muskoka band. The following year at the annual distribution of gifts and the annuity payments in Penetanguishene, a medal, bearing the likeness of the Great Mother (Queen Victoria) was presented to each of them.

In a government report published in 1858, the Sandy Island people are described in terms that say more about the author and his times than they do about his subject:

The Sandy Island Indians are Heathen, and live alternatively on the borders of Lake Huron [Georgian Bay], about 50 miles north-west of Penetanguishene, and in the interior north of that place; they cultivate very small patches of Corn and Potatoes, not as a dependence for food during the Winter but rather as a bon-bouche in the Autumn. . . .

They have hitherto resisted all the attempts made to civilize them, and cling with unaccountable tenacity to the foolish superstitions imbibed from their fathers.

While it is tempting to try to relate something of the fortunes of this band in a simple coherent manner, the scattered records that have survived only add to the confusion. For example, in early October 1855, a number of families of the Sandy Island band travelled to Penetanguishene to dictate a letter to their local superintendent's office. They wanted a new chief appointed. Megis was now acting as the principal chief (Mah-kah-da-mi-zhu-quod had died in 1854 or 1855) and Megis was not, to their minds, acting in their best interests. They had serious problems with different people encroaching on their traditional fishing grounds, but Megis was neither living there (presumably he was settled at Obajewanung in Muskoka), nor was he attending to their concerns.

The petitioners pointed out that Mah-kah-da-mi-zhu-quod's son was willing to assume the position of principal chief of their community. In 1856, however, for reasons that are not clear, the chieftainship was assumed by his nephew, Solomon James,* and Megis once again became the subordinate, or second chief.

In the 1850s the Muskoka band had established a more permanent settlement between lakes Rosseau and Muskoka. Their village, Obajewanung, was located on the

* W. B. Robinson (1797–1873) was the uncle of John Beverley Robinson (1820–1896), Lieutenant-Governor of the province of Ontario, and the first Honourary President of the Muskoka Lakes Association.

MAP 5
Ojibwa Land Occupation in
the Parry Sound District

30

shores of Silver Lake and the Indian River, in what is now Port Carling. It consisted of a number of cleared and cultivated acres and about 20 log huts. In a census from the previous year the total population of this community was 39; the population of the Sandy Island Indians as a whole totalled only 140.

Unfortunately Obajewanung was not located on a reserve; it was established on lands that had been surrendered to the Crown in 1850. Megis, the chief of the Muskoka band, had chosen land at Wasaquising. The band's hunting grounds were located in the interior on the Muskoka lakes, and the treaty made provision for the bands to continue to hunt on Crown lands unless they had been granted to and were in actual occupation of a settler. No one expected that to take place for decades.

Megis died in about 1858 and was succeeded by his brother, Bah-ga-me-gah-bow. Curiously, the Indian Department was ready to impose a system of inheritance on band offices, and simply decreed that Megis's brother would be recognized as chief until Megis's eldest son came of age. It also sent instructions to have Megis's son taught to read and write.

In early 1860 Asa Nah-wah-gua-gezig, a sometime member of the Muskoka band, but then living with the Beausoleil band, argued that he had the best claim to the chieftainship of the Muskoka band; he demanded the medal of the late Chief Megis. He believed that the chieftainship, or the right of succession, belonged to the Birch Bark totem, or clan, of the tribe and not the Reindeer, whose chieftainship had been "transferred" to Rama and was at that time held by Chief Yellowhead. As Bah-ga-me-gah-bow was also a Reindeer, he was therefore a usurper.

At first it appears odd that a man who was a member of the Beausoleil band would claim the chieftainship of a band associated with a different community. But then again, we must remember we are dealing with a number of very small nomadic groups of people. The Sandy Island people were in regular communication with their fellow Ojibwa tribesmen down the Bay, and so of course there was intermarriage and an interchange of members of their extended families.

And as the people were nomadic—dependent on hunting, trapping, and fishing—it was only with the regular presentation of gifts and more importantly the division of the bands' share of the treaty annuities that membership of a particular band became important. Solomon James himself, prior to his becoming the principal chief of the Sandy Island

Band, appears to have been working as a schoolteacher for the Beausoleil band in the early 1850s.

Two interesting points are brought to the fore by Nah-wah-gua-gezig's protest. The first is that the medal and flag customarily awarded to chiefs by the Indian Department had become an unquestioned symbol of authority; two of these emblems had been presented to the Sandy Island band in 1851, one to Mah-kah-da-mi-zhu-quod and the other to Megis. The second is the general question of succession of authority and of the totems of the Chippewa of lakes Simcoe and Huron. These totemic groups were in existence by at least the mid-eighteenth century. The chiefs and warriors signed all documents with a pictograph of their totem, and the Indian agent or translator would sign their names below. The totems were organized patrilineally, that is, the children adopted the clan or totem of their father.

Because Bah-ga-me-gah-bow's chieftainship was challenged, the Indian Department asked Chief Yellowhead, the universally acknowledged chief of all these peoples, who was, in fact, the legitimate chief of the Muskoka band. Fortunately his reply has survived, and it provides a chronological list of the chiefs of this group: Ah-ze-gah-ne-ze, Nah-wah-je-gez-hig, Ne-gah-nah-nah-quod, and finally Megis, who had been responsible for signing the Robinson treaty in 1850. James Bah-ga-me-gah-bow was Megis's brother, and as Yellowhead pointed out, he had Megis's medal in his possession.

Although the Sandy Island people were described as determined traditionalists in their religion and subsistence patterns, they were in fact adapting to the newer ways and the new technologies. Still tied to the seasonal migrations and cycles of hunting, trapping, and fishing, they were gradually becoming more established in particular areas. As we have seen at Obajewanung, log cabins were taking the place of wigwams. In the January 1862 petition that they presented to the Governor General, their attachment to their village is plain.

Reading between the lines, we can also see that the frontier was about to engulf them, that the surveyors were making out lots, that roads were being built, and that lumbermen were beginning to make their mark. A situation they'd thought they wouldn't face for generations was unfolding at an almost bewildering speed.

When John Dennis, the surveyor who had set out their reserves in 1851, was met laying out a new line near Obajewanung in January 1862, Bah-ga-me-gah-bow and the warriors of the Muskoka band decided they would have to make a formal appeal for redress through Dennis. The surveyor in turn immediately drew up their document and posted it to

TOP, MAP FROM *PARRY ISLAND FARMERS* BY E. S. ROGERS AND FLORA TOBOBUNDUNG, 1975. FAR LEFT, INDIAN CHIEFS AT SARNIA, 1860. LEFT, WILLIAM BENJAMIN ROBINSON.

* Converts to Christianity, especially those who became Methodists as Solomon James had, gave up their traditional names and adopted English ones.

MAP OF THE NORTH SHORE GEORGIAN BAY, 1856.

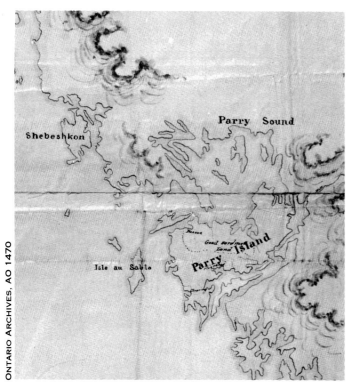

32

In 1845, Canadian painter Paul Kane (1810–1871) visited an Indian Encampment on Lake Huron. While not in Muskoka, this is typical of how its native Settlement at Obajewanung would have looked at the time.

Toronto for the consideration of the Indian Department before forwarding to the Governor General.

The superintendent, W. R. Bartlett, was confused. The previous year, in June 1861, the principal chief of the Sandy Island Indians, Solomon James, had forwarded a petition to the Indian Department, advising the Crown that the band, in council, had decided they wanted to surrender their separate reserves and settle as a single body on Parry Island. Among the chiefs' and warriors' names that were affixed to the petition was found Bah-ga-me-gah-bow. Now Bartlett was presented with a petition signed by the same chief that totally contradicted the previous one.

Bartlett's initial response, though not communicated to either chief, was to allow Solomon James to have Parry Island and let the Muskoka band under Bah-ga-me-gah-bow have the land they wanted between lakes Muskoka and Rosseau. The Muskoka band had advised him that Chief James was simply trying to seize their land when he had no right to it. Their account, which was corroborated by Dennis, stated that when the reserves were being laid out they had successfully requested that their original allocation (chosen by their late chief Megis) at Wasaquising be exchanged for Parry Island; this was readily granted by the government, for at that point, the Crown had not granted any lands in the area.

An additional, though unstated issue may well have had to do with the fact that James had converted to Christianity and become a Methodist. Gathering all the band together and settling them in one place might facilitate the conversion of the rest of the band, who were predominantly traditionalists, and encourage the building of churches and schools.

In July 1862 Bartlett held a council on Christian Island with Chief James in an effort to resolve the issues the Muskoka band had raised. Chief James pointed out that he was the successor of Chief Mah-kah-da-mi-zhu-quod, and as such was the principal chief of the Sandy Island Indians. When the reserves were first laid out in 1850 it had been agreed that all the lands of the Sandy Island peoples would be held in common by all the tribe. The Muskoka band was very much in the minority and were not in a position to alter or alienate lands without the consent of a majority of the whole tribe. Despite that reassurance, the fact remained that James and the majority had signed Bah-ga-me-gah-bow's name to their petition without his consent or knowledge.

The situation became even more complicated when Bah-ga-me-gah-bow explained that his brother, the late chief Megis, had been responsible for the original choice of land at Wasaquising on Georgian Bay, and that neither Bah-ga-me-gah-bow nor the other members in the Muskoka band ever had any desire to remove permanently to the

Bay. He said they preferred to remain where they were at Obajewanung.

Bartlett, understandably confused by the internal politics of the band, initially wanted to attempt to satisfy both parties, but hesitated as "these Indians [the Muskoka] have always been so mixed up with the Sandy Island and Shawanaga People, and have perhaps, held their reserves in common." In brief, the Muskoka band was denied their petition on the basis of the counterclaim of their principal chief, Solomon James.

Within five years James had forwarded another petition expressing the band's desire to give up their lands at Nashko-ta-zing and locate on an enlarged reserve inland at Shawanaga. Bartlett wrote back impatiently asking what had taken place. Why had they decided against Parry Island? What then of the Muskoka band? There is no reply in the files to Bartlett's queries.

In the mid-1860s, however, as a result of James's actions, the Muskoka band gradually began to establish itself on Parry Island. The efforts of Bah-ga-me-ga-bow had all been for naught, and the frustrations of this 70-year-old widower and his small band can only be imagined.

Former Parry Island chief Flora Tobobundung and the late ethnologist Dr. E. S. Rogers identified the Muskoka band's various hunting grounds in the Parry Sound and Muskoka areas during this critical period in the mid-nineteenth century. Most sources agree that the bounds of the Sandy Island Indians were the Moon River to the south and Lake Wawakesh on the Magnetawan to the north, but Tobobundung and Rogers both gave an easterly boundary for the traditional hunting grounds of the band, and delineated within these grounds the different family subdivisions. Five individual groups were identified under the names Waswani, Muskato, Paowis, Manitowaba, and Megis.

In the southern section was found the Waswani, whose winter camp was at Maple Lake. Their grounds were roughly the area bounded by the Moon River, lakes Muskoka and Joseph, and Georgian Bay. Inland was the Muskato, who were found around Lake Muskoka, all of Rosseau, and the easterly parts of Lake Joseph, and to the east, to about the line of Highway 11, including Three Mile Lake. Their winter camp was located at Port Carling, though in some accounts they are described as travelling as far afield as Beausoleil Island and Wasaquising.

A group under Paowis had their winter camp at Wawakesh Lake. They ranged through the north and westerly sections of the Parry Sound District. To the east, toward Ahmic Lake with a winter camp at Lake Manitowaba, was the group under, naturally enough, Manitowaba. The Muskato and Manitowaba "families" were deemed cousins in the sense that they were both of the Otter totem. Lastly was the group under Megis, found between the Wawasani and the Paowis, inland from Parry Sound at the north end of Lake Joseph.

Wading through the Byzantine politics and trying to come to an understanding of the different chiefs and their interrelationships, we tend to lose sight of one simple fact: very few native people lived in Muskoka, and the different bands had only a few dozen families. The land simply could not support a significant or stationary population.

In a census prepared for the annual presentation of gifts to the Indians of Sandy Island in the 1850s, we find enumerated two common chiefs, 34 warriors, 34 women, 19 boys under 16 years old, and 17 girls under 15. The total population of the different bands making up the Chippewa of lakes Simcoe and Huron in 1850 was 699—Sandy Island with 106, Colpoy's Bay with 34, Rama with 182, Snake Island with 153, and Beausoleil with 224.

By the mid-1860s Obajewanung was known as Baisong Rapids or Indian Gardens by the newcomers, and was finally named Port Carling in 1869. The Township of Medora had been surveyed, and the government began granting lots to white settlers. By 1871 all but three Muskoka families had quit Obajewanung as it underwent its transformation into the frontier settlement of Port Carling. The rest had removed to the Parry Island area, but had not as yet taken to the land.

In an 1871 census all gave their occupation as hunter or trapper, with the single significant exception of Solomon James, the principal chief, who was denoted as a trader. Abner Elliott, an Ojibwa Wesleyan Methodist missionary, was living among them by this time and had made his first conversion in 1869 or 1870. In total there were 36 families, living in 21 dwellings on the three reserves in the Parry Sound area; the majority of them were still described as "pagan."

The 1871 census shows the 35 families, excluding the missionary's, reporting that in the 1870 season they had taken 286 beaver, 1103 muskrat, 242 mink, 24 otter, 30 martin, two fox, three bear, and 293 moose, deer, or caribou. As would be expected on Georgian Bay, fishing was a major occupation; 3510 fathoms of nets were reported, and a total catch of 39 barrels of white fish and 22½ of trout. Within a decade virtually all the residents of the reserves were classified as farmers.

By the early 1870s the last members of the Muskoka band had finally moved off the Muskoka lakes. Some returned every summer to sell crafts and fish, others to hunt and trap in their traditional hunting grounds. This is said to have gone on in the traditional pattern till the turn of the century. But for most, the break was clean; their future was on Parry Island and largely centred on the Bay.

Benjamin Hardcastle Johnston, the enumerator for Medora and Wood townships in the 1871 census, noted that a 100-year-old Indian, William King, a pagan, had died the previous year of inflammation of the lungs. In his reminiscences Vernon Wadsworth, the well-known surveyor, talks about Musquedo, the old medicine man who lived at Obajewanung; Wadsworth was convinced that Lake Muskoka had been named for Musquedo. The surveyor also makes mention of Musquedo's son, who was known to the British as William King. Given the frequency of English names being shared by fathers and sons when the proper Indian name was not used, it is hard not to imagine that the old medicine man Wadsworth recalled with such respect was B. H. Johnston's pagan.

Whether or not they were one and the same, after the old man's death it was only a matter of months before the last of the Muskoka Indians gave up and left Muskoka to settle on Parry Island. Muskoka had been thrown open to settlement and to the lumberman. The first hotels catering to that new animal on the frontier, the tourist, had opened and the first islanders had arrived. ▷

MORNING QUIET, SOFT PASTEL, DAVE BECKETT.

36

3

DAVID THOMPSON SLEPT HERE

Muskoka's First Surveyor

BY SÉAN PEAKE

A HUNDRED AND FIFTY YEARS AGO, Muskoka's lakes and rivers were known only to the Indians and a handful of white trappers. To the outside world Muskoka was a blank space on a map. It wasn't until the 1860s, when the region was opened up for settlement, that the first detailed surveys were made to fill in those gaps—or so the surveyors and government officials thought. For, more than 20 years earlier, an accurate survey of Muskoka's lakes was made by a man who has been called the world's greatest geographer—David Thompson. Natural cynic that I am, I become rather suspicious when someone or something is labeled the "world's greatest," but after years of research into Thompson's life, I believe the epithet is valid.

After the War of 1812, the British government wanted to find a route for troops and supplies from the Ottawa River to Georgian Bay that was beyond the reach of U.S. military forces. With a safe route between the two points, Britain would be able to supply and maintain its military posts in the Great Lakes and have access to its western territories. Royal Engineers scrambled over the Severn River–Lake Simcoe area and the surveys in 1826 and 1934 touched upon the shores of Lake Muskoka and the Muskoka River, but the area between here and Lake Nipissing was still unknown. Then, as tensions eased between the U.S. and Britain, so did the need for the water route.

The next call for a route came soon after the completion of the Erie Canal in 1828. From time beyond memory, the main highway from Montreal to Lake Superior and the West was up the Ottawa and Mattawa rivers into Lake Nipissing, then down the French River to Lake Huron. From there, the route followed the north shore of Lake Superior to Grand Portage, or Fort William—the gateways to the Prairies, Hudson Bay, and the Arctic and Pacific oceans. Almost everyone who travelled to the West before the completion of the railroad in 1880 followed this chain of rivers and lakes.

As the agricultural and natural-resource output from new American Midwest states began to swell, this route fell out of favour, as it was ill-suited to the larger craft needed to handle the growing volume of materials and goods destined for American and European markets. The commercial steamships and schooners that sailed the Great Lakes diverted much of the trade away from the Ottawa valley and into the hands of Montreal merchants. And as American goods passed through Canadian ports, Canadian merchants profited and everyone was happy—everyone, that is, except the Americans.

To avoid paying Canadian taxes, duties, and service charges and to capture part of the European trade, the Americans built the Erie Canal, linking Lake Erie with New York City. Almost overnight, much of the lucrative trade that flowed up and down the St. Lawrence evaporated and with it the fortunes of the merchants, not to mention the revenues received by the governments of Britain, and Upper and Lower Canada. The only solution, as some Ottawa merchants claimed, was to build a canal from Lake Huron to Ottawa. While the project would restore a respectable portion of the trade back to the Montreal merchants, it would also open up land for settlement for emigrants trying to escape poverty and unemployment in the U.K. Some of these merchants wrapped their noble claims in the flag of patriotism, but others could not hide their naked self-interest. Land speculation was quite a lucrative business at that time, and some of the Ottawa-valley merchants wanted the government to open up the tracts of land for the simple reason of making money.

To remedy the situation, in 1837 the government of Upper Canada allocated £3000 pounds to explore and record the nature of the country between Lake Huron and the Ottawa River for the purpose of building a ship canal. Commissioners were appointed and three routes of exploration chosen. One was to follow the traditional French-Nipissing-Mattawa-Ottawa route; another was to go along the Shawanaga (now the Magnetawan) to the Ottawa River and back again by the traditional route. The third route was to go up the Muskoka River to its headwaters, then down the Madawaska River to the Ottawa. David Thompson was first appointed to survey the French River route, but fortunately for us, he was later assigned the Muskoka River section.

Born in Westminster, England, in 1770, Thompson landed in Canada in 1784 as an apprentice to the Hudson's Bay

128 One-Tree Island, Lake Joseph   On Muskoka Line

Company in Churchill, Manitoba. Later transferred to York Factory at the mouth of the Nelson River, he made his first inland excursion to the foothills of the Rockies near Calgary in 1787. The journey made a deep impression on Thompson's young mind and forever shaped his character. The following winter while at Cumberland House on the Saskatchewan River, near The Pas, he learned the science of surveying from the best surveyor of the time, Phillip Turnor. In the years between 1790 and 1812 Thompson surveyed by canoe, on foot and horseback over 55,000 miles of the Northwest from Hudson Bay to the Pacific, and the Missouri River to Lake Athabasca. As he worked to fill in the map of North America, he endured a minimum of comforts and often terrible conditions. Much of his work was stolen by the English cartographer Aaron Arrowsmith, keeping Thompson in obscurity until he was "discovered" in the late 1880s by J. B. Tyrrell, a Canadian mining engineer and geologist.

At the time that Thompson was chosen for the Muskoka survey, he was 67 years old and struggling to make a living for himself and his family. While there was no one alive who was as experienced as he, Thompson was viewed with some skepticism by Captain Baddeley, the commanding Royal Engineer in Upper Canada and one of the survey's commissioners. Baddeley wrote to John Macaulay, a member of the legislative council of Upper Canada and the official in charge of the survey, saying that rumours were circulating that Thompson was "not trustworthy as to the reporting of facts" and that the Speaker of the House, Archibald Maclean, could provide him with more details. Whatever Maclean had to say to Macaulay, it obviously did nothing to sway his opinion of Thompson's ability to perform the survey.

While it is impossible to find out what those rumours were, one incident some 10 years earlier stands out as a probable source. During the international boundary survey between Britain and the U.S., Thompson was the chief surveyor and astronomer for Great Britain. A controversy erupted over the cession of Barnhart Island in the St. Lawrence River to the Americans. The British, wanting to keep intact its military establishments on Wolfe Island, agreed to cede the island to the U.S. in return for total control of Wolfe. Barnhart residents—some were Loyalists who fled the U.S. during the American Revolution—protested and searched for someone to blame. As Thompson was the only member of the survey team who lived in the area, rumours

sprang up that he had been taken and imprisoned in Quebec, then shipped to England to be tried for treason. Macaulay, who was quite familiar with the boundary survey, would have known the truth and quickly dismissed the charge.

Thompson had another disagreement with Baddeley when it came time to choose the survey's mode of transport. The Royal Engineer thought tin boats were best for surveys, but Thompson wanted a canoe made of cedar. Baddeley may have been a competent surveyor and engineer, but he certainly didn't have Thompson's wilderness experience. The advantage of a birch or cedar canoe was that repairs could be made at anytime simply by going into the forest.

Thompson was well aware of the problems one faced when trying to repair or build canoes with inferior materials. When he first crossed the Rockies to the Columbia River in 1807, he had hopes of being able to build a canoe from the birch trees growing on the other side of the mountains. It turned out that the climate was more moderate on the western side of the mountains than on the east, and so the rind on those trees did not grow thick enough to be useful. Instead, he had to make a canoe out of the materials around him, namely cedar. The chances of stumbling across an open tin mine while surveying Muskoka seemed rather remote, and taking rolls of tin would be just unnecessary baggage—especially on portages. Baddeley wrote to Macaulay that Thompson "seemed so pressing on the point that it [was] conceded to him." As events unfolded, it was the right decision.

Thompson's Muskoka journal, entitled *Journal of Occurrences from Lake Huron to the Ottawa River,* 1837, is the first written description of Muskoka lakes. Throughout most of his life, Thompson kept meticulous track of weather conditions—often three observations a day—daily events, the abundance or lack of game, geological features, and any landmarks of note, and the Muskoka journal is no exception. His writing is typically objective and quite void of emotion, for rarely does he give us his personal reflections. Nevertheless, it provides us with the day-to-day routine of being on the land.

On August 1 he set off with five men in a 25-foot cedar canoe from Christian Island, in Georgian Bay near Penetanguishine. His outfit, when measured by today's standards, was quite meagre and included: one 50-fathom net of five-inch mesh, a twilled-cotton tent (which soon became mildewed and riddled with small holes), 450 pounds of salt pork, 100 pounds of beef, 300 pounds of biscuit, two bushels of peas, one pound of tea, eight and a half pounds of butter, five gallons of whisky, five pounds of nails, two yards of towelling, tin mugs, almost seven pounds of tobacco, and a tea kettle. No Gore-Tex rainsuits, no sunscreen, no flashlights, and certainly topographic maps. By August 5 he'd reached Beausoleil Island and begun the search for the

39

MANY FINE PHOTOGRAPHERS HAVE PLIED THEIR TRADE IN MUSKOKA OVER THE YEARS. ONE OF THE EARLIEST AND BEST WAS JAMES ESSON OF PRESTON, ONTARIO, WHO TRAVELLED THROUGH THE DISTRICT IN 1880S SHOOTING STEREOGRAPHS, WHICH HE LATER SOLD IN SETS.

Guests at Currie's Bala Falls House Bala Muskoka. 1861

mouth of the Muskoka River. Buried in a labyrinth of islands and channels, its exact location was not precisely known at the time, but by the afternoon of the next day, he had entered the river and was on his way upstream. On August 13 at 11 a.m., after ascending 12 waterfalls and portaging 2180 yards, he reached Lake Muskoka, or as he called it, Swamp Ground Lake (from the Indian name Muskako-skow-oo-sakahagan) and set up camp at the head of Bala Falls.

By relying on Thompson's journal, I have retraced his route through the region and pinpointed landmarks and campsites, particularly on the three lakes I know best—Muskoka, Rosseau, and Joseph. To provide a glimpse of what Thompson saw during his 12 days on these lakes, I have selected passages from his journal of that time. Because the journals also record his surveys, much of what he wrote was a series of courses and distances or changes in a river's elevation. For clarity I have omitted these and indicated their removal with three-dot ellipses. As well, I have expanded some abbreviations and replaced his symbols for right and left with words.

AUGUST 14, MONDAY. At 9:32AM set off, came to Swamp Ground Lake and held on to 11AM, put ashore. Rain came on and we dined. At 12:10PM, set off and held on to 1:35PM, when very heavy rain with loud thunder came on and we had to keep under the shelter of a point of rock and let it fall on us to 3:15PM when we crossed N46E to an islet 500 yards and camped where the Indians have been [the southeastern point of Charybdis Island]. At 3:30PM, the rain ceased but the weather cloudy and threatening. By 4:15PM, got to writing up my journal. Everything again wet and my papers for drawing wet. From the camp about due south there appears a fine body of hardwood and gentle rise of land, but all the shores and isles hereto are bound with grey sienite rock, as per specimens, with red fir and pines and have a soil of worth except for red oak, which is everywhere in the bays and on all the Carrying Places, but often of low growth. Cloudy weather and in the evening 6PM showers of rain. Wind SE and East 1 to 1/8. Several loons about us. Showers of rain in the night but somewhat cool.

AUGUST 15, TUESDAY. Wind Southerly, cloudy. Breakfasted and at 7:10AM set off. Sketched the lake about us, many islands &c [etc.]. Course South. At 7:53AM put ashore to examine the woods and the soil at a place not looking favourable. About 30 yards within is a small

WHEN THOMPSON BEGAN HIS SURVEY OF THE MUSKOKA LAKES IN 1837, DID HE ENVISAGE THE CHANGES TO COME? SIXTY YEARS LATER, BALA WAS A BUSTLING RESORT TOWN, THANKS IN LARGE PART TO THE UNTIRING EFFORTS OF ITS FOUNDER, THOMAS BURGESS.

meadow with white birch and beech, very fine woods of that kind, but yellow sandy soil. Many showers with dark dirty weather and gusts of wind to 11AM, then tolerable fine. At 12:23PM dined. At 1:15PM set off, all grey sienite and quartz sienite. Examined the soil. About 2 or 3 in. black vegetable mould, then a good rocky, sandy clay, basswood &c &c, good land. Saw an Indian lodge and in hopes of getting information went to it about 1 1/2 miles off, but no person, suppose they have gone to Lake Huron for presents &c [the southeast tip of Eileen Gowan Island]. They have left a cat and many utensils &c with many rolls of very good birch rind for canoes. I asked my men if they would have a birch rind canoe made, they said not, as it would not stand the required rough usage which our business must have. We returned to where we came from and continued the survey of the lake. At the Indian lodge, fine ground and hardwood and small patch of potatoes look well but the potatoes are yet very small. At 2:50PM, we commenced the survey, when finding no camping place, we returned from the bay to near the end of N2E, course 250 yards [Firebrand Island], grey sienite.

We have had a day of wild weather. Showers of rain, gusty wind with thick dark mists to 11AM, then moderate and fine with changeable winds to West and NW. Loons calling all night. Most of this day, the lands have been very good in soil and timber, but all the points and most of the shores have a ledge of yellow fir and red oak on grey sienite rock and look very forbidding, but about 50 to 100 yards within, the land is good and mostly all hardwood. The islands are mostly yellow fir and rock of no use to the farmer, but for the timber for building which is small and handy. About full moon. But the land is very poor, as well as the water. We haven't heard or seen a squirrel and hare or a mouse, yet there are many tracks of deer in the hardwoods &c.

AUGUST 16, WEDNESDAY. A calm night, lightly cloudy. Musketoes. Heard a few birds singing, quite a novelty. At 6 3/4 AM set off, having breakfasted went to an islet of N2E and began the survey of to day. At 8 1/2 AM examined the ground. At a distance it looked well but the shores are all pines and rocks, except a few bays, about 4 or 5 in., sandy black vegetable mould, then approvedly deep reddish sandy clay. Warm, but not rich. Hardwoods good as usual about 80 to 100 yards from the water. At a narrow [Lighthouse Narrows] which leads to the Matchedash River by a CP [carrying place, or portage] &c &c found a piece of birch rind with several names of 1831 but could not make them out. Further in the narrow, about 300 yards, small horns of deer on the left, we then examined the bay and found the CP leading to the Matchedash River of about 1000 yards length, a small brook crossed the path twice or thrice and entered a small lake at end of the CP, the brook is from this lake. Returned and about 1/2 m from

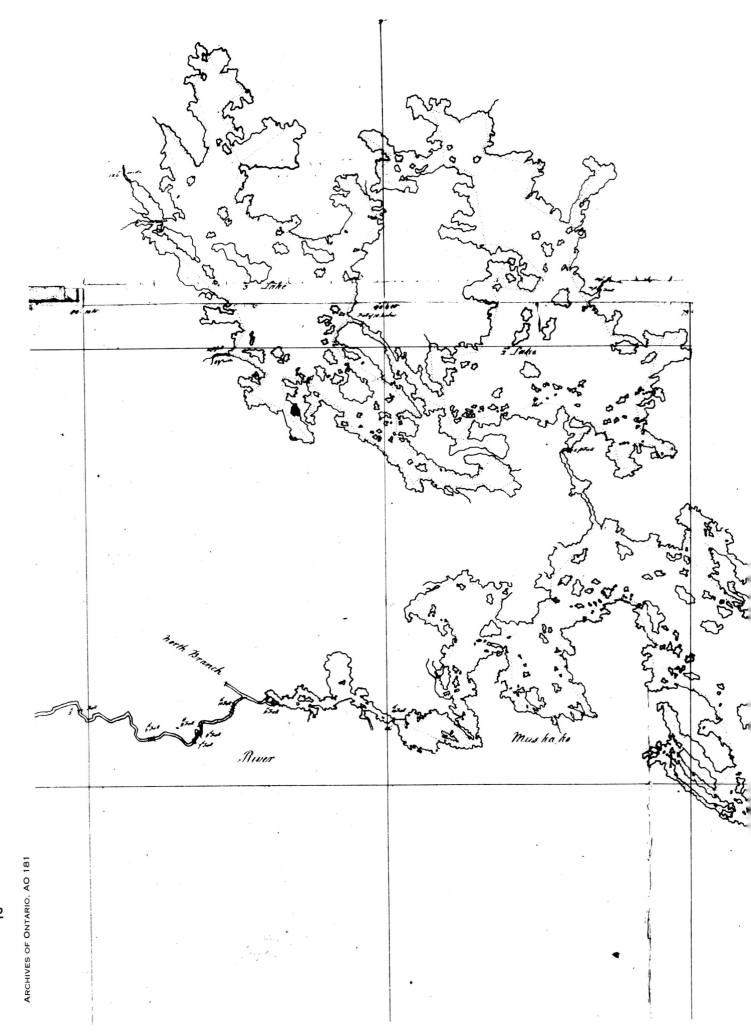

North Branch

River

Muskako

CP, passing the horns, observed for latitude, double meridian altitude of the sun 116°.51'50" . . . [on Greavette Island]. Observed for variation by the plumb line but gave no variation as before. Held on and camped at the Indian lodge [at Eileen Gowan Island], bad campment, at 6:10PM, the cat but no person. Many flies. Thank God we have had a very fine day and employed it well. The country appears as barren of berries as of everything else. Agriculture may do well here but nothing else will. The whole of the large islands on which we camp is mostly good land. The river we have to go up is about 3/4 miles from us.

AUGUST 17TH, THURSDAY. All night SE wind and cloudy. Musketoes bad. At 5:35AM set off. At 7:25 put ashore to breakfast. Wind NE and cool, cloudy but fine, soon changed to SE 1 to 1 1/2, threatening rain. At 12:20PM put ashore to dine, we have caught 3 fine bass. Rain and close misty weather came on with a side wave and seeing the weather apparently set in, we camped at 1PM, the place low smooth rock and safe [in Scarcliffe Bay]. Killed a small collar snake, bluish colour with a ring of yellowish red about its neck, close to the head. It was about 1 foot in length and

girth in proportion. Evening SE wind, sultry heat with showers of rain. +74. The lands about us appear when about 1 to 2 acres within very fine, with good hardwood of fine growth and soil about 2 to 3 in. of vegetable mould and a brown warm subsoil. Very good for agriculture. Set the net.

AUGUST 18, FRIDAY. Cleared in the night, wind North about +64. Took up the net, not a single fish. These lakes do not seem to have much fish. All we can get is a chance bass with the hook.

Breakfasted. Woods within mostly hard maple and some fine basswood. At 6:46AM set off to a river, course up it . . . Came to a strong rapid [at Port Carling] about 2 ft descent and about 260 yards above it a strong shoal rapid of large stones of about 2 ft descent, in all say 5 feet descent, across the rapids 15 yards or so. The CP is on the left N60E 50 yards, very good to a bay of stale water. Easy to make a lock. Soil shallow upon grey sienite as usual. Woods of hemlock, cedar, maple, red oak &c. We now left the cargo and only taking what we thought necessary for a few days, took the light canoe over the rapids and set off at

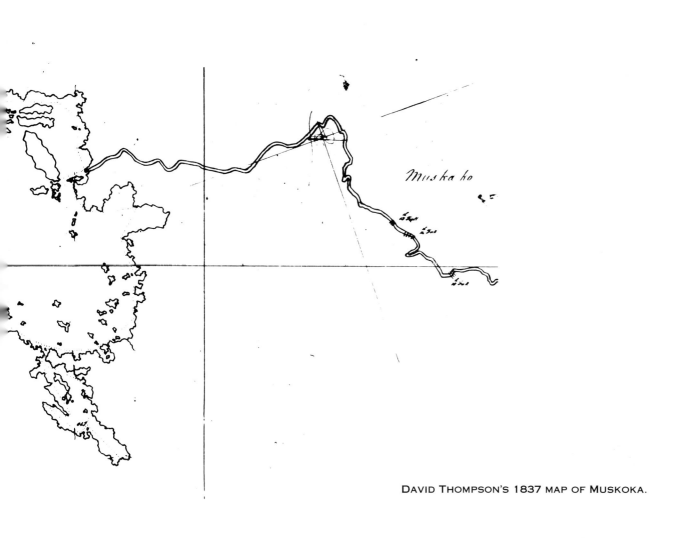

DAVID THOMPSON'S 1837 MAP OF MUSKOKA.

10:38AM and surveyed a fine lake, bordered to the water frequently with fine hardwoods and scarce brown subsoil, to near noon, when we put ashore and I observed for latitude, double meridian altitude of the sun [on Edith Island] . . . ther[mometer] +74. Examined the lower end of an island as per map, set off. A superstition prevails that a crooked knife, however keen it may cut when set of a handle of wood, will not cut well if handled with deer's horn and that the horn acts upon the edge of the knife as tobacco does. At 3:40PM, at a small fall [at the upper rock-cut, Joseph River] of the same river. Descent about 18 in, about 50 ft wide with from 4 to 8 in. of water over a smooth rock of grey sienite. Handed the canoe up it. The CP is on the left of a few feet, say 4 or 5 yards into still water and to a lake, which we surveyed on the left and the bays seemed to bring us almost back to the 1st fall. At 6PM, we camped on an islet of small yellow fir, clean and tall, as most of the firs are, but only 4 to 10 inches diameter [Sunset Island]. A WNW wind has blown fresh since noon, clear and cool. So far the whole of this lake appears surrounded by good land and fine hardwoods often to the water edge, especially all the bays. The points as usual have a border of rock and woods of yellow fir with some birch, red oak &c &c, but the border is not wide, 50 to 100 yards or so. A few musketoes.

AUGUST 19, SATURDAY. A very fine calm night and morning. At 6:20AM set off. At 7:08AM came to a CP of a good path of hare and otters up a steep bank across an isthmus of this great point [Port Sandfield], a large arm of this lake we left on the left[hand side] this morning, the CP is N20E 60 yards [across] it and appears to lead parallel to the line of survey of this morning, fine hardwoods all along it. At 7¼ AM put ashore to breakfast and examined the land. As usual a border of rock and yellow fir, then birch then maple &c &c. Vegetable mould and a warm sandy brown clay or light brown some places appears a brown yellow, but all support a fine healthy vegetation. At 8:35AM set off. At noon observed for latitude, double meridian altitude of the sun LL 114°.30'.0", error +6.20" +60. At 1:07PM put ashore and dined. Speared 5 bass, saw many to day, but they will not take bait such as we have, a bit of salt pork. At 6PM, put up on an islet where Indians have formerly been [Turtle Island]. A very fine day, thank God, and as usual well employed. The men foolishly took only 2 days provisions of pork. +60.

AUGUST 20TH, SUNDAY. +56, calm and clear. Observed for longitude and time. Clouds came on but afterwards cleared. Set off to examine the appearance of two brooks

in the bay before us. Found they both came from the same lake. The brook on the left [in Portage Bay} has a good short CP of about N70W 100 yards, about 3 to 4 yards wide, but blocked up with fallen wood, to a fine lake bearing N60W 1½ m, as per sketch. Returned and went to examine the brook on the right bay [Smith Bay]. It is about 8 yards across from 6 to 8 inches deep, current about ½ m per hour, but blocked up with fallen wood and has no CP. It comes from the same lake with the other brook and has a fall of 18 or 24 in. near the lake, about 300 yards to the lake. The grey sienite is in strata, easy to be raised and a lock made. But as the waters of this river are already so far lost and the land about the lake so far as we could see had not a favourable appearance, I did not think it worth while to survey any further, especially as I was informed by Paul la Ronde, a native of this country, that a route by a chain of lakes &c with long C Places led to the Beaver Lake and the route to be the same lake by the main river with much more water but longer. I therefore returned to the island. Observed for latitude, double meridian altitude of the sun . . . +74, all very good. Set off, course S85E, held on the survey to 6:10PM to the end of course S10W where not finding a place to camp, we returned about 400 yards and camped on smooth rocks [see map]. A very fine day and evening. SEly wind at times a little fresh. The rock of today has changed to hard quartz and sienite with strata from 6 in to 8 ft, with steps and perpendicular walls like basalt, rising 20 to 50 ft above the lake, in many places a curious appearance. Took specimens in 5 places as per map &c. All has a most barren appearance, a scanty growth of yellow fir, but within is the same good land and hardwood forests and soil, though in places removed further back. Much had been formerly burnt and have young woods with spins and small w birch &c &c. At 8:30PM, heavy gusts of wind and showers of rain from the westward which ceased in the night. +70.

AUGUST 21ST, MONDAY. +68, cloudy and calm. Put up the specimens, breakfasted and at 7:40AM set off and continued the survey. At noon observed for latitude, double meridian altitude of the sun . . . +70. At 12:43PM, at the 2nd fall [Joseph River], handed down the canoe &c and the men's provisions being out, set off for the 1st CP where we left the cargo. On the way detained about ½ hour with rain and the men dined on soup and biscuit. At 3:30PM arrived at the 1st CP [Port Carling] for the last ½ hour a heavy storm of wind and rain. We got all wet when we arrived at the CP, it was some time before we could camp for the violence of the weather from the south. By 5PM, the weather changed to gusts of wind and showers of rain, some very heavy, which continued all night. +56. Men 1 box of pork.

AUGUST 22ND, TUESDAY. Night and morning of bad

MUSKOKA LAKE.

weather, wind a heavy gale from WSW, ther. +52 with showers of rain which mostly ceased about 9AM, but the wind high and cloudy weather continuing. Writing my journal, the courses &c &c. The rain soon returned and continued all day. Bad weather, the night more moderate. 2PM +56, 9PM +52.

AUGUST 23RD, WEDNESDAY. 5AM +53, wind North and veering NEward 1/4, dark, cloudy, threatening weather. Examined the provisions, a box of biscuit had got partly wet and so mouldy that we had to throw away about half of it, supposed to have got wet in the rain coming across the Nottawasauga CP on the waggon. Put up the specimens &c. The weather clearing up a little at 8:45AM set off and went to the place of the Deer's Horns [Greenridge Point] and surveyed the right side of the lake. Bad weather now detained us to 9³/4 AM, set off and held on. At 12:30PM dined &c. Set off and held on against a WNW wind to 6PM, when we camped upon a point of rocks, bad but no better in view. We have come about 2 miles along a bank of rocks which rise about 180 ft in height above the level of the lake where highest, and come to the lake in rude slopes. Cold chilly day, suffered from it. Killed 2 young stock ducks. All the mainland and some of the islands good hardwood and good land, but almost every where the lake &c is bordered by rude rocks and firs with a few red oak and aspins &c. The last 2 miles have been burnt some years ago and have young woods of fir and aspins. At 6:05PM camped [near north entrance to Skeleton Bay]. Cloudy day and night, 2PM +58, 9PM +56.

AUGUST 24, THURSDAY. +55, wind NW 1/2, cloudy. At 5:55AM set off and held on all day. At dinner some showers of rain. At 5:30PM camped [at Kingsett Point]. We are now close on what has been surveyed and few places on which we can camp. At breakfast took specimens, the same hard rocks prevail every where and show no regular dip. The land, except the points, very good, strong soil and fine hardwoods. A moderate NW wind all day, cloudy mostly. 2PM +60, 9PM +56.

AUGUST 25, FRIDAY. +53. A fine calm night and clear morning. Light airs from eastward. At 5:41AM set off course S30E to a point we came to on the 1st survey of this lake [Elarton Point] and we now follow on to the place of observation and put ashore for fog, we could not see. Breakfasted. At 7:30AM cleared and we set off and surveyed to the point of Deer's Horns and proceeded to the CP, the weather fine but light thin clouds did not allow me to observe for longitude. At 9AM arrived at the CP and found all well. Took the canoe down the rapids, loaded with *every thing and at 9:32AM set off. Met 2 Indians, very old man and a sick boy. They are on their way to the 2nd lake. Held on the survey to the islet on which we camped the first day from the 12th fall [Charybdis Island]. Dined and set off for the upper river at 1:30PM. At about 1½ miles from this mouth of the upper river, camped at 5:06PM [near St Elmo] as there is no camping for some distance up the river. Many flies. A steady SE wind all day and cloudy weather but fine for work. +68, 9PM +62. Took specimens of quartz &c.*

AUGUST 26, SATURDAY. Rained in the night in showers, SbE wind, dark cloudy weather, wind fresh, ther. +59. Early, a few showers. At 8:06AM ventured to set off to the river [Muskoka River]. At 8:23AM entered the river, about 50 yards across, appears very fine, deep alluvial soils with fine hardwoods, very fine meadows . . . examined a marked line which crossed the river, the line runs N10W and S10E, blazed trees on both sides the line &c, course cont'd . . . to the forks. The right fork having great body of water and by a strong rush of current cuts across the left fork, course up the right fork [south branch of the Muskoka River] . . . a kind of channel goes off on the left . . . end of course a marked line of blazed trees cross the river. Examined it on the left, it leads up a high bank of earth among fir a picket set, but no writing on it. The direction of this line appears N20W and S20E. The bank is about 50 ft high, it then descends to rise another bank still higher. All along steady current at 1½ m per hour, our rate 100 yards per minute, South wind, dark cloudy weather . . . current about 2 miles per hour. Land rising on left and right with firs . . . to a rapid . . . to a rapid from S70E 300 yards, heard a fall. Land rising in both sides with firs &c . . . Course up the rapid S70E about 1 ft descent, went up on the left with the line, across 60 yards. The rapid about 30 yards. This brought us in view of a high fall, S70E 300 yards to right point, S45E 500 yards to the foot of the fall at ½ PM on the right side in still water. Paul la Ronde now finds that it was the branch of this river that we left to day, up which he once passed a few years ago in the winter. Carried all over by 3:30PM, we had to clear the path for the canoe. The path is over very uneven stony and rocky ground, roots of trees and wet places from small springs and high at times on the right of the path, which leads as near the fall as possible. This fall rushes down a great height thro' a rift or crevice in the rocks, in places very narrow. The rock is sienite in thin layers of about 2 to 6 in, dips about N20W at an angle of about 20° to 30° below the horizon. Appears easy to work. From the drift wood piled at the upper end, it appears the water at times rises about 7 to 8 ft perpendicular above its present level. A considerable body of water forms this fall. Very dark weather with showers of rain, we camped. The CP is 300

yards, very uneven and the fall descends about 122 feet perpendicular, the general course of CP S70E or so . . . About the middle of this CP, near the edge of the fall is a hemlock tree marked on four sides, one blank, 2nd, William Hawkins D.S.; 3rd, 20th August 1835, God Save the King, and a line not readable. The 4th side 23 miles NE corner of Mara. This line come from S10 E to N10W. 2PM +72, 9PM +62, dark cloudy weather. Wind SbE.

To Thompson, Muskoka seemed a barren place, and compared to the lands in the Northwest, it was. Even a bird's song was an event worth recording in his daily journal. From a fur trader's point of view, there was little point in establishing a trading post—Muskoka was essentially trapped out. The scarcity of beaver was thanks to the introduction of steel traps and a new bait called castorum in the mid-1790s. The combination of the two was so successful that the Iroquois, Algonquin, and Nipissing Indians virtually eliminated the beaver from their lands. With no means left to procure the goods they needed for trade, they began to migrate to western Canada, some stopping around Lake Winnipeg, others continuing to the foothills of the Rocky Mountains and the Peace River district along the Saskatchewan River in pursuit of beaver skins.

The impact of the new traps and bait was not lost on native elders. Indeed, in this partially published account of his years in the West from 1784 to 1812, Thompson relates what an old Indian told him during his survey of the area just west of Lake Winnipeg:

"We are now killing the beaver without labour, we are now rich, but [shall] soon be poor, for when the beaver are destroyed, we have nothing to depend on to purchase what we want for our families, strangers now run over our country with their iron traps, and we, and they, will soon be poor."

Thompson's own observations continue:

The Nepissings, the Algonquins and Iroquois Indians having exhausted their own countries, now spread themselves over these countries, and as they destroyed the beaver, moved forwards to the northward and westward. The Natives, the Nahathaways [Cree], did not in the least molest them; the Chipaways [Ojibwa] and other tribes made use of the traps of steel and of the castorum.

For several years all these Indians were rich, the women and children, as well as the men, were covered in silver brooches, ear rings, wampum, beads and other trinkets. Their mantles were of fine scarlet cloth, and all was finery and dress. The canoes of the furr traders were loaded with packs of beaver, the abundance of the article lowered the

BALA FALLS, WATERCOLOUR, PAM TURNER-WONG.

48

London prices. Every intelligent man saw poverty that would follow the destruction of the beaver, but there were no chiefs to control it; all was perfect liberty and equality. Four years afterwards [1801] almost the whole of these extensive countries were denuded of beaver, the Natives became poor, and with difficulty procured the first necessaries of life, and in this state they remain, and probably forever. A worn out field may be manured, and again made fertile, but the beaver, once destroyed, cannot be replaced; they were once the gold coin of the country, with which all the necessaries of life were purchased.

As for the annual sales of beaver furs to the European market, Thompson makes no bones about his position on the matter:

It is a work worth while for some person curious in these matters, to examine the sales, but this properly belongs to some intelligent gentleman of New York who will not disdain to examine how many millions of these animals have been destroyed for the sake of their furrs. This animal, once so very numerous, it is now being eradicated from this continent.

Thompson's comments in his journals about the poor state of fishing may seem puzzling, since the region later became a magnet for anglers, and many praised its fine fishing. Again, though, Thompson thinks like a trader. Before a post could be built, the area had to have a secure food source. For the traders living on the Canadian shield and in the forests, whitefish was the mainstay of the winter diet, so an abundance of fish was crucial for the post's survival; so was an abundance of game, but to a lesser degree. To procure enough fish for the winter, nets similar to the one Thompson had were placed across suitable bays; these were checked twice a day and mended and cleaned every two weeks. When the fish stocks were exhausted, the post was abandoned, and the trader moved on to a more hospitable place. The scarcity of whitefish Thompson reported, though, is a result of the greater depths and rocky bottoms of Muskoka lakes—whitefish are partial to shallower and softer-bottomed lakes.

The map he produced to accompany his report appears somewhat distorted; many of the islands are not recorded or have shapes that in no way resemble their actual shapes. The purpose of his survey, though, was not to provide a map for settlement, but to determine the location and elevation of the highest point of land between the Ottawa River and Georgian Bay. This may explain why Thompson's survey ended up buried in a government file. His official report to his superiors outlines only the distances between falls and carrying places, the elevations gained to the height of land and lost to the Ottawa River. None of his observations about the state of the land and its suitability for agriculture was mentioned. Only when Thompson was searching for survey work in 1842 and 1843 did he outline to the governor general that "there is a very interesting section of Canada almost unknown yet deserving attention from the goodness of the land and its immense water powers for every purpose useful to the future inhabitants, on which section at present there is not one cottage." In typical bureaucratic fashion, it took the government almost 20 years to look into the matter.

After this survey work in Muskoka, Thompson took up the issue of the Oregon territory. In 1846 the British government completely ignored Canada's historic claim to the territory and appeased the Americans by settling on the 49th parallel as the international boundary. Thompson, who had spent six years in the area and single-handedly mapped the entire region, was outraged at the decision and lobbied hard to reverse the decision. Also, to support his family, he began writing his memoirs. He'd hoped to publish them in two or three volumes, but by 1850, failing eyesight and ill health forced him to abandon the project. He spent the remaining years of his life in hard times, although not in the abject poverty some historians put forward. He died in 1857 and was buried in an unmarked grave on Mount Royal; his wife of 58 years survived him by three months and lies at his side. A monument now marks the site, erected in 1927 by the great Canadian historian and the first editor of a portion of Thompson's memoirs, J. B. Tyrrell, in tribute to Thompson's outstanding efforts to unroll the map of Canada. ▷

4

IN THE FOOTSTEPS OF THE MAPMAKERS

Explorers and Surveyors

BY SUSAN PRYKE

We will not cease from exploration
And the end of all our exploring
Will be to arrive where we started
And know the place for the first time
— T. S. Eliot

MUSKOKA'S TERRAIN makes explorers of every weekend hiker. You feel it in your calf muscles when you heft yourself up a particularly steep incline. You taste it in the wintergreen berries picked along the way—that chalky, chewing-gum taste that reminds you of childhood hikes, when your father showed you how to tell the safe red berries from the poisonous ones.

You walk until you reach one of those impenetrable hemlock swamps, where the sunlight never reaches the ground. Just when you can't imagine going farther, you find a square surveyor stake, grey with age and lichen—proof that someone had once gone farther . . .

EARLY EXPLORATIONS

It took explorers a long time to discover Muskoka, yet they danced around its edges for almost two centuries. The native people and fur traders who crossed the district in the early years left little evidence of their comings and goings. The only maps they used were in their heads.

The very first European to venture this far west was a young Frenchman named Etienne Brûlé. The year was 1610 and he was on orders from Samuel de Champlain to cement France's alliance with the Hurons. The trip took Brûlé to Huronia, just south of Muskoka. Champlain himself came this way in 1615, again circling Muskoka, via the Mattawa and French rivers, then heading south along the shores of Georgian Bay.

While the French made no official forays into Muskoka, they knew of the extensive system of lakes. Two early maps, the 1656 map by Sanson—mapmaker to the French king—and the 1657 *Novae Franciae Accurata Delineatio*, show lakes in the Muskoka region. René Robert Cavalier Sieur de la Salle, better known for charting the Mississippi from its headwaters to the Gulf of Mexico, paddled the Severn River to Georgian Bay in 1680.

In the minds of the Europeans, Muskoka had grown from a blank area on the map to one with a series of interconnected lakes. Dr. John Mitchell's 1755 map of the British and French dominions in North America shows Muskoka sprinkled with amoebalike shapes that somewhat resemble lakes Muskoka, Rosseau, and Joseph.

The French regime ended in 1763 with the Treaty of Paris, which ceded Canada to the British. The new regime took little interest in the northern wilderness until hostilities with their American neighbours—the War of 1812—demonstrated the value of having an alternate water route to Georgian Bay. Lakes Ontario and Erie were, at times, a little too close to the American border for comfort.

In 1819 the British, determined to link up existing waterways with a series of canals, sent Lieutenant Joseph Portlock of the Royal Engineers to explore the Severn River. He travelled all the way to Georgian Bay and reported—wrongly as it turned out—that the soil was good for growing crops.

The first recorded exploration of Muskoka happened almost by accident. Lieutenant Henry Briscoe, also of the Royal Engineers, had orders to explore the Talbot River in 1826, but his guides never showed up. So he hired a man who took him to a large river farther north. That large river turned out to be the Muskoka.

He journeyed up the Severn River, across Morrison Creek to Muldrew Lake, and then overland to Lake Muskoka, landing about where the Gravenhurst wharf is today. His superiors weren't happy with his efforts, however. The Duke of Wellington, whose idea it had been to explore the inland waterways, accused Briscoe of wandering over the country and reporting on any old thing he felt like, "excepting what they were sent to examine and report upon."

Commerce was behind the second documented excursion into Muskoka. Entrepreneur Charles Shirreff, of Fitzroy Harbour on the Ottawa River, saw the lumbering

HUNDREDS OF MUSKOKA TREASURES ARE ON DISPLAY AT THE MUSKOKA LAKES MUSEUM IN PORT CARLING, INCLUDING FIRST EDITIONS OF CAPTAIN JOHN ROGERS'S MAPS.

51

potential of Muskoka, but reckoned they'd need people to work in the lumber camps and a reliable way to get the logs to the market.

In the autumn of 1829, he sent his son, Alexander, to see if a water route could be set up between Georgian Bay and the Ottawa River, and to judge the land's suitability for settlement. Alexander gave the first good description of Muskoka:

The singular facilities which this plain country possesses for water communication must be evident. Were there any possibility of leading a population into it, the channels and basins of still water, intersecting in every direction, might quickly be completed into a ramification of waterways, which for general utility and natural beauty could scarcely find a parallel. Sufficiently deep and expansive for the largest steamboat and yet too small, or too well sheltered by the bold shores, to be dangerous for the smallest skiff.

But without some main line of navigation from the inhabited parts of Canada, this pleasant and commodious region must, for obvious reasons, remain a desert.

Alexander Shirreff came to Muskoka from the east, following the Oxtongue, South Muskoka, and Musquash rivers all the way to Georgian Bay. He is the first explorer to record the name Muskoka, citing the traders as the originators of the name, after an Indian chief who hunted in the area. Ojibwa Chief Mesqua Ukee, or Musquakie, lived at the Narrows, near Orillia, but claimed all the land in Muskoka as his hunting ground.

EARLY SURVEYORS

Military men, surveyors, and local personalities all had parts to play in plotting the lines of longitude and latitude that slice through Muskoka today. Their exploits bear little resemblance to the swashbuckling adventures of the explorers you may recall from your grade-school history books—remember Radisson and Groseilliers, La Verendrye, Joliet and Marquette?

Far from searching for a passage to India, they had the arduous task of charting straight lines across land that was forever throwing up impassable walls of rock or presenting dense mosquito-and-blackfly-infested swamps.

Vernon Wadsworth, who accompanied John S. Dennis on his survey of Muskoka from 1860 to 1865, made these observations in his journal:

The blackflies and mosquitoes now made their appearance

and in such swarms that we were badly bitten by them. I never saw such swarms of flies in all my six years' experience in the woods.

In 1835 Lieutenant John Carthew directed a survey north from Lake Couchiching, through Muskoka (crossing Skeleton Lake), and culminating in what is now Parry Sound District. The line his group plotted was called the Hawkins line, after William Hawkins, one of the surveyors.

The group nearly perished at the aptly named Distress River, however, at the point where it joins the Magnetawan River. Years later, Vernon Wadsworth told the story in his journal:

[Distress River] was rightly named for the Carthew party reached there with no provisions, expecting to receive them from the Georgian Bay, 60 miles distant, by canoes passing up the Magnetawan River.

The provisions never arrived and the surveying party abandoned their belongings and camp equipment and surveying instruments and travelled through the forest to try to reach the Georgian Bay, as they supposed they would meet with the Indians there who would rescue them from starvation.

I later met an Indian at Nascoutaing and he informed me that the Carthew party, nearly dead from starvation and fatigue, had reached the Georgian Bay near their village and by a great chance they were discovered and brought to the village where they fed them carefully with soup from deer meat at first and then with stronger food until they were well enough to be taken by canoe to Penetanguishene where at the time there was a small British garrison.

And so the group lived to see the completion of the first north-south survey line in Muskoka—the line from which all others were drawn. When Carthew returned from Georgian Bay, he passed through Lake Rosseau, and was the first to mention the lake by its name.

While Carthew led the north-south survey team, his associate, geologist Frederick Baddeley, explored the South Muskoka River from Purbrook down and took a side trip up the North Muskoka as far as Bracebridge Falls—the first recorded visit to that site.

In 1860 surveyor John Dennis declared that he'd discovered Lake Joseph. He hadn't. For, unknown to him—and practically everyone else at the time—explorer/surveyor David Thompson had charted its shores more than 20 years before.

Possibly the greatest explorer to jot down the longitude and latitude of locations in Muskoka, Thompson is legendary. His name evokes images of rivalries between the Hudson's Bay Company and North West Company to

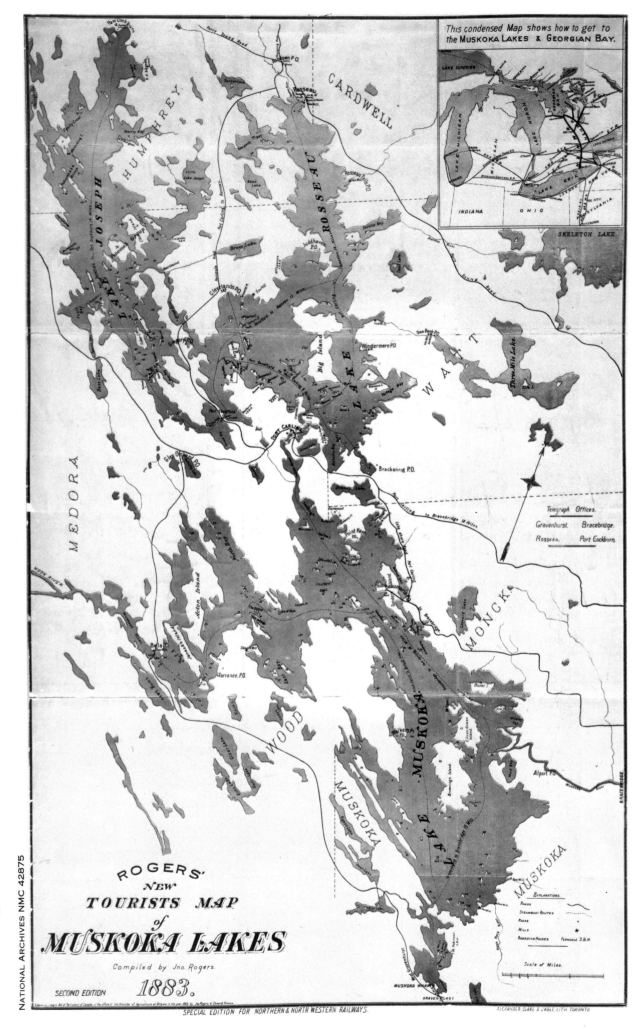

54

This condensed Map shows how to get to
the MUSKOKA LAKES & GEORGIAN BAY.

SKELETON LAKE

Telegraph Offices.
Gravenhurst.   Bracebridge.
Rosseau.   Port Cockburn.

ROGERS'
NEW
TOURISTS MAP
of
MUSKOKA LAKES

Compiled by Jno. Rogers.
1883.

SECOND EDITION

Explanations.
Roads
Steamboat Routes
Rocks
Mills
Boarding Houses   Ferndale S.B.H.

Scale of Miles.

SPECIAL EDITION FOR NORTHERN & NORTH WESTERN RAILWAYS.   ALEXANDER, CLARE & CABLE, LITH. TORONTO.

claim land in Canada's West, for he mapped thousands of miles of it for the North West Company. His efforts were so painstaking that his maps became the basis of all future maps.

One of his least-known exploits was his survey of the Muskoka River in 1837, when he journeyed from Georgian Bay to the Oxtongue River, spending time on all three Muskoka Lakes and Lake of Bays. His was the last of the "canal" expeditions and the best. He liked the look of the land and was impressed with the waterfalls as possible mill sites. He suggested immediate and further surveys.

For some reason, Thompson's fine maps and accounts of the area seemed to disappear for decades, buried perhaps in a government file by some judicious clerk. Or maybe the problem was that the federal capital was moved a number of times, or that Thompson was a bit of a renegade and did not fit in the polite circles of society.

At any rate, this led surveyor John Dennis to think he'd discovered Lake Joseph, which he named after his father, Joseph. There's a double irony here because the lake had been identified and regularly visited in the 1830s by Jean-Baptiste Rousseau, a fur trader from Penetanguishene who had named it after *his* father, also Joseph. (Lake Rosseau, too, is named for Joseph Rousseau.)

Among other assignments, Dennis had the job of locating a harbour on Georgian Bay (the spot he chose became Parry Sound) and to survey a road to link that Harbour with the Muskoka Road at South Falls. Before he did that, however, he travelled the Muskoka lakes to accurately position them.

His men fought their way through the bush, packing 100-pound sacks of supplies. For the most part, they ate salt pork, supplemented with bear, porcupine, and sea-gull eggs.

When equipment broke, they fashioned replacements using only axes as tools. A man who could fix things was a great asset. John Dennis once remarked: "A good contriver is better than a great eater."

The job demanded stamina and ingenuity. Of the crew, Wadsworth wrote:

They were great axe men, packmen and canoe-men, and prided themselves on their walking powers.

I have known them to walk or run between daylight and dark on their journeys on the ice of the Georgian Bay, 60 to 80 miles, and then dance all night, and if occasion required they could do without food for long periods and travel with heavy loads.

I have seen two men I often had on those surveys, William Parling and Cozac Cote, each carry 200 pounds of flour or bacon a measured mile on snowshoes breaking their tracks and without resting.

Wadsworth was just 16 years old when he accompanied the survey party. His mentor, Dennis, went on to became the surveyor-general of Canada and deputy minister of the interior.

John Dennis's survey was commissioned because, in the late 1850s, government officials finally began giving serious thought to opening Muskoka for settlement. The idea got a boost when the district's parliamentary representative, Angus Morrison, explored the lakes around Gravenhurst. On the strength of his enthusiastic report, the government started to build the Muskoka Road, one of many so-called colonization roads, in 1858.

"Road" is perhaps too generous a term for this first pathway into the forest. It was little more than a blazed trail, with rocks and stumps cluttering the way. No wonder Muskoka's early settlers chose travel by water over land transportation. The creation of a good, reliable steamboat line probably did more to boost settlement in Muskoka than anything else.

The man who created the Muskoka Navigation Company, A. P. Cockburn, studied the waterways from his canoe in 1865. He was sufficiently impressed to put a steamboat on the lakes the following year.

MAPPING THE LAKES

Once public transportation was available, the lakes began attracting both settlers and tourists alike. It was at this time that Muskoka's great mapmaker arrived on the scene—and he wasn't supposed to come here at all!

Captain John Rogers had Hamilton in mind when he set off from England in 1871. But he met a couple aboard the ship who told him such wonderful stories about Muskoka that he changed his plans and went with them. He had no money to speak of, just a willingness to try new things. He helped clear land for settlers when he first arrived in Port Sandfield.

After a year and a half, he went to Toronto to work for a book distributor, but he kept up his ties with Muskoka—mainly through his relationship with the Cox family, where he boarded (he eventually married one of the Cox girls, Edith May). For on Rogers's reports, Enoch Cox rented property in Muskoka, then later built Prospect House on land he'd purchased at The Cut in Port Sandfield.

Rogers persuaded a Chicago publishing company to publish the *Guide Book and Atlas of Muskoka and Parry Sound Districts*. In mapping the district, he tramped all across Muskoka, pinpointing churches, schools, and settler's locations. He marked each jog in the road, each noteworthy creek and river, sometimes walking 40 miles a day. After the book was printed, Rogers had the job of selling it.

His maps of the lakes, which he also published and sold, survive to this day, proudly hung with regatta trophies and bits of driftwood in cottages across Muskoka.

07 Brig on the Shadow River   On Muskoka Line

Seymour Penson, who did the sketches for the 1879 atlas, said Rogers was a young good-looking lad when he arrived in Port Sandfield, and one who had a fund of knowledge on every subject. And well he might have. Before coming to Canada, Rogers had worked for the railway, studied law, then joined a London firm that specialized in building diving and condensing machines.

His expertise in distilling seawater took him to Arabia and the east coast of Africa. Before coming to Canada, he'd spent three months as the engineer on a clipper ship.

Penson also said: "Certain places seem to fit certain natures, and Muskoka certainly suited John Rogers. The freedom from restraint; the ever-changing climate, with just enough of harshness to be piquant; the natural beauty of the place and the abundance of material for scientific experimenting . . . all these things and many others must have appealed strongly to a man like John Rogers, and they threw over him a spell that has never been broken, for he is chained to the place to this day, and is likely to be for the rest of his days."

John Rogers and Edith May settled on Hemlock Point, Lake Joseph, and later moved to a spot on the Peninsula Road, just north of Port Sandfield. His second home on this site—Birchwood—is still standing, and has been the home of his grandson Maurice.

Today, Rogers's atlas is a godsend to every recreational explorer, who strikes out from the back door, climbs the humps of rock, and crosses deep ravines. You return wanting to know who strung the fence lines now embedded in the bark of old trees (surely cows couldn't have gone this far afield!) and who built the foundations that have left rectangular scars on the land.

The bush is full of old roads that once went somewhere, and old survey pegs that prove yours aren't the first feet sunk in sphagnum in this very spot.

So you push on, watching for telltale slash marks on tree bark, crouching and crawling your way through the undergrowth. Ahead is a view you've never seen before, across the lake, over the islands, to the horizon piled high with clouds. The effort has been well worthwhile. ▷

DATES OF TOWNSHIP SURVEYS

1857

John Ryan surveyed Macaulay Township. The name honours Chief Justice John B. Macaulay, who fought in the War of 1812 and was prominent in provincial public affairs.

Charles Rankin of Owen Sound surveyed Muskoka Township, which is named for Chief Mesqua Ukee.

1864

W. H. Deane surveyed Monck township. Viscount Stanley Monck was Governor General of Canada.

1865

Thomas Webb Nash surveyed Watt Township, which takes its name from James Watt, the inventor of the steam engine.

1866

T. A. Baldwin completed the survey of Cardwell Township. Viscount Cardwell, secretary of state for the United Kingdom, assisted in bringing about Confederation in 1867.

1869

Thomas Byrne surveyed Medora Township, the only township named after a woman. She was Medora Cameron, niece of Stephen Richards, commissioner of Crown lands.

1870

A. B. Scott surveyed a portion of Wood Township, named for Edmund B. Wood, a provincial treasurer. The township is the only one where the concessions are numbered north to south, rather than south to north.

1877

James K. McLean completed the survey of Wood Township.

57

ANOTHER IN THE JAMES ESSON SERIES SHOWING EARLY ROAD AND BRIDGE CONSTRUCTION. LITTLE WONDER PEOPLE PREFERRED TO ROW.

PORT CARLING MUSEUM, WATERCOLOUR, LYNN HAGEY.

5

THE PROMISED LAND

Early Settlers

BY PAUL KING

ON A MAP OF CANADA, Muskoka is a mere dot. It covers barely one-third of one per cent of Ontario. Much of it is water. Within its 1585 square miles are 1600 lakes and 17 rivers.

And much of the rest, as the first settlers found, is rock.

Which is why, within a century, Muskoka's evolution from farmland to cottage country was inevitable. For over the rock stretched a carpet of scenic splendour. It was a land created not for struggle but serenity—and escape from city life. If its granite terrain proved hostile to farmers, it could still provide hospitality.

And, since the building of Muskoka's first inn at the hamlet of Severn Bridge by shrewd Irish settlers in 1860, it has.

The American Revolution, which saw a colonial victory in 1783, brought a surge of United Empire Loyalists into Upper Canada. But it wasn't until the War of 1812 that the British government was spurred into conducting surveys of its northland. The waterways leading to and through Muskoka became of vital interest to statesmen, traders, and soldiers alike. Not only was a route needed between the Ottawa River and Georgian Bay for troops and supplies, which would keep them out of reach of American military forces, but land was needed for settlers.

Along with the surge of United Empire Loyalists, Upper Canada of the early 1800s saw an influx of British, German, and Dutch immigrants, which swelled its population to 150,000 by 1824. Yet roads were dreadful, and nearly 15 per cent of the prime land was reserved for Protestant clergy and the Crown. The anger fomenting at provincial administrators finally erupted with the Upper Canada Rebellion of 1837.

A vastly unamused Queen Victoria dispatched Lord Durham to investigate the Upper Canada turmoil. He arrived to find that the population had swollen to 400,000 and that it appeared next to impossible for a person with no influence to obtain public land. And so, the surveying of new land for settlements began in earnest.

But the survey reports on Muskoka were, for the most part, negative. The land, with its rocky terrain, was declared unfit for agriculture, and one report even suggested that the government not incur further expenses trying to divide it into townships and farm lots. No potential settler, alerted to these reports, could fail to be alarmed.

Yet the legislative assembly paid the reports little heed. It was already committed to colonizing the Ottawa-Huron Tract, as the region between the Ottawa River and Georgian Bay was then called. With emigration increasing to the U.S. and the prairies controlled by the Hudson's Bay Company, Upper Canada needed a new frontier—and the only land available lay north. After all, the region was blanketed by forest, and beneath tall timber had to lie rich soil. All that was needed now were roads to get there.

In 1850 the government cajoled the Ojibwas into ceding most of the Ottawa-Huron Tract, and began to build the famous colonization roads. Not surprisingly problems cropped up with every mile. Straight lines were impossible. Lakes, rivers, and rock cliffs caused massive detours. Waterways needed bridges. Swamps required causeways.

At first the work was done by contract. But contractors often bid so low they either went broke or built only rutted lanes of mud. Many roads were soon ploughed into quagmire by wagonloads of timber, while numerous bridges and causeways were accidentally burned by settlers clearing their land. When the government finally took on the job of building roads itself, wages were so low—99 cents a day—that workers were hard to find. And although all settlers were required to keep finished roads in repair, few bothered.

Nevertheless, the routes snaked slowly northward. Costing less than $200 a mile, many were the so-called corduroy roads, made of split trees laid side by side with the flat surfaces down. But during spring runoffs, the logs often floated away.

Still, the major northern artery, the Muskoka Road, did fulfil the dream of its planners—and determined the direction of traffic and the location of Muskoka's towns. It began in Washago in 1858, with boats from Orillia delivering workmen and supplies. One year later, the first location tickets were issued for lands along its route, accompanied by the optimistic notice: "From [the northern tip of] Lake Couchiching to the Great Falls of Muskoka—a distance of 21 miles—all streams have been bridged and the road has been levelled."

In fact, the road was opened only to Gravenhurst and was so rough that no more than 800 pounds could be hauled along its surface. Nevertheless, scores of road workers stopped off at Irishman Hugh Dillon's Severn Bridge inn, making the Dillons not only Muskoka's first homesteaders, but its first commercial hosts.

By 1863 the falls in Bracebridge were finally bridged, with the road stretching a further 24 miles to the present site of Huntsville. Then, as settlers streamed in through the following decade, new access roads were slashed through virgin forests where sunlight seldom reached the soil. Muskoka's wilderness was becoming accessible.

Before the Ojibwas ceded their massive Ottawa-Huron Tract to the government, it seemed likely to be taken over by a private land company. In the early 1830s various groups, often with the same officers, pressured the British government into granting them land. While the motives of most were greed, their arguments were compelling: unemployment and poverty in Ireland and the British Isles; the despair of immigrants arriving homeless in a new land; the flow of emigrants from Upper Canada to the United States, where wages were higher and land cheaper; the necessity of a northern route made safe by settlers.

Although no one knew where the actual route would run, or the speed with which it could be developed, it looked as if the requested land grant would be made. But in 1835 Lord Aberdeen advised London that it was "not expedient to establish any new Land Company whatever in Canada." And there the matter rested for nearly 25 years.

During that period, a number of traders lived in Muskoka; traces of cabins with stone fireplaces were later discovered on the Muskoka River, and on Yoho Island and Chief's Island in Lake Joseph. The enormous house with the collapsed roof found on Yoho is believed to have been built by a prominent fur merchant named William B. Robinson, who bartered with Indians near Midland. Robinson's Montreal bookkeeper, who moved to Penetanguishene in 1825, was Jean-Baptiste Rousseau—from whom Lake Rosseau got its name.

Yet the northland seemed mainly forgotten until 1853. In that year, when the City of Toronto completed a railway up Yonge Street to Lake Simcoe, the government passed its Public Lands Act, which provided for the sale of 100-acre land lots in Muskoka at fixed prices, plus free grants to settlers in the vicinity of a public road—if they promised to keep it repaired.

Five years later, land in a number of townships was up for sale. Within three months an amazing 54 location tickets had been issued along the Severn and Muskoka roads.

When the agent R. J. Oliver gleefully reported that some settlers were not only pleading for postal services but planning to buy extra Crown land behind their lots to build churches and schools, the euphoric government launched a massive campaign to lure more settlers.

Problems swiftly developed. Immigrant greenhorns who'd never handled an axe before were suddenly required to cut forests, build flat-roofed, moss-chinked log shanties without windows or fireplaces, excavate massive boulders, till ground with shared oxen, fight backflies and bitter winters, sleep fully dressed in overcoats, and walk as far as Barrie for a sack of flour. For in the bush there were no stores, no horses, no mail, and no doctors. While some townships grew, others stagnated. Some speculators bought land, stripped its timber, then abandoned it. Many settlers who bought land on instalments had no way to pay.

Finally the council of Simcoe County—to which the Muskoka Township had been added—stepped in. In 1865 it warned the governor general that the way in which the lands were being sold "retards the progress and settlement of the country." The council urged the giving of free land under set conditions to encourage rapid settlement and an increase in the number of taxpayers; it also suggested that speculators forfeit their land if payment was in arrears.

As a result, the following year the first session of Ontario's new parliament passed the Free Grants and Homestead Act, which enabled the lieutenant-governor to "appropriate any Public Lands considered suitable for settlement and cultivation as Free Grants to actual settlers."

Greeted with mass approval—except by settlers who had already bought land and still owed payment—the act said any settler 18 or older could select 100 acres in a surveyed township; any family head could select 200 acres; and extra land would be given to compensate for rocky sections.

Strict conditions were attached. Applicants had to swear they believed the land was suitable for settlement and cultivation, and would not be used for lumbering or mining. Settlers were required to: have 15 acres under cultivation within five years, of which two acres had to be cultivated annually; build a house fit for habitation that was at least 16 by 20 feet; and live on the land for a minimum of five years, "not being absent more than six months annually." Settlers meeting these requirements would hold their estate without limitation.

To the poor in Britain, Europe, and Ontario itself, the act seemed a godsend. Within five years Muskoka's population had reached 5360. Two decades later it had swelled to 15,666. By 1901 it was almost 21,000.

Much of this early settlement can be attributed to England's numerous emigration societies. In the year the Free Grants and Homesteads Act was passed, a dozen such

DID THE THRILL OF OWNING YOUR OWN LAND OUTWEIGH
THE HARDSHIP OF MAKING SOMETHING GROW ON THAT
ROCK-INFESTED LAND? FOR SOME IT DID, BUT FOR MANY
IT WAS SOON TIME TO PACK UP AND MOVE ON.

groups existed in London alone—although accusations were made that a few of these, founded by rich families, sought mainly to remove the poor and unworthy from their neighbourhoods and foist them off on Canada. Yet most performed an exemplary role in sending skilled workers to the New World while relieving the Old World of overpopulation.

The St. Paul's Church Emigration Society of London, for example, was comprised of artisans and labourers who subscribed to a weekly fund enabling members to emigrate. Its founder, Rev. A. S. Herring, was instrumental in sending 3000 members to Canada in four years alone. Visiting his Muskoka settlers in 1870, he was given the honour of christening the Port Sandfield cut that September, and during a Bracebridge reception he said, "Many who were in misery are now comparatively in a state of comfort."

The Ontario government was also striving mightily to populate Muskoka. Ever since receiving agent R. J. Oliver's glowing report of settler enthusiasm in 1860, it had advertised free land grants in pamphlets and posters throughout Canada and Europe, and had even sent an emigration commissioner to England. From the British Isles, Germany, France, Norway, and the United States, hundreds of families—though few from Canada—accepted the offer.

But although growth continued until the turn of the century, there was growing discontent with the land. To many the promised land proved most unpromising. Muskoka's rock broke not only backs but dreams. Farms were put up for sale, and some homesteads were simply deserted. A number of disgruntled settlers headed west to the Prairies, where more wheat could be produced than Canadians could consume. Even so vocal a Muskoka supporter as A. P. Cockburn, a member of the provincial legislature, admitted at a settlers' association meeting in 1867 that "very often people had come here with exaggerated ideas of the country and had left in consequence of the disappointments they had met with."

Social snobbery was also evident. In 1871 ardent Muskoka enthusiast Thomas McMurray admitted there were cases of poverty, "but such is the exception, not the rule. If the right class will only come," he sniffed, "they will do well." Echoing his sentiments, an Utterson settler named Mrs. King wrote of the harsh existence of "poor ladies and gentlemen . . . who form the worst, or at least the most unsuccessful, class for emigration." Muskoka, she said, offered a hard life "for the lower classes."

But receiving the greatest swell of criticism was Muskoka's soil—or lack of it. In his pamphlet, Canadian Lands Grants in 1874, Joseph Dale attacked every aspect of Muskoka from its bad roads, ramshackle shanties, absentee ownerships, and cost of settlement to, above all, its hated rock. "I have known instances," he fumed, "where a

mound of earth has been sought for, and looked upon as a treasure."

Muskoka's defenders pointed out that settlers got extra land to compensate for rocky fields and claimed that certain crops equalled those of southern counties. While the soil atop the Precambrian rock was often thin, they allowed, it was made of richly fertile leaf mould built up over centuries.

But as the Canadian Press Association pointed out, "In too many instances the settlers made the mistake of clearing off the timber from the rocks. The result is that the soil, no longer held by the fibrous roots of trees, is readily washed away by rains."

The erosion, however, wasn't due solely to settlers. Lumbermen were also stripping its dense forests. For the trees that proved a bane to farmers were a boon to others. By the 1850s Britain's demand for square timber—thick pines squared by axemen for shipbuilding—made Ontario's lumber industry soar. When transportation costs grew, the market shifted to the U.S., which had depleted its own pine forests and craved sawn lumber for its westward growth.

Scattered licences for cutting in Muskoka had been granted in 1856, allowing some companies to employ up to 1000 men. But the big lumber companies didn't really move into Muskoka until a public auction of timber berths in 1871 brought sky-high prices. At the same time, ironically, the government was making its major push to settle and cultivate the area. Conflict was inevitable.

Like the rivalry between cattlemen and sodbusters in the West, the clash between lumbermen and homesteaders in Muskoka was acute—particularly after the government sold lots to both in the same area. Settlers were infuriated by the sight of licensed lumbermen cutting pine on their land with no compensation. Lumbermen were equally angered when settlers cut and burned forests for farmland. While timber merchants asked to have special zones set aside, the government rejected their requests in favour of farming. For agriculture was viewed as permanent, and lumbering as temporary.

By 1870 the argument became moot as the opposing forces found they were dependent on each other. The settlers provided the produce, meat, oxen fodder, and often labour that the lumbermen needed. The lumbermen offered both a market and paid employment. Often, in fact, when a lumber camp moved on, settlers had to abandon their farms and follow.

As railways fast replaced waterways, the timber trade grew. By 1872 the railway had reached Washago, and three years later, Gravenhurst—which soon became the hub of Muskoka's lumber industry with 14 humming sawmills. Finally even the government realized that Muskoka's future was not in farming. By the 1880s, with the area opened

FRANK MICKLETHWAITE WAS ANOTHER OF THE GREAT
PHOTOGRAPHERS WHO SPENT TIME IN MUSKOKA. THIS
PICTURE OF PORT CARLING WAS TAKEN IN 1887, ON
FRANK'S FIRST TRIP TO THE AREA.

and towns springing up, colonizing efforts were quietly abandoned.

Although surveyors chose Muskoka's first town sites, they didn't always succeed. In 1847, for instance, Muskoka Falls was picked as a future settlement. But when steamer service started on Lake Muskoka, it was swiftly eclipsed by Bracebridge, far better located for navigation. Basically, towns such as Severn Bridge and Huntsville sprang up where major roads crossed navigable rivers, or at natural navigation terminals such as Gravenhurst and Port Carling; a waterfall, a means for powering mills, was also a factor. And when the railways arrived, many villages deprived of rails declined or died.

When the Muskoka Road spanned the river in 1859, Severn Bridge became Muskoka's first community. Hugh Dillon built his inn, and within five years the hamlet had a sawmill, post office, shops, tavern, and schoolhouse—with stables below. But despite its water power, Severn Bridge was soon surpassed by a town farther up the road on Muskoka Bay—Gravenhurst.

The first settler to recognize the value of this location was Irishman James "Micky" McCabe and his Scottish wife, Catherine, who built the Freemason's Arms Hotel there in 1861. A rustic log structure with a large dining room/tavern downstairs and mosquito nets on the feather beds upstairs, it was a popular place with travellers and lumbermen. The tavern was famous for "Mother" McCabe's water, and vinegar-and-molasses "stirabout." At his dock on the bay, called McCabe's Landing, Micky kept a leaky scow with one oar and a pole. Within four years the location had a handful of homes and shops, as well as a post office and Anglican church, and the village of Gravenhurst, also known as Sawdust City, was born.

In 1861 four Scotsmen—McMurray, Beal, Leith, and Cooper—settled in the area that was to become Bracebridge. McMurray wrote in his journal: "There was not a tree cut, nor a road. All was dense forest." The log huts they erected and the potato patches they cultivated sat near Hiram Macdonald's small brick tavern on the south side of the river, which could be crossed only by a log. Within months, Macdonald and Cooper had opened a sawmill and grocery store to supply the lumber camps. Before the decade ended, the town boasted a court, registry office, several churches, sawmills, hotels, schools, a newspaper, and even a jail.

In 1862 Augustus J. Alport, a prosperous New Zealand immigrant, moved his family to Muskoka, where he'd bought a large block of land on the mouth of Muskoka River. After erecting a house and several barns, he called his home Maple Grove and set up life as a gentleman farmer in the hub of a settlement he named Alport.

Although the Huntsville area had known trappers' shanties since the 1850s, its first permanent home was built by James Hanes, an Utterson farmer, in 1863. Six years later Captain George Hunt and his family arrived with other settlers, even though the last three miles of the Muskoka Road were incomplete. Under Hunt's supervision, the corduroy road was finally finished in 1870, and the new post office was named Huntsville in his honour.

In 1965 Daniel Cockburn paddled up from McCabe's Landing to the Indian River. He found only the Ojibwa village Obajewanung with 20 log huts, and plots of corn and potatoes. But noting that the river connected lakes Muskoka and Rosseau, Cockburn set up a trading post. Soon joined by two Méti brothers, Alexander and Michael Bailey, the three men and their families were Port Carling's first white settlers. When the lock at the falls was completed in 1871, Cockburn became the village's first lock master.

Alexander Bailey was a tall dignified old man known for his soft words of wisdom. Arriving from Quebec with his Méti wife, who was skilled in the use of medicinal herbs, he built a house in the Ojibwa village itself and began to cultivate the land. Their son, George Bailey, was a wheelsman on the steamer Wenonah.

Michael Bailey, who arrived with his children and extremely plump and ebullient Irish wife, was the exact opposite of his brother: impetuous and hard drinking. Knowing a lock was soon to be built at the portage, he erected a log house on the site to take in boarders when the work began.

Farther downriver lived John Thomas, a former member of the Confederacy rumoured to have done something during the Civil War that made him persona non grata in the United States. He'd arrived in Muskoka with his Canadian wife in 1868 and purchased a 10-acre clearing from John McKinlay—a man who made a living by squatting on a piece of land, clearing the property, then selling it.

In the same year, Joseph Tobin brought his wife and their extensive brood from the area of Glengarry on the St. Lawrence River. As the family had always lived in the woods and were used to native customs, they had no problem adjusting to Muskoka. When Tobin saw the big 1200-acre island in Lake Rosseau, he instantly recognized it as a prime location. The island hadn't been sold before then because the Indian Village claimed it as a burial ground.

But, speaking the native tongue, Tobin convince a village leader named Billy King to let him to build a house on one end. He paid King the grand sum of five dollars for the privilege, and soon, to King's amazement, Tobin was clearing land and apportioning farms lots among his children.

Seymour Penson remembered the Tobin takeover well. As he wrote many years later in his autobiography, "the Indians made some objection," but the island "was

This is the Mortimers' farmhouse (later Wingberry House) in 1887. Like many early Muskoka settlers, the Mortimers soon realized there was more money to be made renting out rooms to visitors than scratching a living from the Precambrian shield.

somehow all absorbed amongst the Tobins." Penson was 18 in 1869 when he emigrated from London, England, with his parents and built a house named Ferndale on Lake Rosseau. He recalled his fellow Muskoka settlers the year he arrived as a diverse and colourful lot.

Benjamin Hardcastle Johnston, a blustering man with a black beard and thick Irish brogue whose pugnacious manner disguised a soft heart, was a middle-aged widower with four sons. He came to the Brackenrig Bay area in 1866 and with the help of his sons erected a log house, which he called Wildgoose Lodge. A couple of years later he moved to the Indian Village (Port Carling) and became postmaster. About the same time, 35-year-old William Davidson, a tall aloof Scot, also enlisted his four sons to clear the bush on the farm he called Brackenrig, while his countryman Sandy Fraser, a young bachelor who craved solitude, built his house and farm single-handedly at the mouth of Brackenrig Bay.

Another lonely bachelor was the gentlemanly William Smallbones, a rake-thin man of 75 with flowing white hair and beard whose solitude had more to do with his eccentricities than his age. After inviting neighbours to tea, for instance, he'd pour them a bitter homemade brew of hemlock leaves; few returned. His neighbour on Lake Rosseau was an old English soldier by the name of William Dawson. He married a local widow with several children, and the family soon became famous on the lake as butter makers.

Frank Forge, powerfully built, deeply religious, and always cheerful and kindly, was one of the best-loved settlers in Muskoka. He'd come to Canada from Yorkshire in his youth and worked on a farm in Markham, where he married a local girl, before settling in Muskoka. The Forges arrived with $18 and nearly half as many kids, and lived off fish and potatoes. Later, when he got a job as a hired hand for a family on Three Mile Lake, Forge would trudge through the bush to the mill at Severn Bridge and lug home a 100-pound sack of flour on his back, crossing the Muskoka River on a log. The 70-mile round trip took three days. Bread, in Muskoka, was obviously a luxury.

Penson recalled: "When [Forge] took his oxen to do a day's work, he worked harder than any man I knew." Forge was also one of the best, at a time when almost every Muskoka transaction was by trade, at driving a bargain whenever he sold, as he'd say, "a coo or a hox."

Thomas Atkins, a solemn widowed Scot of 30, came to Lake Rosseau in 1860 and cleared a section on the shoreline. He was accompanied by his sister and her husband, David Fife, as well as a married cousin, Scott Atkins, who each cleared farms in the bush.

An adjacent section of the shoreline was cleared by Archibald Taylor, also 30, who built a sawmill at the mouth of the Dee River where it dropped into Lake Rosseau. He called his place Windermere and opened a post office, which was later moved to Tom Atkins's land. Taylor's mill had a single circular saw that could cut pine logs of any size into one-inch-thick lumber, which sold for $8 per 1000 feet.

Farther west, where the Royal Muskoka Hotel later stood, lived the Wrenshall brothers, bachelors Frederick and William, who'd arrived from Liverpool in 1865.

KATE MURRAY

ECHO
ROCKS

BEFORE A SYSTEM OF ROADS DEVELOPED IT WAS EASIER
TO MOVE PEOPLE AND GOODS THROUGHOUT THE AREA BY
WATER. THE *KATE MURRAY* WAS BUILT IN HAMILTON FOR
CHARLES VANDERBURGH OF PORT CARLING, WHO USED
HER TO TOW LOGS TO HIS SAWMILL AND FERRY TOURISTS
AROUND THE LAKES.

69

THIS LOG BUILDING WAS THE FIRST SCHOOL IN WOOD
TOWNSHIP. THERE WAS PROBABLY SOMETHING TO
BE SAID FOR HAVING EIGHT GRADES IN ONE. PUPILS
COULD MOVE ALONG AT THEIR OWN SPEED.

Boat-builders by trade, they turned easily to farming—and cultivated their land in a cunning way. After advertising in British newspapers for young men with capital to learn farming in Canada, they soon had a string of strapping lads out tilling their fields. Most came from families who paid the Wrenshalls the required $200 for their sons' apprenticeship—which consisted of handing them a hoe or axe as soon as they arrived and putting them to work.

Although most of the youths were quickly disenchanted and moved on, the Wrenshall brothers prospered—mainly because the ads continued and boys kept coming. (George Fox was the only farm apprentice who stayed with the brothers for more than a year, but by all accounts he "was not very bright.") And since their ads also attracted English settlers to the area, the Wrenshalls inadvertently played a major role in the district's development.

Another Scot, William Norris, arrived in Muskoka in 1868 after working on a Hamilton farm for several years to build a grubstake. The same year also saw the arrival of Charles Minett and his bride, both 25, who had married just before leaving their village of Bishop Cleeve in East Anglia, England. With his hometown friend, Josiah Callard, Charles selected lots and built shanties for their respective families to live in.

Josiah Callard and his wife, having no children of their own, adopted a 16-year-old girl named Ida, who deeply impressed the Muskoka settlers with her striking face and figure and strong religious bent. Whenever neighbours visited, Ida always sang hymns. She caused one of the community's first scandals when, a few years later, she ran away with a married man and was never seen in Muskoka again.

And so began Muskoka's first communities. Settlers were soon followed by schoolteachers, merchants, travelling salesman, government assayers, saddlebag preachers, itinerate showmen—and, inevitably, tourists.

Muskoka's first tourists became its first cottagers. After centuries of trapping, lumbering, settlement, and farming—mighty endeavours that all eventually died out—a new era began.

Muskoka finally found its true purpose—and greatest wealth—as cottage country. ▷

BY NECESSITY, MOST SETTLERS WERE INDEPENDENT,
SELF-SUFFICIENT TYPES, BUT THERE WERE SOME JOBS
THAT REQUIRED THE GOODWILL AND STRONG MUSCLES
OF THE NEIGHBOURS.

There might be rocks, stumps, mosquitoes, runaway pigs, wet hay, small potatoes, and no sugar, but oh, what a view!

CLEAR CUT LOGGING IN MUSKOKA, WATERCOLOUR, LYNDA LYNN.

6
TIMBER!

The Lumber Trade in Muskoka

BY RICHARD TATLEY

THE MUSKOKA LUMBERMAN! Six foot three in his stocking feet, all bone and muscle. Tough as an axe-handle. The man who could stride for miles through the bush and cut down 110 pine trees every day in any kind of weather. The man who could endure great hardship, provided he got his daily fare of pork and beans and tea. The devil-may-care man who could "birl," or spin, a log amid gushing white water or spring from one timber to another with his pike-pole, oblivious to the fact that he couldn't swim. The coarse, rough man who couldn't write his own name and was always ready for a fight. The proud man who believed in himself, feared no one and strode forth with his head held high. The lonely man, without home or family, who worked hard all his life with little to show for it in the end, but who wouldn't have had it any other way. The Muskoka lumberman.

The above stereotype may be slightly exaggerated. Lumbering in Canada, as in the United States, has always projected a powerful mystique that has both fascinated and frightened onlookers. The mystique of the rugged outdoorsman who, willingly or not, forgoes the comforts of home and the joys of family life to live amid the rigours of the bush, facing the frigid temperatures of winter and the blackflies and mosquitoes of summer. The mystique of the camp fire and of evenings spent in a smoky log camboose, or bunkhouse, miles from civilization, chewing the stem of a pipe or a wad of tobacco and clapping to the fiddler's song about the ghost of a brave comrade crushed under a log-pile or drowned in a turbulent chute in some river, or about some legendary foreman who demanded and got miracles from his men, or about the fantastic feats of "Purple John" or the brawls at McIlroy's Hotel. . . .

While not discounting all these colourful myths, we must remember that lumbering in Muskoka, as elsewhere, was always undergoing gradual change. In time it discarded much of its coarse, rough-hewn image and became quite respectable—and a lot more comfortable. But at the same time it lost most of its fascination for outsiders and became just another bland and boring, if strenuous, way to earn a living.

In fact, there was a considerable degree of specialization within the industry. Operating a lumber camp, and the depots from which it was supplied, called for tree markers, cutters (axemen), log scalers and stampers, timekeepers, cooks, road levellers and graders, teamsters and their horses, blacksmiths, and of course the foreman and his clerk. Log drivers—sometimes known as river hogs—were required to guide the logs down the rivers and over rapids. Crews were needed for the boats and tugs, and sorting jacks were used to move and sort the logs on still lakes. The mills required millhands, sawyers, planers (if the mill had a planer), yardmen, slab drawers, and lumber pilers to stack the sawn lumber and load it onto railway flatcars. A small sawmill might employ two to 10 men; a large one might need 100. Similarly, a small lumber camp might engage about 20 men, whereas a big one might need 100 to 150 hands, plus about 200 horses. The industry also created its own transport routes and even its own towns. According to the 1881 census, nearly 900 men in Muskoka (about half the adult male population) were involved one way or another in lumbering, which at that time dominated the Muskoka economy.

Why was this? Basically, the reasons were threefold. For one, during the nineteenth century Muskoka supported huge stands of white and red pine, cedar, spruce, tamarack, balsam, black ash, yellow birch, maple, beech, basswood, oak, and hemlock—despite the occasional forest fire. For another, markets for some of these woods were opening up, both in Great Britain and the United States. And finally, the Muskoka pineries were becoming accessible, by one means or another. Under these conditions, the invasion and spoliation of Muskoka's forests was inevitable. The only questions were: how, when, and by whom?

Lumbering did not touch the forest solitudes of Muskoka until the mid-nineteenth century, mainly because there was no need; before then, the lumber companies were busy laying waste the forests of the Ottawa Valley, the Kawartha lakes, the Lake Simcoe watershed, and the peninsula of southern Ontario. At the time there was little demand for wood products in Canada, with the exception of firewood, because the population was sparse and the forests

66 Lumbering at Wilson's Falls, Muskoka River   On Muskoka

abundant, and south of the Great Lakes the Americans still had plenty of timber of their own.

The main demand came from Great Britain, which had been granting a preference to Canadian timber ever since the Napoleonic wars. The British, however, wanted square timber—usually whittled down by skilled axemen right in the bush—rather than sawn lumber, mainly because square-timber beams could be conveniently packed aboard sailing ships at Montreal and Quebec City without shifting. Nothing less than perfect pieces satisfied them; each "stick" had to be flawless, without a single bruise or knot or trace of rot. This meant that each pine had to be at least 21 inches in diameter and that many a noble tree was cut and then left to rot in the bush, just because it contained some slight defect. When one considers also that much of the wood from acceptable trees was destroyed as the logs were squared, the trade appeared to be extremely wasteful. But by about 1865 British importers began to accept consignments of four-inch-thick sawn planks known as "deals," and then square-timber trade began to decline. In any case, most Muskoka lumber went to the United States rather than Britain, and seemingly little square timber was cut in the district after 1880.

The American invasion of the Muskoka pineries started as early as the 1850s, as the forests of Michigan, Wisconsin, and parts of Minnesota receded before the axe, but it did not make serious inroads until the 1860s. By then, however, cities such as Buffalo, Detroit, Chicago, and Cleveland were expanding rapidly and developing a ravenous appetite for softwoods. As Professor Arthur Lower has observed in *The North American Assault on the Canadian Forest*, "it was inevitable that demand should reach across the lakes." Unlike the British, the Americans wanted sawn lumber, not square timber, and were prepared to accept more or less whatever they could get; after all, defective planks could always be used for firewood. The results were to revolutionize the entire Muskoka economy.

By the 1850s sawmills were sprouting on the fringes of Muskoka. In 1852 Quetton St. George, an émigré French nobleman, built a mill at Washago. In 1857 J.&W. Gibson and Company of Willowdale opened another mill on the lonely shores of the harbour of Parry Sound, which was sold to the J.&W. Beatty Company in 1863, and it was at this point that Parry Sound really came to life. In 1856 licences were first issued for cutting along the Severn, Moon, Musquash, Seguin, and Black rivers to such firms as Quetton St. George, Andrew Heron, George Caswell, Joseph Smith, Peter Christie, and the Gibsons. In 1861 licences were also issued for cutting in the new townships

of Morrison, Muskoka, Ryde, Draper, and Macaulay, and as early as 1864, years before the rise of Huntsville, we are assured that Hunter's Bay was already full of logs, destined for the Moon River. The first sawmill within the Muskoka District itself was built by 1854 at the first falls on the Musquash River, about two miles inland from Georgian Bay. Owned by W. B. Hamilton of Penetanguishene, it exported mainly across the Great Lakes to Chicago, but also to Owen Sound and Collingwood.

Until the coming of the railways, however, the Muskoka timber limits were of little value because of the difficulties in exporting the lumber; indeed, the only way to do so was down the Moon and Musquash rivers, both of which are bedevilled with rapids and waterfalls, and neither of which has a decent harbour at its mouth. In May 1868 a letter printed in the Orillia Expositor contained the following lament:

Mr. Alex Bailey has almost unlimited water power, and facilities for manufacturing lumber at Bracebridge, but in consequence of the large outlay attendant on the land carriage is unable to bring the material to market, consequently he is compelled to saw just what is required for home consumption. Messrs. Willson and Holditch are at present building a mill a short distance east of this village, they also are naturally concerned in finding means of transit to market for what they will be able to cut. There is another mill somewhere near Lake Rosseau, but as there is no means of disposing of the surplus quantities which could be sawn, these mills will have to confine themselves altogether to local demand.

Access to markets was not the lumbermen's only problem. Another was the growth of settlement, which by then was being encouraged by the government as a means of arresting the drain of population from Canada to the United States. The first European settlers began arriving by 1859, following the newly opened Muskoka Road, which was started at Washago in 1858 and gradually crept northwards. It was inevitable that the interests of the settlers would clash with those of the lumbermen, because the settlers wanted complete freedom to do what they liked with the timber on their lands, whereas the lumbermen wanted the pineries reserved for themselves. Having paid cash for their limits, the lumbermen complained bitterly when they found settlers at work within those limits, often burning the brush to clear their lands and frequently starting forest fires in the process—which in turn ruined many a fine stand of timber. They also indignantly protested that many so-called settlers were taking up land for the sole purpose of stripping it of all valuable timber, selling it, and then moving on—a sorry situation that was all too often true.

No fancy machines on this job site, but the result is the same.

WEISMILLER LUMBER YARD, BALA, WATERCOLOUR, LORNE JEWITT.

But the government at the time favoured agriculture, because farming was expected to produce permanent settlements, while lumbering was viewed as merely a passing concern, albeit a very profitable one, in that the government derived a lot of revenue from licences and timber dues. Indeed, the Act to Amend the Law for the Sale and the Settlement of Public Lands (1853) gave settlers unrestricted control of the pine on their lots, whether they were inside timber limits or not. In short, the settlers were given a free hand, while the lumbermen were heavily taxed and regulated. The lumbermen argued that the lands of the Canadian shield were mostly sterile granite, quite unfit for farming; but this cut no ice with the government, who wanted to believe the opposite. We should note, however, that in these matters some lumber barons were their own worst enemies, in that many of them acted as if they had a divine right to do whatever they wanted with the forests, and consequently had few friends in high places.

There was, of course, another side to the situation. More and more, the settlers and the lumbermen began to realize how useful each could be to the other. Some early lumber firms saved a lot of timber by buying logs from the settlers (who were otherwise prone to burn them); Peter Cockburn of Orillia, father of the more famous A. P. Cockburn of steamboat fame, was the first to do this, starting in 1865. The early settlers in turn raised hay, vegetables, and foodstuffs, which the lumber camps badly needed, and frequently the farmers themselves contracted to "cadge" these supplies to the camps, mainly in winter, using horses and sleighs. Indeed, many struggling settlers could sometimes find no other markets for their crops, given the dreadful state of most pioneer roads, and no doubt they were grateful for some hard cash. In time, too, many settlers, having little to do during the winters, began turning to the lumber camps for seasonal employment, which did not make life any easier for their wives and children back home. In many cases agriculture in Muskoka became so dependent on the lumber trade that when the lumbermen moved on, settlers found they had no choice but to follow.

Gradually these realities began to percolate government officialdom, and the regulations were rewritten. The Act Respecting the Sale and Management of Public Lands (1860) specified that a settler's rights no longer covered the disposal of pine if his lands lay within a lumber company's timber limits, while the Free Grants and Homestead Act (1868) went even further: under its terms, until a settler had fulfilled all the terms of ownership of his lot, the Crown reserved all the pine for itself, and the settler was entitled only to such timber as was needed for clearing the land, or for building and fencing. This was meant to curtail the abuse of timber stripping by speculators posing as settlers. Legally, then, a settler could not try to raise a

little cash by selling his timber unless he was prepared to pay dues to the government of 75 cents per 1000 feet, which was exorbitant. Meanwhile the lumber crews could cut all the timber they wanted on the settler's land until the settler formally secured a deed, while the settler could do nothing about it. Oftentimes the lumbermen simply ignored the rights of property owners and carried on. Typical is the following complaint in a local newspaper of the period:

The lumbermen in these districts have for a long time imagined they possessed the powers and the functions of the Provincial government and have been in the habit of treating the settlers as if they were dirt under their feet, knowing full well that the lumbering firms backed up . . . by Messrs. Pardee and Company can afford to laugh in their sleeves at the efforts made by the settlers to free themselves from the yoke. And indeed there are very few farmers who have the means or the pluck to fight the saw kings in the courts.

In fact, though, both sides commonly ignored the rules if they found it in their interests to do so.

By 1870 Gravenhurst, Bracebridge, Bala, and Port Carling were all on the map—just barely—and a couple of steamboats were available to tow booms of logs across the Muskoka lakes or scow provisions to the lumber camps; but as yet very little logging was being conducted beyond the rivers. The lumber companies were feeling confident, however, perhaps because they sensed that a railway was coming to Muskoka, and by 1871 several prominent firms— A. G. P. Dodge and Company of New York; Clarke, White and Company; Hotchkiss, Hughson and Company; the Cook Brothers; and the Bell Ewart Company—were entering high bids for timber berths in Muskoka and Almaguin. Prices fetched an average of $241.62 per square mile—a considerable amount!—and brought revenues of $118,646 to the Ontario government. The Dodge Company alone purchased eight limits totalling 94,000 acres, started building the Nipissing Road from the village of Rosseau up to the Magnetawan, and opened a depot at Port Anson on Ahmic Lake. Soon it had more than 800 men working in its camps, and this was not exceptional. All went well until the autumn of 1873, when the sudden collapse of a number of banks in the U.S. triggered the worst depression in the century, unequalled until 1929. The *Report* for the Ontario Commissioner of Crown Lands in 1875 glumly confirmed that both the square-timber and sawn-lumber trades were stagnant, with cash sales almost nonexistent. Professor Lower has noted that Canadian lumber exports declined from $29 million in 1873 to a mere $13 million in 1878. The hapless Dodge Company, among others, went out of business, while the survivors had to retrench drastically. In

his *Memoirs*, Captain Robert Dollar, who later became a shipping tycoon on the Pacific, recalled the events of 1872:

At that time I . . . went to a new country, the Muskoka district . . . where in partnership with Mr. Johnson, we bought timber on land owned by farmers and started lumbering for our own account, making our headquarters at Bracebridge, Ontario. It was a new country just opened by the Government, and there was a good opportunity. Business was booming at this time and we did not sell our logs, expecting to get a higher price when we would deliver them at the market the following summer; but at that time along came Black Friday [September 17] in New York, which paralyzed business throughout not only the United States but Canada as well. When we came to sell our logs we found we had made a loss of what little money we had put in as well as about $5000 more . . .

In order to pay up the debts, my partner and myself had to go to work on wages . . . it took three years' hard work to get even with the world again.

Captain Dollar eventually managed a comeback in 1876, when he formed a new partnership with Herman Henry Cook, the former Dodge Company agent. To quote him further:

He furnished the money and I the brains and hard work. Having the experience of previous years I was extremely cautious and careful, and made a success of the new venture from the start . . . In 1876 I had started eight camps in Muskoka district, and besides these I started a camp to get out saw logs on one of the islands of Georgian Bay. . . .

Amid all this gloom were a few heartening developments. In 1876 the government agreed to slash the dues demanded for licences in Muskoka and Parry Sound. Besides that, the Northern Railway of Canada, which had been deriving substantial profits from hauling wood from Barrie to Toronto, now felt constrained to follow the lumber trade northwards as the Lake Simcoe basin was logged out. By the time the depression of the 1870s hit, the line had reached Washago, but despite this it managed to extend its tracks to the Severn River by 1874 and to Muskoka Bay (Gravenhurst) by November 1875. This was too good an opportunity for the lumber companies to miss, and though all of Muskoka benefitted from the railway's arrival, the lumbermen made the most immediate gains, and with them the town of Gravenhurst.

With a fine, spacious harbour capable of sheltering up to 50 million feet of logs at the foot of a watershed extending

A HARD DAY'S WORK NEAR TORRANCE.

north as far as the heart of the modern Algonquin Park, and with plenty of level land around western Muskoka Bay for sidings and millyards, Gravenhurst was ideally suited to become a major lumber town. In addition, the railway officials were assuring the lumbermen that they had no intention of extending the line farther north for at least the next 10 years. As a result, many lumber companies began vying for millsites along the shores of what soon became the village of West Gravenhurst, even before the railway arrived.

Before 1875, apparently, Gravenhurst had only one steam-powered sawmill: a small portable, built near the future site of Muskoka Wharf by Peter Cockburn and his sons in 1870. In 1876 the Cockburn Company shifted its operations from the Musquash River to Gravenhurst and built another mill where the concrete towers of the stone-crushing plant would later be erected. In 1888 this mill went to the famous Rathbun Lumber Company of Deseronto, which later acquired a second mill on Muskoka Bay. By 1877 the Hotchkiss and Hughson Lumber Company built a mill on the bay, as did the firms of Caldwell and Perkins, William Tait of Orillia, James Brydon, and the Hill brothers of Gravenhurst. In 1878 Messrs. McBurney and Laycock of Woodstock founded the Woodstock Lumber Company mill in West Gravenhurst, soon to be flanked by Joseph Chew's mill, the DeBlacquiere mill, and James Brydon's second mill, which around 1890 went to the Snider Lumber Company of Waterloo.

Meanwhile, shingle mills were being erected by such men as Henry Delong and Henry King. By 1880 the Thompson and Baker Company acquired the former Cockburn mill. So crowded did Muskoka Bay become that one company, Crone and Patton of Toronto, which arrived in 1880, had to locate its mill outside the bay, at the mouth of the HocRoc River near Muskoka Sands; this forced the firm to scow its lumber to the railhead, but gave it the advantage of not having to pay taxes to the town. At about the same time two more mills were built on Gull Lake. By 1878 Gravenhurst had a total of 17 saw and shingle mills, and by 1883 it was exporting 50 million board feet of lumber and 35 million shingles annually, to say nothing of logs and square timber, and that was more than any other town in Ontario except Ottawa and perhaps Midland. Not uncommonly, the whir of the bandsaws could be heard nonstop, day and night. The railway soon had to build more than 20 miles of sidings through West Gravenhurst to service the millyards. Gravenhurst had now entered its glory days as the "Sawdust City."

Undoubtedly the greatest of all the Muskoka lumber firms was that of Mickle and Dyment. This concern started inconspicuously in 1877 when Charles Mickle of Cargill, Ontario, arrived at Gravenhurst and formed a partnership

GRACE M.

Micklethwaite 1905.

THE TUG *GRACE M.* WAS BUILT IN GRAVENHURST IN 1905 TO PULL LOG BOOMS FOR THE MICKLE-DYMENT LUMBER COMPANY.

with William Tait of Orillia; together, they built a sawmill near the old Muskoka Wharf. Within just a few years, however, Mr. Mickle bought out Tait's interest and soon acquired a second mill. In 1884 he made another partnership with Nathaniel Dyment of Barrie, and soon the empire of "M.D." was showing its might. The firm gradually bought up to 200 square miles of limits, partly in what is now Algonquin Park and partly in an area east of Kawagama (Hollow) Lake; and in time it was employing more than 1000 men. By 1890 it owned five mills, including some at Bradford, Severn Bridge, and Fenelon Falls. In 1894 it pioneered by adding a planing mill, which allowed it to produce smooth "dressed" lumber, for such purposes as doors, sashes, and interior building trim. By 1910 it was still exporting 12.5 million feet annually (when many other firms were shutting down), and these totals rose to 20 million feet in 1912, the peak year. Five tugs were required to tow all the logs, while the portion of West Gravenhurst closest to the mills became known as Mickletown. The company did not cease operations until 1933, long after all the other Gravenhurst sawmills were gone.

While the big mills like Mickle and Dyment's cut primarily for the American market, those up the lakes were still left with only the local trade. They included the Burgess

family mill at Bala (built in 1868), and others at East Bay (1876), Rosseau Falls (1877), Rosseau proper (1879), Brackenrig, Windermere, Bracebridge, and later, Walker's Point and Port Sandfield. For a time it seemed likely that the big companies might log out the whole district and leave nothing for the local mills, though as of 1869 the small mills were given the right to appeal to the commissioner of Crown lands to have timber reserved for them.

By 1878 the depression had lifted and the industry entered its heyday, which lasted till the turn of the century. In 1878 the government built a large timber slide at Muskoka Falls to allow logs to shoot down past the falls without damage. After 1880 the newly formed Muskoka Slide and Boom Company started building additional slides at Bracebridge and along the Musquash, charging user fees to the lumber companies. By that time, too, with the advent of the industrial age, cities in Canada were starting to expand rapidly, and soon demand was also increasing in Europe and South America. As a result, the lumber trade flourished for decades.

The next big development was the extension of the railway north from Gravenhurst to Callander by January 1886. The result was that wherever the line crossed a major river or tapped an important lake, a new lumber town sprang up. Good examples of this are Huntsville, Burks Falls, South River, and to a lesser extent, Bracebridge. Logs that formerly were shepherded all the way down the rivers to Georgian Bay could now be sawn up at the railway crossings and shipped directly south to Toronto. Huntsville in particular sprouted three new sawmills on the Vernon River and Hunter's Bay after 1886, collectively cutting up to 160,000 board feet every day; by 1889 the three mills had expanded to six. For that matter, a number of temporary villages sprang up close to other mills built beside the railway tracks, and died when the mills shut down. For example, at one time Martin Siding and Parkersville each had more than a hundred residents.

Bracebridge derived fewer benefits, since it lacks a really spacious harbour in the river, and in any case few companies wanted to move their mills from Gravenhurst. Even so, the famous firm of Singleton Brown and J. D. Shier opened a large combination mill in 1885, just as the railway came through. (Of course, the usual spur was built down to the yards.) Within just a few years Singleton Brown went into business by himself and developed the first shingle mill in Canada equipped with a double-cutting bandsaw. The mill, on the south side of the river below the falls, was soon turning out up to 20 million shingles annually, some of which went to Britain, Europe, and the U.S. (A collapse in prices in 1898 forced the plant to close.) The Shier Company in turn bought several limits east of Dorset and up the Oxtongue River, remaining in business until the 1920s, before evolving into Northern Planing Mills Ltd. Other mills were built by Mathias Moore at Falkenburg and Roy Green near Fraserburg. Baysville likewise had a water-powered mill by 1892, soon to be followed by a steam sawmill and shingle mill, while Dorset was briefly the regional headquarters of the famous Gilmour Lumber Company of Trenton.

As a rule, the lumbermen used the lakes and rivers to reach their camps and brought in their supplies on punts, rafts, tugs, and scows. "Tote roads" were built as required in the late summertimes (especially around portages), using horses, scrapers, and hand labour; during the winters these roads were tramped down and sprinkled with water to form ice, making a very solid surface. As an added precaution, horses' hooves were sharpened for better traction. Much of the teaming was done under contract by local farmers or urban merchants, using wagons, sleighs, and stoneboats. Everyone prayed for cold weather, since mild temperatures turned the roads into quagmires.

The camps themselves were usually built beside the lakes and streams. One might consist of a stable for the horses, a blacksmith shop, an office, cookhouse, and one or two cambooses for the men. Generally the buildings were of squared logs, with pole rafters and peaked tarpaper roofs, and usually dirt floors. The cambooses had no stoves, and only fireplaces for warmth or cooking; the men slept two to a bunk, with their feet to the fire, and as a rule, the older employees were given first choice of bunks. The men wore blanket coats with red sashes and capes and high boots, and seldom removed their clothes all winter. All cooking was done in huge iron pots. The main fare was pork and beans, supplemented by peeled potatoes that were frozen and stored in barrels—but sometimes the cooks treated the men to fruit pies if the ingredients could be obtained. Tea was commonly available and might be flavoured with sugar or maple syrup. It is said that the roughest, toughest, and brawniest lumberjack never dared to quarrel with the cook, but the cooks were expected to be good. No talking was permitted at mealtimes, which were usually after dark, and commonly the men were roused before sunrise to begin their day. The foreman's word was, of course, law.

In the bush, the trees to be cut were always scaled or marked in advance, and each "jack" was expected to cut 110 pines a day—or else! Usually a camp fire would be started, and the men might get a little hot tea and perhaps a sandwich around noon. Horses were used to drag the logs to the nearest river or lake, where they would be piled on the ice to await the spring breakup. Leisure hours in the evenings would be filled with story-telling and singing, usually to the strains of a fiddle or mouth organ; sometimes there would even be an impromptu dance, with men taking the parts of women. Most of the jacks chewed tobacco or smoked pipes; cigars and cigarettes were not allowed because of the fire hazard, and liquor was positively prohibited, for an inebriated axeman was prone to injury. There were no doctors nearby to deal with a severed limb or artery, or a man crushed by a log. The camps tended to be exceedingly isolated, especially in winter, and though they might be visited by the occasional preacher or peddlar, some companies forbade visitations. To us such conditions may seem unbelievably harsh and primitive, but few complained then—not as long as he was adequately fed!

Once cut, the logs were stamped with the company's identification marks, sometimes using ink that ran through the wood to discourage any thought of cutting off the ends and stealing them. In the spring the river drivers took over, feeding the logs downriver with only peavies and pink-poles to guide them or pull them apart if a jam developed. Loosening up a pile of sawlogs at a rapids was extremely dangerous work, and despite his dexterity many an ill-fated logger found an unmarked grave beside the swift-flowing waters. During the drives the men lived in tents mounted on rafts, which also featured a cookhouse. It was not uncommon for rival company gangs to meet on the rivers, and naturally each would try to get a head start on the others—which sometimes led to fights.

At the river mouths, boom timbers consisting of logs chained together were laid out across the channels and secured to the shores at both ends to "bag" the logs and

TREES WERE CUT IN THE FALL AND SKIDDED TO THE
NEAREST LAKE IN WINTER. IN SPRING THEY WERE
ROUNDED UP AND TOWED TO THE SAWMILLS, OFTEN
MAKING NAVIGATION ALL BUT IMPOSSIBLE.

form a loop around them; this constituted a "tow." Unless a favourable wind happened to be blowing, the tows then had to be "warped," or winched, across the lakes. This was done by fitting out a raft with a treadmill, around which was coiled a heavy steel cable with an anchor attached. The raft would then be poled out in front of the tow and anchored, then poled back and attached to the tow. Then the men had to turn the treadmill and winch in the cable, thus dragging the tow forward. Large gangs were required for this slow, back-breaking work, which had to be performed, rain or shine, winter or summer. Fortunately, by the 1880s horses were commonly substituted for human muscle power, and by 1893 they in turn began to be replaced by "alligators," or warping tugs, which were basically large scows with deck cabins, paddlewheels, and winches powered by steam engines. Besides being tireless and requiring only three or four hands to run them, alligators had few problems towing against the wind. They were also amphibious and could be winched overland from one lake to another, using the anchor cable; hence the name "alligator." Only on the larger lakes were there likely to be conventional steam tugs available to boom the logs and tow them to the mills. Occasionally a tug and an alligator might work in concert; for many years the Mickle and Dyment firm used a big 'gator called the *John Bull* to winch several tows at a time from Dorset across Lake of Bays to the Baysville Narrows, while a little tug called the *Niska* composed the tows, took charge in confined waters, and "swept up" any stray logs left behind.

Predictably, many sawlogs owned by different companies were apt to become mixed up in the same tow. To get around this problem, devices known as sorting jacks were anchored across the rivers, or in waters close to the mills; here pike-men armed with poles would prod the various logs into the correct slots. For many years one such device was used on the south branch of the Muskoka River near the railway bridge to separate the logs bound for the Shier, Weismiller, and Mickle-Dyment mills. Another was positioned at the mouth of the Muskoka River, and a third for a time at Parker's Point, near Gravenhurst. I should add that confined channels such as the Gravenhurst Narrows were a real nuisance to the tug crews, who had to bring the booms to the entrance, open them in front, and use cables to drag the booms (and their logs) through the passage, meanwhile setting another boom to collect the logs as they spilled through. So extensive were the operations that for years Gravenhurst residents were frequently able to walk right across Muskoka Bay over the logs!

The log drives were not conducted without controversy. People complained that they speeded up erosion along the riverbanks, causing channels to fill with silt. Bracebridge merchants grumbled because shipments by steamer were

often held up. Cottagers, who were becoming quite numerous by the 1890s, were frustrated in their attempts to get to town to shop by boat, often having to wait for hours for a log drive to pass through the Muskoka or Indian rivers. And a passenger steamer always ran the risk of breaking a propeller or splintering its hull while trying to force its way through the logs. The authorities supported the navigating interests and insisted that no one had the right to obstruct the waterways, but as a rule the lumbermen did what they pleased—or what they had to do—and it was hard to take any action against them beyond the imposition of fines. The log drivers generally knew when the passenger steamers were coming and tried to leave a passage clear for them, if only because the passenger ships could, and sometimes did, ram and break the log booms, which resulted in logs being strewn all over the lake. But the lumbermen showed scant consideration for private launches and motorboats, and smart cottagers soon learned to follow the passenger steamers if they wanted to get to town.

But undoubtedly the loudest complaints arose after the log drives were over and the jacks emerged from the bush with money in their pockets. Then, as people said, all hell broke loose. Full of bravado and high spirits and spoiling for liquor and excitement (and women), the loggers—sometimes dubbed the press gang—would march into the towns, especially Gravenhurst, and practically take over. Veritable orgies of drinking, singing, swearing, chewing, wrestling, brawling, and wild spending ensued, chiefly in the hotels, while the townsfolk barricaded themselves in their homes and stayed off the streets. Police constables were few in those days, and often the only recourse open to the townsfolk was vigilante action. After a few wild days and nights, many an exuberant logger would wake up in the gutter with a crashing headache and empty pockets, and realize he'd been rolled—relieved of all his earnings during the previous night's bash. Then, unless he had a family to return to, he would have to hang around cheap boardinghouses until he could find a job in another camp.

Such antics happened only on occasion, however, and tended to diminish as the years went by. Tourists travelling by train and steamer seldom encountered any lumbermen, unless perchance they spotted a hardy little tug puffing along with a boom in tow. Still, the smell of fresh-cut pine, the endless rows of stacked lumber, the shriek of the band-saw and the hum of the engines in the towns were sure to attract the awe and attention of visitors. More commonly, one might find hundreds of mill-boys from West Gravenhurst thronging the dusty streets with their sweethearts on a Saturday evening in June, ambling past the stores, or lounging on a spacious wooden verandah, discussing the latest lacrosse or baseball game, or a recent moonlight excursion, or their heroes—men such as the one and only

CHARLES MICKLE, MUSKOKA'S LUMBER BARON, SURVEYS
A PORTION OF THE 14 MILLION FEET OF LUMBER HIS
GANGS CUT EACH YEAR—UNTIL THERE WAS NOTHING
LEFT TO CUT.

Gill Boyd, who could swing an axe like no one else; or the
Grant boys, Tom and Jim, the champion crosscut sawyers
of the whole north country; or the Jenkins boys; or Silver
Dan McDonald and young Jack McCrae. They were the
giant lumberjacks and fondly described as big men with big
hearts, always ready to back up a weaker brother.

"Those were the days that made Gravenhurst the envy
of the north," recalled an oldtimer in 1929. "Those were
the days when men were men. Girls were peaches and not
painted dolls, and snobs were an unknown animal."

In the same vein, it seems appropriate to point out that
many lumber barons became the leading men in their hometowns, and that several—including Singleton Brown, J. D.
Shier, and Charles Mickle—sometimes served as mayors.

Nonetheless, lumbering was a risky enterprise. There was
always the danger of a sudden drastic fluctuation in prices.
Competition was intense, and sometimes lumbermen found
rival firms stealing their timber, which could lead to expensive lawsuits; for example, in 1895 Herman Mutchenbaker,
who ran the mill at Rosseau Falls, unsuccessfully sued the
Rathbun Company for infringements.

A chronic danger was fire, both in the bush and worse,
in the millyards, sometimes caused by sparks blown from
a sawdust incinerator. Many firms were ruined this way.
On October 14, 1891, two mills in Gravenhurst were wiped

out in a single fire; only one was rebuilt. Likewise the Woodstock Lumber Company lost its mill to a blaze, and later
its entire millyard, and never recovered from the loss. The
Shier mills in Bracebridge were devastated by fire in
September 1925. The Weismiller planing mill at Bala was
destroyed six years later, but was rebuilt. The list is long.

Other firms ran into trouble for different reasons.
William Thomson of Orillia, owner of the Longford Lumber Company, acquired the "white mill" in Gravenhurst
around 1890, and enlarged it into the biggest in town,
with a capacity to cut up to 100,000 feet a day, this at a time
when timber was starting to dwindle and the average daily
cut was only about 50,000 feet. Having overestimated the
supply, Thomson was soon obliged to sell the mill to the
Rathbun Company. Similarly the Gilmour Company, unwilling to move its mills from Trenton, was eventually forced
to cut hundreds of miles away from its home base. In 1894,
having entered high bids for limits in Algonquin Park, outside the Kawartha watershed, it decided to build a very
expensive tramway and jackladder to move its logs from
Lake of Bays over the height of land, only to find that it
took two seasons to move out a single season's cut, and
worse, that the logs were in very poor shape by the time
they reached Trenton. Not surprisingly, the tramway wasn't
in use for long.

Despite individual setbacks, the Muskoka lumber trade
was at its height from about 1883 until 1890. The drives
on the Muskoka River in 1887 alone were estimated to
total 60 million board feet, and in 1891 the output was
reckoned as the second highest in Ontario—and that didn't

even include Gravenhurst! The census of 1901 assigned Muskoka a production total of 32,774 cubic feet of sawn lumber and 21,545 logs valued at $1,591,696.

But the industry carried the seeds of its own destruction. No one was concerned about reforestation in those days because, after all, the forests were limitless, weren't they? By 1910 the great stands of white pine were largely wiped out, and in 1911 the output was valued at merely $367,533. The outbreak of war in 1914 took many men overseas, and by 1920 most of the sawmills had shut down—for good.

In an effort to delay the inevitable, some firms started to cut tanbark (peeled from hemlock) for the tanneries in Bracebridge and Huntsville. Others tried cutting hardwoods. Maple and birch had been ignored during the glory days, not because there was no demand for them, but because hardwoods usually sink when efforts are made to float them. However, in 1901 a Huntsville businessman named George Hutcheson established the first integrated hardwood mill in Canada on Hunter's Bay, and opened several camps in the bush. The "experts" ridiculed the idea and insisted it would never work, but Hutcheson's firm, the Muskoka Wood Manufacturing Company, proceeded to peel its logs in the bush, and then to build them into 60-foot rafts supported by softwood booms, which kept them buoyant long enough to reach the mill, and as a result the operation paid. Soon the company became famous for its veneers and hardwood flooring. The men usually left for the bush in September and stayed until March, but they were allowed to go home for Christmas and New Year's. At first the firm hired free-lance tugs to tow on the lakes, but by the 1920s, suspecting that the crews were deliberately thinning out the logs to prolong the season, it began using men in small boats called pointers instead. The drivers were proud of their work and were well paid.

Other operators, including George Tennant of Bracebridge, the Boyes of Vankoughnet, and the Weismiller Company tried imitating the Hutcheson firm, though not always successfully. The Shier Company turned to hardwoods during the 1920s, but many of the logs were lost while under tow. The firm also tried hauling them out of the bush using trucks, but the roads were often flooded out. When the banks refused to advance any further credit, the company ceased operations, and Mr. Shier, like Herman Weismiller and others, turned to the wholesale business. The result was the birth of Northern Planing Mills, which is still in business today.

By the 1920s the industry was a ghost of its former self, but luckily for Muskoka, the tourist trade had already emerged as the mainstay of the economy. By about 1935 the surviving operators were able to use bulldozers, backhoes, trucks, and graders to build gravel roads to their camps, which were usually on high ground; such roads

could be used year-round, and soon the river drive became a thing of the past. The new mobility also allowed the remaining bush crews to come and go more freely and visit their families more often. The camps were enormously improved, radios helped to diminish the isolation, and eventually chainsaws largely supplanted the axe. By now, however, lumberjacks were more likely to be Polish or Finnish immigrants or French Canadians, rather than local men.

During the Second World War, some Muskoka firms provided specialized products for the war effort. The Tennant Company helped produce Spitfire wings and maple and birch caskets, while the Brackenrig sawmill (still in business today) cut tamarack roots into seat frames for lifeboats. After the war, small-scale cutting of second-growth timber continued in inland areas, but the emphasis was now on trying to preserve what was left of the forests, and most companies found it more profitable to retail imported lumber.

Today, only a few genuine sawmills survive in Muskoka. But the industry has made its mark. On the negative side it stripped and nearly scalped the whole district in its rapacious and insatiable search for pine. The devastation allowed insect enemies of the trees to spread faster, speeded soil erosion, and almost ruined Muskoka's scenic beauty. On the other hand, the timber trade saved the region from destitution after the failure of farming became manifest. It created thousands of jobs, made fortunes for a few, and kept the district afloat until the tourist trade took up the slack. Not without reason did the oldtimers claim, "Those were the days!" ▷

7

THE MUSKOKA CLUB

*The First Islanders**

BY D. H. C. MASON

IN JULY 1860, TWO YOUNG TORONTO MEN, James Bain, Jr., and John Campbell, employed in the publishing firm of James Campbell and Son, were planning their one week's holiday. They were 18 and 20 respectively and they wanted adventure. They would pack the necessities of life in homemade knapsacks, take a gun and powder and shot flasks, a box for botanical specimens and fishing gear, and go north.

The Toronto, Simcoe, and Muskoka Junction Railway was completed only to Barrie. They left it at Belle Ewart on the west shore of Cook's Bay of Lake Simcoe where they took the little steamer, *Emily May*, to Orillia. From there they went in a rowboat up Lake Couchiching to Washago, walked to Severn Bridge, and put up at the Severn Bridge Hotel, kept by Mr. and Mrs. Hugh Dillon. The next day they set out up the new Muskoka Road. No journals of this trip is available, but we have a letter written by James Bain more than 40 years later that says that they reached Lake Muskoka where Gravenhurst now stands, that not a tree appeared to have been cut along the shore and that two Indian wigwams stood on the beach.

In 1861, Bain, Campbell, and a friend called Crombie—and the latter's dog—did the trip again. Fortunately a full journal of this expedition survives, from which it appears that, on August 5, they set out from Toronto by rail and the *Emily May* took them to Orillia where they put up at a hotel for the night. The next day, in a rowboat and taking turns at the oars, they headed for Washago where they arrived after dark and walked through the woods a couple of miles to Severn Bridge and its hospitable hotel.

The next morning they walked up the Muskoka Road. They were greatly troubled by mosquitoes and black flies, against which they had no protection but their handkerchiefs and leafy boughs; and also, strange to say, they suffered from thirst, for it appears they had not thought the water of the streams they passed fit for human consumption. Their journal reads:

But at the end of twelve miles, we came to a log hut of peculiar construction which we concluded to be Micky McCabe's tavern. We entered by a slight stoop through the doorway and we were greeted by the illustrious Michael, a long spare party of about 50, who promised us something to refresh the inner man, when a voice, shrill and commanding, came from a bed in the corner where Mrs. McCabe signified her intention of getting up . . . Not wishing to be spectators of a backwoods toilet, we bolted into the fresh air and held a committee on our future course. The landlady, who was all right now, despatched Micky to dug up the murphies.

While Mother McCabe, as she preferred to be called, carried out the cooking outside the house, she questioned them on their occupations: "Yez'll be measuring and surveying, I suppose." "No." "Yez'll be preachers then?" Their protests that they were pleasure bent simply did not register with her. They were thirsty so she mixed them a drink they christened "stirabout," which was "a quart of water mixed with a cupful of vinegar and another of molasses."

The McCabes' tavern, the Freemason's Arms, must have been on the Muskoka Road near the point at which the wooden arch now stands at the entrance to Gravenhurst, the Gateway to Muskoka, for our pioneers then marched off two miles to the nearest point on Muskoka Bay known later as McCabe's Landing, and later covered by the Muskoka Navigation Company's docks.

Here they found McCabe's scow. There was only one paddle to which they added a pole cut out of the bush, and set out as the first navigators, for pleasure, of the Muskoka lakes. The scow leaked like a sieve and they were kept busy bailing to keep her afloat. Twenty-five years later John Campbell wrote and sang "The Quarter Centennial song":

'Tis five and twenty years ago,
Thought I've forgot the day,
When three youths launched a rickety scow
On fair Muskoka Bay.

89

* *This chapter is extracted from* Muskoka, The First Islanders and After, *by D. H. C. Mason.*

One was a bluffer, the other a duffer
And the third who sings this lay
Tonight is just the kind of man
That anyone cares to say.

And ever since then all kinds of men
And women and girls and boys,
And lots of those strange non-descripts
Best known as hobbleboys,
Have left their homes homes in the wilds to roam
Through all these changing years,
To go in the track of that kitless pack,
The hardy pioneers.

Somehow they propelled the leaky scow up through Muskoka Bay and out through the narrows about two and a half miles, though they thought it was five. They were thrilled with the beauty of the lake, then undesecrated by man, and by the botanical specimens they collected on some of the islands.

On the return journey the wind was against them, and after two hours' work, they gave up the attempt to reach McCabe's and landed, probably on Daisy Island, where they spent the night. After a frugal meal of the remains of a ham bone and some seed cake, their only provisions, they sat around a blazing fire "and songs beguiled the hours till 9:00 o'clock." It is amusing to read that they took turns in keeping watch through the night and that they considered the brown water of the lake scarcely drinkable.

The next morning, after a little more knawing of the ham bone, they launched the scow and, the lake being calm, paddled back to be warmly received by Mother McCabe.

Such was the first pleasure trip on the Muskoka lakes by its first summer visitors.

THOMAS M. ROBINSON

Among the settlers moving into the newly opened Muskoka was an English sailor, Thomas M. Robinson. In his later years, Mr. Robinson wrote his memoirs, which throw an interesting light on conditions in the new territory and also on the early summer trips of Bain, Campbell, and their companions.

In July 1860, Mr. Robinson arrived in Toronto seeking information about Canada's Free Grants and Homestead Act of which he had heard in England. His inquiries led him to Barrie where he met an agent for Muskoka lands and was supplied with a map with lots marked for settlement. By stage he reached Orillia and, by rowboat, Washago, where a sawmill was in operation. Severn Bridge was the only post office in Muskoka—the postmaster walked the 12 miles to Orillia and back every Saturday with the mail. Robinson walked up the Muskoka Road. Long after

dark he found the home of a Dutch settler, Frank Webber, who put him up for the night. Next morning, accompanied by Webber, he continued his march, finding Micky McCabe's inn a mile farther on. The McCabes, he says, were the settlers farthest north at that time. Half a mile farther they took an Indian trail to Muskoka Bay, or McCabe's Bay as it was then called, where they found a bark canoe, which they borrowed to paddle up the east shore. A mile or two north he fell in love at first sight with the land surrounding Cliff Bay and extending to the narrows, and decided to make it his home. (Many years later it became the site of a famous sanatorium.)

Robinson then returned to England and, in January 1861, set sail from Liverpool with his wife and all their household possessions to take up life in their new home. Whatever may be thought of his judgment in choosing midwinter for the venture, no one could question his courage.

They reached Severn Bridge by road from Orillia. There he left his wife at Hugh Dillon's hospitable inn and the next day walked to McCabe's where a Mr. Mercier offered him a nearby lot with a building on it for $25. He closed the deal and set to work to make a more habitable dwelling.

Since his visit of the previous summer, a number of settlers had moved in and taken up land along the road, one even going as far as Muskoka Falls, the end of the road.

In the spring Robinson finished his log shack, brought his wife and their goods from Severn Bridge, settled in and began clearing his lot on the lakeshore for their permanent home. He bought a small punt to use for reaching his land and was later engaged to take a party of surveyors by lake to the North Falls (Bracebridge). He had no knowledge of the lake but managed to find his way. Soon after this trip, seed corn was urgently required in the little community, and reports said it was to be had at the Indian Village of Obajewanung (Port Carling), somewhere to the north of Lake Muskoka. Robinson, in spite of the fears of his anxious wife, volunteered to find the village and set out with another man to row there. They worked up the east side of the lake, exploring every bay and inlet. At last, near sunset, they entered the Indian River and so reached the village with its log houses and cultivated lands. By sign language, for they spoke no Ojibwa, they explained the object of their visit, got their corn, and held out their money from which an old man selected a moderate number of coins. Most of their return journey was made in the dark with a thunderstorm brewing, but with luck and perseverance they reached home. These two trips made Robinson the most experienced navigator of the lakes in the neighbourhood.

About this time Hugh Dillon began to run a large sailboat between Washago and Orillia connecting with the steamer *Emily May* from Belle Ewart. Robinson was engaged as captain with a young man as crew, and the passengers usually took turns at the oars when there was no wind. Settlers were beginning to swarm into the country. Robinson wrote:

Among the passengers not looking for land were two young men, the pioneers of that class who have made the name of Muskoka famous the world over. The young men in question were students at the University who, with adventurous spirits, were the first to go into the wilds of Muskoka as tourists. They were John Campbell, famous in Theology and for years professor in a college in Montreal, and James Bain, for years Chief Librarian of Toronto and eminent as a scholar. On this occasion they walked to McCabe's and stayed for the night and borrowed a boat and slept under it at night on a sandy beach and on their return walked back to Severn for the night and carried a lot of botanical specimens to Washago and took the boat with me to Orillia the next day. This proved the pioneer tourist trip which has brought thousands and is still bringing multitudes annually to that picturesque locality.

It must be noted that Mr. Robinson, writing many years later, blended together the walking trip of Bain and Campbell in 1860 with that of Campbell, Bain, and Crombie in the following year. Neither of them was a student at this time.

By the autumn Robinson had built his new house, which was to be his home till replaced with a larger one 20 years later.

THIS ISN'T THE MUSKOKA CLUB, BUT IT COULD HAVE BEEN. REEF ISLAND, LAKE JOSEPH, 1887.

In June of the following year, 1862, Robinson received a letter from Campbell and Bain, who hoped to return that summer for a longer trip if Robinson could act as guide. This he welcomed, as he was eager to learn more of the unexplored country and also urgently needed some ready money, for he was on his last few silver coins.

Unfortunately Campbell and Bain's log of this trip has disappeared. However, Robinson fills the gap. He gave a very detailed account of such a trip, which he says was made in that year, though he includes in his account one or more incidents that certainly occurred in following summers. He was one of the party in at least three successive years, though his journal describes only one.

THE 1862 EXPEDITION

According to Robinson's recollection, he, Campbell, Bain, Crombie, and Robert Morrison manned the boat (though there is strong evidence in the journal of the 1863 expedition that William Tytler, who wrote it, was also present in 1862). They spent the morning of a lovely day in late July loading their boat, a barrel of biscuit causing considerable difficulty, and pushed off after a hearty dinner provided by Mrs. Robinson, whom they left on the shore full of fears for her venturesome husband and "too sad to say good-bye." The wind was fair and they carried a small sail, and making good time, camped on Eight Mile Island where they passed the night in a thunderstorm in which the biscuit barrel and some of the blankets suffered.

The next morning broke fine and clear. They climbed to the top of the island and were so enchanted with the beauty of the scene that, according to Robinson, English failed them and they took to Greek. After a swim, breakfast, and much picking of the abundant huckleberries, they got

OFF FOR THE HOLIDAYS, WATERCOLOUR, AUDREY MATHIESON.

under way again, stopping at a sandy beach near the mouth of the Indian River where they spread out the blankets and biscuits to dry. About sunset they reached the Indian Village and hauled their boat up the rapids, not knowing there was an easy lift-over where the locks are now. It was dark by the time they reached Lake Rosseau and they were now in country unknown even to Robinson, so they made for the first low point. They set up camp with some difficulty, and it was nearly midnight before the tent was pitched and supper eaten and they could settle down.

The mosquitoes woke them early and their only protection was the smoke of their fire. Again the morning was clear and still and they pulled to the west, for all they knew of Lake Joseph was that it lay in that direction. This course should have taken them directly to the mouth of the Joseph River, but somehow they missed it, though they searched, as they thought, every bay and inlet for the channel to that elusive lake. The Indians called it Obwadgwajung, and said it was the most beautiful of all the lakes. After spending a

few hours fishing, bathing, and huckleberry-picking, they turned south into a long bay on the western shore of which they saw thinner woods on a sandy ridge, the future site of Port Sandfield. They climbed the ridge and beheld water on the other side, unsure if it was another bay or Lake Joseph. However, the spot was just the place for a permanent camp, so they unloaded the boat and pitched the tent. Laying poles on the sand, they hauled the boat up and over the ridge and launched her, the first craft other than a canoe to float in Lake Joseph.

After an early supper they set off to explore their new discovery. As they went west, the bay opened to their right till they saw the full long sweep of a lake opening toward the northwest. They knew then they had found the elusive Lake Joseph, "last, loneliest, loveliest, exquisite, apart" as it then was. They pressed on toward the setting sun and "the picture was too grand," wrote Robinson, "to be described." The captain turned the boat about and, in the dark, they found their camp by the light of the fire. With thankful hearts they lay down, resolved on a long day of exploration on the morrow.

The weather, however, ordained otherwise, for it rained all day and they stayed in camp.

The next day Crombie was left in charge of the camp, though why they thought this necessary is not clear, and the remainder set out to explore their new discovery. The day was fine and clear with a west wind. With the object of exploring the lake and finding the outlet to Lake Rosseau, they coasted up the east shore till they came to Loon Island, where the lake "seemed to divide in two." They struck to the northwest, explored either Gordon Bay or Hamer's Bay, and finally reached the lake head, the future Port Cockburn. On their return they seem to have explored Little Lake Joseph and actually entered the Joseph River, but thought it a bay with a log lying across the bottom of it. As night was closing in they made for camp, after a full and arduous day's work, for they must have covered well over 30 miles. But they'd failed to find the outlet and decided to try again from Lake Rosseau.

All the next morning was spent in getting the boat back over the sand ridge, a difficult job, for the western slope was much steeper than the eastern one. They accomplished it by placing her broadside to the water and lifting first one end and then the other. In the afternoon they rowed north and found a bay not previously explored. This led to the long-looked-for outlet, the Joseph River, for they came, after several miles, to a small two-foot waterfall beyond which lay the log they had seen on the previous day. They had now achieved both their objectives and set out on the return journey to Muskoka Bay, which they reached in good time the following afternoon, camping on Daisy Island in front of Robinson's house.

So ended the first real pleasure trip on the Muskoka lakes. It was to be repeated summer after summer for many years. The composition of the parties varied, but two were always present: John Campbell and James Bain, who had first walked to Lake Muskoka in 1860, looked on its untouched beauty, and resolved to return.

THE 1863 EXPEDITION

In his journal, William Tytler lists the members of the party as follows:

1. Captain – R. Morrison	for short, Captain
2. Chaplain – W. M. Smith	for short, Pills
3. Steward – J. G. Fraser	for short, Star
4. Geologist and Secretary – W. Tytler, B.A.	for short, Hanns
5. Fisherman – J. Bain	for short, Finn
6. Curate and Botanist – J. Campbell	for short, Curate
7. Boy – Jos. Campbell	for short, Boy
8. Guide – T. M. Robinson	for short, Ducens

Their journals were evidently kept as aids to memory rather than as dull logs and are more concerned with amusing incidents than geographical detail. One must therefore read a good deal between the lines, sometimes, to be quite sure of what actually happened. The first few lines of Tytler's journal give an idea of his peculiar style:

MONDAY, JULY 20TH—Rush to station. Fall of about 15 drops of rain. Finn with the gun rushing like the wind. Whistles. Hats. Pipes. Baggage car full. Smoking extraordinary. Fraser will you pass the rosy. Rain. Belle Ewart. Emily May waits for excursionists. Packing the traps. Train arrives, red coats and blue jackets. Ladies fair, disheveled hair. Hands full of sandwiches and other beverages.

However, it appears they were met at Orillia by Robinson, took passage in a boat to Washago, and walked to Dillon's at Severn Bridge where, after supper, they sang half a dozen songs apiece, said prayers, then went to bed.

On Tuesday they procured a team of oxen and a wagon, in which they loaded their boats and traps. All went well for five miles, at which point they reached the home of the oxen, who promptly headed for their stable, breaking the wagon tongue around a stump. Ducens made a seamanlike splice and, after a short stop at McCabe's, they reached the landing, 14 hours after leaving the Severn, a distance of 13 miles. The boat was launched and loaded, and they arrived long after dark at Robinson's hospitable house where Mrs. Robinson awaited them with an excellent supper.

The next afternoon they set off up Lake Muskoka and camped on Eight Mile Island. The following day, July 23, they passed the Indian Village, this time portaging their boat instead of pulling her up the rapids and, with a fair wind, made their old camping ground (Port Sandfield). The day ended, as most did with: "Supper, concert in the evening, lots of jokes and repartee. Turn in early after prayers."

On July 24, all but the Curate and Hanns rowed up the Joseph River (they called it the Katago) and back to camp via Lake Joseph. It rained the next day and they only did a little exploring and botanizing, but the day finished with "a great evening of song, jest, quip and crank," the Chaplain making a great hit with a new song, "Vive la Companie." The grog was issued and after prayers they turned in about midnight.

On the next day, Sunday, the Sabbath was strictly observed. A pulpit was rigged up and the Curate conducted morning service with the Steward as precentor. After a dinner of fried ham, rice, and huckleberries, afternoon service was held, also by the Curate. A bathe and tea were followed by a reading by Hanns, a good deal of sacred music, the shorter catechism, issue of grog, and then to bed.

126 Camping on Yohocucaba, Lake Joseph   On Muskoka Line

On Monday they were up early, struck camp, and set off up Lake Joseph against a very stiff headwind. They landed on an island inhabited by the Indian chief Pegamegabo and his family. It is fair to assume that this was the little island just south of Yoho which was named after the chief and is now known as Peggy. They obtained some geographical information from the old man, who spoke a little English. Camp was made near the head of the lake where they stayed all next day, exploring, fishing, picking huckleberries, and receiving a visit from "our old friend Peg." That evening there was a double allowance of grog and they didn't turn in till one o'clock. It was a good night.

Wednesday was fine with a fair wind down the lake. After a little difficulty they found the Joseph River, made the portage in 10 minutes, and then on to the Indian Village where they portaged in the dark in 15 minutes. They were obviously becoming more expert. At 11 o'clock they camped on an island in Lake Muskoka, and Tytler records "a jolly day and splendid moonlight night."

The next day they started late but lunched at the mouth of the Muskoka River and went up to the North Branch Falls. To quote Tytler's cryptic notes, "Saw mill, make boat fast, McDonald's hotel, sleep no go, up at 2, breakfast, start at 4 for South Falls, over in boat, arrived at McDonald's, trout fishing, stage full." (Muskoka was developing by then—hence the "stage.") Apparently they parted here with the Captain and Boy and pulled down river and around to Robinson's house on Muskoka Bay. After supper, some of them attended "McCabe's concert, the last of the season." Much is left to the imagination.

On Saturday, August 1, they were awakened at three in the morning to be in time to catch the stage to Washago. The Robinsons produced breakfast and they started for McCabe's Landing at four, said goodbye with "three cheers for Ducens and another for the bairn," got themselves somehow to Washago, and so home by way of the steamer *Fairy*, which then seems to have been running on Lake Couchiching.

Dramatis Personae

At this point it may be well to give some account of these men insofar as records allow.

The captain of this expedition, Robert Morrison, was a young Scotsman in the employ of James Campbell, the father of John Campbell and head of the publishing firm of James Campbell and Son. He married John Campbell's eldest sister, Christina, and his grandson, Herbert C. Barber, now has a cottage on the north end of Yoho Island.

AS EARLY AS THIS PICTURE LOOKS, IT WAS TAKEN AT LEAST 20 YEARS AFTER THE MUSKOKA CLUB GAVE YOHO ISLAND ITS NAME.

Of the Chaplain, W. M. Smith, I know nothing. The Steward, J. G. Fraser, was, I believe, a bookkeeper in a wholesale drygoods house. The Geologist and Secretary, William Tytler, was a tall, spare individual with a delightful sense of humour suggestive of Mark Twain. He was born in 1841 and graduated with a B.A. from Toronto University in 1862. In 1924 his alma mater conferred on him the degree of LL.D. He was first a teacher and later chief inspector of schools in Guelph, Ontario. In his 80s he still retained his charm, his humour, and much of his vigour.

Finn, the Fisherman, James Bain, Jr., was born in London, England, in 1842 and, at the age of four, arrived in Canada with his father who, some years later, established a book and stationery business on King Street just east of Yonge Street in Toronto. James, Jr., began his career in his father's business but later entered the firm of James Campbell and Son, where he became a close friend of John Campbell. In 1872 he was sent to represent the Campbell firm in the city of his birth. Here he established a publishing business of his own in conjunction with J. C. Nimmo. In 1882 he returned with his family to Toronto and became private secretary to Professor Goldwin Smith at the Grange. When Toronto's first public library was formed he was made librarian, a post he held with great energy and ability until his death in 1908. The establishment of the Public Reference Library on College Street was chiefly due to his untiring efforts. He was deeply interested in early Canadian history, and the collection he made of early Canadian records and documents is unique and of great historical value. He was honoured in 1902 with the degree of D.C.L. by Trinity University.

The Curate and Botanist, John Campbell, was born in Edinburgh in 1840, and after a stay in Alsace, where he was sent at the age of 14 to perfect his French and German, he joined his father's firm in Toronto, but later entered the University of Toronto from which he graduated brilliantly in 1865. He was university prizeman in English verse in 1863, and in English prose in 1863 and 1864. He was Prince of Wales prizeman in arts, gold medallist in metaphysics, and gold medallist in modern languages in 1865. At the same time he was sufficiently up in botany and geology to give the lectures during an illness of the professor. In the following year, while at Knox College, he took his M.A. In 1867 he graduated in divinity from Knox College and in 1868 from Edinburgh University. From 1869 to 1873 he was minister of Charles Street Presbyterian Church, Toronto, and was then appointed professor of church history and apologetics at the Presbyterian College in Montreal, a post he held till 1904. His great love, however, was languages, both living and dead, of which he had a very broad knowledge, and he devoted himself untiringly to his ethnological and archaeolgical investigations. The number and variety of

MLA 1984 YEARBOOK

THERE'S NOTHING LIKE A BRISK THREE-MILE ROW, FOLLOWED BY A LEISURELY PICNIC LUNCH ON ONE OF MUSKOKA'S MANY ISLANDS. STRANGE HOW IT ALWAYS SEEMED TO BE UPHILL GOING HOME.

his publications listed by the Royal Society of Canada, of which he was elected a fellow, is extraordinary. These and his work in deciphering archaeological inscriptions brought him an LL.D. from the University of Toronto, the Order of Merit of Roumania, and the Bronze Medal of Honour of the French Republic.

His work, however, was all done in seven months of the year. During the long summer months in Muskoka, he worked with the same vigour in his garden, scarcely ever opening a book.

The Boy, Josia Campbell, was John Campbell's younger brother, and at the time of this second expedition was 15 years old. He died in 1870.

Perhaps the outstanding characteristics of these men were a keen sense of fun and humour, a love of the wilds, a great capacity for good fellowship, and an artistic nature, which enabled them to make their own amusements, write their own songs, and later, even to write and act in their own plays and operas. They enjoyed their evening "grog," which in no way conflicted with their strong religious principles. Many of the deep friendships cemented in their Muskoka trips lasted the rest of their lives.

THE 1864 EXPEDITION

This third expedition is the last for which we have a journal. It was composed of the following:

1. Captain — J. G. Fraser (alias the Star)   ex Steward
2. Chaplain and Naturalist — John Campbell   ex Curate
3. Steward and Secretary — James Bain (alias Finn)
4. Armourer — Master Jos. Campbell (alias the Boy)
5. Armourer No. 2 — Master Ewart
6. Ducens — Mr. Robinson

It should be noted that Morrison, Smith, and Tytler are missing and that Master Ewart (later J. S. Ewart, K.C.) has been added. Also, some promotions have been made. Fraser becomes Captain, Campbell becomes Chaplain, and Jos. Campbell is appointed Armourer.

This time the Chaplain seems to have preceded the others by two days, leaving Toronto on Saturday, August 6, and arriving at Severn Bridge at seven that evening. On Sunday he walked to Robinson's "preaching at two stations" on the way. ("Stations" were private homes lent to itinerant preachers for services.) Next day he botanized and met the party at McCabe's. The rest of the journal was kept by James Bain.

On August 9, they reached Robinson's house, put off at once up the lake, and camped on an island four miles above the narrows. Next day they sailed and rowed into Lake Rosseau and camped on an island. "Tea, good concert, drinks and to bed—hard day's work."

The following day, August 11, was terribly hot and they didn't get far up Lake Rosseau. The next was better but recorded as a quiet one with numerous amusing incidents; on August 13 they set out for the head of Lake Rosseau where they found signs of a river, presumably Shadow River, but were unable to get through the marsh at its mouth. There was much shooting at ducks by the two boys, Campbell and Ewart, which was invariably unsuccessful, but they found a delightful camping place where they had "the finest night yet" and a concert.

On Sunday there was a "general perusal of religious literature by all hands and a morning service conducted by the Chaplain." After lunch reading was resumed and the day finished with a sacred concert.

On Monday a portage was found and the river entered and followed, till the way was blocked with snags. Later they came across a bark wigwam. The two Indian men they met gave them some geographical information, but the women seemed "without the faculty of speech." Josia Campbell, it was recorded, fired at a bittern in a tree and brought down a porcupine, a successful shot at last.

On August 16 they rowed, taking 40-minute spells at the oars to Sandfield, where they camped. Next day there was an expedition to Lake Joseph up the Joseph River and back again, followed in the evening by games, a concert and a "general bend." The captain gave a double allowance.

On the following day the party set out for home, passing, in Lake Muskoka, several fires and tremendous smoke over the lake, but camp for the night was made on Daisy Island again. The next day the swamp at the Black Hawk Rock River (now known as the Hoc Roc) was explored for botanical specimens, and for the first time the journal mentioned the name of Gravenhurst.

On Saturday, August 20, the party walked to Washago, caught the little steamer *Fairy* to Orillia, where dinner at the Queen's was "very good and cheap," had a stormy passage in the *Emily May* to Belle Ewart, and then went on by train to Toronto.

THE FORMATION OF THE CLUB

In September 1864 the Muskoka Club was born with seven members: Robert Morrison, D. Cowan, John Campbell, James Bain, J. G. Fraser, W. M. Smith, and W. Tytler. Its goals were "to provide an annual expedition for its members, to preserve the records of past expeditions, and to receive information on subjects of interest to its members." It had a president, vice-president, secretary-treasurer, editor, and curator whose duties are set out in the constitution. The membership fee was one dollar a year.

From 1865 to 1871, we have no written record, but much happened in those years. The earlier trips were exploratory expeditions, and so for some time the club had no fixed abode. To quote from one of their songs:

From Island to Island like sea birds we roam,
The Lake is our pathway, the forest our home.

Muskoka was gradually changing from a wilderness to a summer resort area. In 1866 Mr. A. P. Cockburn launched the first steamer to ply the lakes, the *Wenonah*, by which the Indian Village could be reached much more quickly than by rowing. In 1869 she was manouevred up the Port Carling rapids (where the small locks now are) by building successive coffer dams behind her. She then plied Lake Rosseau and was replaced on Lake Muskoka by the *Waubamik*. A steamer had begun to run from Orillia to Washago while the 14 miles from there to Gravenhurst were covered by stage in four hours. The passengers usually arrived rather bruised and battered.

In 1865 or 1866 the club selected Chaplain's Island, near the entrance from Lake Joseph to the Joseph River, as a permanent camp. They brought up some lumber and built a shed to cook under. They took Cowper's phrase "Oh! for a lodge in some vast wilderness" and called it Ophir Lodge.

It must have been about this time that the first ladies intruded on the hitherto monastic club. One summer, John Campbell was packing his kit when his younger sister, Elizabeth, my mother, standing by, said, "Oh, how I wish I could go with you!" "Why shouldn't you?" he answered. At that time it was a revolutionary idea. Ladies going into the wilds for fun? However, that year or the next, Mrs. Young, wife of Professor Young, who later became a member of the Muskoka Club, offered to chaperon. Elizabeth, her sister Jessie, and their friend, Louise Ewart, a sister of Armourer No. 2, the future husband of Jessie Campbell, made the trip. They took their sketching material with them, for they were all members of an art class of which Ernest Seton Thompson was also a member.

This must have been in the late 1860s, because in 1871 it was recorded that ladies had been with the club for several years. Later the chaperon's duties were performed by Christina, the eldest of the Campbell sisters after her marriage to Morrison, the Captain.

In 1871 the locks at the Indian Village were completed and a cut made to connect lakes Joseph and Rosseau at Port Sandfield, thus opening the upper lakes to steam navigation. This and the extension of the railway to Washago brought about revolutionary changes. The Muskoka Club

EVERYBODY LOVED TO COME TO YOHO ON A SUNDAY
MORNING TO LISTEN TO JOHN CAMPBELL PREACH
WITHOUT NOTES OR TEXT. EVEN THE YOUNG BOYS
WEREN'T BORED BECAUSE THEY COULD WATCH
CATERPILLARS FALL OUT OF THE TREES ONTO THE
LADIES' FANCY HATS.

by this time had guests, both ladies and gentlemen, as
well as members, who came and went during the season.
Among the guests was "Signor Sandi, our musical director,"
the charming and most tuneful Scot, William Alexander,
whose granddaughter Miss Bertha Alexander occupied
Yoho for many years. The fisherman of this year was
"Signor Thomas Campbello," another of John Campbell's
brothers. Another famous fisherman was Dr. W. H. Ellis,
the author of one of the most beautiful of the Muskoka
songs written in 1870. How long before that date he joined
the group I do not know, but he was a very frequent and
welcome guest at Yoho for 40 or more years after it. His
wonderful obituary on John Campbell in *the University of
Toronto Monthly* has been much drawn upon in this story.
For many years he was professor of applied chemistry at
Toronto and was succeeded by Prof. Watson Bain, the son
of his old Muskoka friend.

The era of the summer hotel was ushered in by W. H.
Pratt, an American, who opened the Rosseau House at the

head of Lake Rosseau in 1870, and charged the then fabulous
price of five dollars a day for rooms and meals on the American plan. The club did not appreciate the change. Perhaps
another of their songs best conveys their point of view:

Peace and plenty in our dwelling,
Beef and biscuit in our store,
Oatmeal, all oatmeal excelling,
Where's the wretch would ask for more!
Let him go and live at Pratts'es
Roost a while with Dugald Brown,
Where mammas with noisy brats-es
Long to pack their traps for town.

Far from gasolier's and lustre's
Sickly artificial light,
Every eve our party musters
Round the camp fire burning bright,
None may sleep while Signor Sandi
Leads the philharmonic din,
While we raise our voices and he
Plays upon his violin.

It should be realized that though for 10 years settlers
had been flocking into Muskoka, some of the civilization so

introduced was pretty primitive, as Frederick Delafosse shows in his book, *English Bloods*. On one occasion, the club spent Sunday in Gravenhurst and attended church in a body. The minister was duly impressed and, to do justice to the occasion, preached a sermon he felt to be a little over the heads of his flock, for he concluded, "You, my brethren, may not understand the words I say, but they is men here that understands them, men of gigantic intellect, men as goes on an unrolling and unrolling of their thoughts and committen on 'em to paper."

Some time in the early 1870s a settler by the name of Frank Forge, who lived on the east shore of Lake Rosseau near the present site of Windermere, inaugurated the first supply-boat service. He rowed a large 20-foot boat loaded with eggs, milk, fresh vegetables, and so on, around the upper lakes. Later he bought a small steamer, the *Ethel May*, and in the early 1890s he was still calling twice a week at each cottage, alternating with the *Mink*, operated by W. Hanna, Port Carling's leading merchant.

In 1871 Chaplain's Island was considered inadequate to the needs of the Muskoka Club, and on August 22 a select expedition set out to find a more suitable home—a larger island with a good harbour, a beach for the ladies, and ground for a garden. Luck was with them, for they found all these two miles westward across the lake. The name they gave it, Yoho Cucaba, was formed by taking the first two letters of each of the names of five of their members— Young, Howland, Cummings, Campbell, and Bain—and it has been known ever since as Yoho.

A rough survey was now being made of the lakes, and islands were numbered and offered for sale by the Department of Crown Lands. The first such sale was made in 1872 to James Bain, the club secretary. It included, besides Yoho, its satellite Peggy (on which Pegamegabo had been camping when they first met him), Burnt Island, Bungay Mena, and Litchie Mena (Little Huckleberry and Big Huckleberry). The price was, I believe, one dollar an acre.

Of the five men who gave Yoho its name, three are new to the record. Prof. George Paxton Young, M.A., LL.D. was a professor of logic, metaphysics, and ethics at Knox College, a man of striking appearance with an enormous white beard. He was universally loved and respected for his sense of humour, great earnestness, and a profoundly reverent nature. As Prof. Hume said in the university *Monthly* in 1927, "He was a great soul." Around the rough plank table his was always the seat of honour, the cheese box. He died in 1889. William H. Howland was a son of Sir William Howland and was later mayor of Toronto. Montgomery Cummings, a student at Toronto University, hailed from the Deep South to which he returned after graduation to practise law. I know little of him except that he was known

as Long Cummings, to distinguish him from the cat, Shortcomings, a sister of Sins.

THE KAMPHIRE KALEIDOSCOPE

From 1871 to 1876 we have a written record, but although it reveals much of the spirit and character of the club, it's rather baffling for the historian. Each year the Muskoka Club provided itself with a nicely bound folio book in which the members seem to have been encouraged to inscribe whatever their muses inspired in them, either in prose or verse. There are a very few serious words in any of the contributions so that actual facts have to be searched for and usually are found by inference. As literature it ranges from the worst of doggerel to charming, if rather ponderous, prose and some of the more beautiful songs. None of the entries are signed.

From the *Kaleidoscope*, from the *Doomsday Book* in the Parliament buildings, the Parry Sound Registry Office, and from family records, the following facts emerge.

In 1873 the club's nearest neighbour, a settler called Pilkey, was engaged to erect a building on Yoho. It was a rectangular affair of modest proportions, probably with a cook shed at the back. The members slept in tents, so it seems it was used as a dining room and a wet-weather refuge. It bore a large sign reading Yoho Cucaba Lodge.

The next year, the club numbered six honourary members and 33 ordinary members. As well, there were 18 gentlemen guests and 35 lady guests. They came and went throughout July and August.

There were also four guides recruited from the Indian reserve at Rama on Lake Couchiching—John Moses, George and Richard Snike, and Joseph Yellowhead.

The literary style of the period was decidedly verbose. The writers did not believe in using one word where two or three would do. For example, on August 18, 1871, the *Kaleidoscope* editor wrote:

Friend after friend departs. We are sorry to be compelled to announce that two more of our party have left Chaplain's Isle to return to civilization. Mr. Burns and Bone's Boy are gone! Yes gone! We stood this morning at the summit of the isle watching the boat as it carried them away. We waved our handkerchief in response to the waving of theirs and, when the boat rounded the last point at which it could be seen—you may say it was folly and deem us weak, but we were unable too repress our emotions. We sobbed aloud. Even now as we write, what is this trickling down our cheek? It is a tear.

There is a long description of the acute distress of Signor Sandi on finding that he had burned the porridge, only relieved when it appeared that "the slight brownness had

FRANK MICKLETHWAITE TOOK THIS PHOTOGRAPH OF JOHN AND MARY CAMPBELL'S COTTAGE IN 1887.

added to its charm just as the sunburn on the ladies' cheeks added to theirs."

Some of the poets have a soul above the rules of metre and would stop at nothing for a rhyme. Here is the beginning of one of the better efforts:

> Tell me oh! Muse who on Chaplain's Isle
> At the catching of fish is the cleverest fellow
> The fair muse replied with a radiant smile
> 'Tis Signor Thomasso Campbello.

> As Signor Sandi's without a peer
> In drawing sweet sounds from the violincello
> So none in the fisherman's art can compare
> With Signor Thomasso Campbello.

The news items have such headings as:

ASSAULT ON A LADY BY A MINISTER OF THE CHURCH (referring to a pillow fight between the Chaplain and a lady guest)

and

OPENING OF PARLIAMENT ON YOHO (followed by an account of the arrival of the governor-general in state, the disgraceful behaviour of the leader of the Opposition, and the general confusion and rioting that followed).

One writer fills several pages with an eloquent argument for the continued presence of ladies, "not only for their refining influence but for their culinary ability." One item headed official gazette reads: "Cooks for tomorrow are Miss Maggie Young and Miss Campbell. Assistant, the Chaplain."

OTHER ARRIVALS IN LAKE JOSEPH

The club's purchase of its group of islands in 1872 was soon followed by others. In 1873 George W. Strange bought two islands farther north and James McLennan bought three, but it seems that they did not immediately build on any of them. In 1875 Mr. Oldright bought the island now known as Elsinore. The following year James Campbell visited the club on Yoho and presented it with a flag. He was the father of John Campbell and six other members or guests of the club and the employer of several more. To the young members he seemed a rather staid and dignified old Scot, and not unnaturally they dubbed him the Chieftain, or Chief. He fell in love with a large island across the lake from Yoho. He bought it that autumn and it became Chief's Island.

Next spring, he had a gang of men at work building a modest family cottage, the first on Lake Joseph. It contained one living-cum-dining-room 15 by 13 feet and two small bedrooms plus a kitchen and store room, and was an object of amusement for the wry inhabitants of Yoho.

For 10 years James Campbell's daughter, Elizabeth, my mother, kept house for him at Chief's Island. In 1881 she married J. Herbert Mason. He had been a guest at the island, which apparently had been a rather frustrating experience. Aboard the *Nipissing* on his way back to town, he wrote Elizabeth explaining that during his stay she had been so continually occupied he'd had no opportunity to speak to her alone. He was therefore driven to propose to her by mail.

After their marriage she continued to manage Chief's for her father until she and her husband bought the island four years later. The way of life changed little and James Campbell was an honoured guest until his death.

END OF THE CLUB

Just when, how or why the flourishing Muskoka Club came to an end I have been unable to find out. But in 1877 John Campbell bought the five islands that the club had owned for only five years. Two years earlier he had married Mary Playfair and, for the rest of their lives, Yoho was their summer home. Much of the spirit of the old club days remained, the devotion to plain living and high thinking, the scorn of luxury and modern conveniences and, not least, the camp fire that burned every evening at the corner of John Campbell's hospitable verandah. There he welcomed old friends and new, and men of letters from many lands, and the jokes and the good talk were seldom lacking.

To those who knew them, the memory of John and Mary Campbell is interwoven with that of Yoho. There he worked indefatigably in his garden as only a lover of nature could. There every Sunday morning he donned his "blacks" and his Glengarry cap, betook himself to the wharf and greeted each boat and canoe as it arrived for the morning service. There in a little hemlock grove he preached his inimitable sermons. There his wife ruled the household with a firm hand and heart of gold. She ran a post office to the great benefit of the neighbourhood because, she said, she would go to no one else for *her* mail, and on Yoho their family

of three boys was brought up, as were also several of their nephews and sons of the old Muskoka Club members.

No account of John Campbell would be complete without a reference to his Yoho sermons and his preparation of them. After breakfast each morning he walked in his garden and no one disturbed him. Well before church time he had drawn from his memory, without reference to any book or notes, a story, allegorized in a few closing words. His sources were the legends of many peoples, including the Egyptians, Irish, French, Polynesians, Jews, Babylonians, Wyandot Indians, the Greeks, and the Buddhists; he drew also from the Norse eddas and the Sanscrit classics of India.

At the conclusion of the service, as the ladies were brushing the hemlock needles from their dresses, he disappeared to reappear again in a few minutes wearing his grey shirt and slacks with a small red tie and his Glengarry, and just as he had greeted his congregation, so he bade them goodbye at the dock.

In July 1904, John Campbell passed quietly away in his sleep on his beloved island, and for years his widow carried on much of the old traditions, as did her niece Bertha Alexander after her. The island has since passed on to three of their grandchildren. ▷

A VIEW OF THE LIVING ROOM ON CHIEF'S ISLAND, 1914.

PORT CARLING CIRCA 1915, CHALK PASTEL, JACKIE CARROLL.

8

THE LAST WALTZ

Life in the Golden Era of Muskoka Resorts

BY BARBARANNE BOYER

OR A GOOD MANY YEARS it stood vacant and forlorn in derelict solitude on a wooded hill beyond the lake. And in this time-weary state of neglect it gave very little indication of being anything but a decrepit old building that had known better times.

Its chimneys were collapsed, its roof beyond repair, the wide verandah sagged and rotting. The dozens of windows that banked the facade were cracked, and clouded with years of grime. What shutters remained hung drunkenly at odd angles, and there was not a single trace of white paint left on the exterior.

The once lavish interior was as ramshackle as the exterior was shabby. Splintered glass, broken china, and odd bits of furniture littered the well-worn floorboards laid down more than a century ago. The years had flown by, new owners had come and gone, and yet even after decades of disuse its silent rooms still whispered softly of long-forgotten events and the people who graced them. . . .

The first time the girl saw the hotel was from the railing of a Muskoka steamboat as it churned through the sparkling blue waters. It was nestled on a hillside surrounded by towering virgin pine and old maples, bathed in brilliant sunlight, dappled by cool shimmering green, all smiling and radiant in pristine white. She shaded her eyes against the glaring afternoon sun and leaned out over the railing, anxious not to miss a single detail. She'd not seen anything lovelier in all her 17 years.*

Even from this distance she could see the gracious sweep of the long verandahs and the elegant wide staircase leading down to the lawns where gentlemen in flannels and straw boaters strolled the winding paths with ladies in billowing long gowns and picture-frame hats. She could also see quite clearly the fancy gingerbread trim outlined in the gables and eaves and along the tops of galleries as delicate as Mother's lace doilies. And beyond the tangled web of flowering vines, the rows of wicker rockers invitingly placed just so, with uniformed waiters dancing attendance.

* The girl and the hotel are composites, drawn from the impressions the author gained from interviews with families who have long-standing traditions of summers in Muskoka. They are cottagers now, but their forebears were an intrinsic part of that golden era of Muskoka's hotels and lodges.

As she stepped back from the railing and adjusted her new straw hat, she noticed with a smile of satisfaction that she was not the only one captivated by the hotel's charm and coquettish air. For indeed it appeared that nearly everyone on the upper deck was straining for a better look at the newest hotel on the lake.

The girl's family, like most well-heeled late Victorians, cherished home and hearth, but delighted in the intrigue of adventure and romance. Family members were much concerned with their health and well-being, and being at one with nature held great appeal. And so, with record numbers of other families, they travelled to the Muskoka lakeland, firmly believing that the crisp fragrant air would heal their bodies and rejuvenate their spirits and fortify them for the winter to come.

They craved adventure and the sense of freedom changing one's day-to-day routine gave. They wanted to "rough it," but only to a degree, for they still expected to find most of the amenities of civilized society. And they wanted a jolly good story to tell family and friends back home, and were determined to have it. Stifling hot summers, black flies and pesky mosquitoes, the dreaded poison ivy, and fishing trips with leaky boats—nothing deterred them. Nor did getting there, for contrary to popular belief, getting there was not always half the fun.

First, Father had to attend to his business. The girl was involved in the tedious chore of closing up the family's city dwelling. Oh, not for a few days or weeks, but rather the whole season, sometimes May to September. And then there was the packing. Steamer trunks had to be lugged down from the attic or up from the cellar and thoroughly cleaned. The aunts' favourite rockers were made ready to send, along with fishing paraphernalia and a carefully straw-packed case of private stock. Picnic hampers included a set of good china and silver, table linens and napkins, a folding table and chairs, as well as a striped canvas awning. The selection of proper clothing was vital and so never left to chance. The younger family members, therefore, required the assistance of older, more knowledgeable family members.

Clothing for the ladies, young and old, was assembled

104

IN 1870 AN AMERICAN, HAMILTON FRASER, CONSTRUCTED
SUMMIT HOUSE, ABOVE, AT PORT COCKBURN. THE PICTURE
AT LEFT SHOWS THE INTERIOR.

in the large trunks. Morning gowns, tea gowns, evening attire, bathing garb, tennis and yachting outfits, as well as a suitable selection of hats, gloves, shoes, parasols, jewellery, and of course ones "whites." In many smaller trunks, a dozen in all, the family carefully packed toiletries and linen, the ivory and silver-plated brush sets and accessories. Daily journals and writing implements and other precious items no one could bear to be without.

All this required weeks of preparation, of course, and the result was often frayed nerves and short tempers, notably the aunts'! As the day of their summer exodus approached, the flurry of activity grew to fever pitch as everyone scurried about on last-minute errands and fare-thee-well teas with friends and family members who weren't partaking in this grand summer exodus.

The day of departure was an event in itself. At Union Station Father took charge of all the possessions while Mother kept track of the boys, never an easy task. The aunts perched regally in a relatively quiet corner fanning themselves, but all the while keeping a stern eye on the groups of boisterous young dandies bound for the lakeside tent colonies.

As the station's regulator clocks ticked off the minutes, anticipation mounted, and when finally the signal was given and the gates swung open, a cheer went up from every corner. Uniformed porters surged forward, dodging through the crowds, weighted down with the personal belongings of holidayers. Laughing and jostling one another, the college boys awkwardly balanced valises and racquets and fishing gear. The wide-girthed aunts, experts in travel, determinedly hiked up their heavy skirts, hoisted bird cages, bandboxes and all, and artfully, using the pointed tips of their black parasols on the unsuspecting, sailed off down the platform like two great ships under sail, porters and servants following in their wake.

Her father and younger brothers enjoyed the "steam train" journey north tremendously, and Mother could now finally relax. The aunts, on the other hand, found the trip tedious and uncomfortable, and twittered complainingly most of the way. As for the girl, she relished the time. She could ponder, daydream, plan her Muskoka adventures, for surely there would be many.

The summer of 1894 was an especially memorable one for the family, because it marked their first season in Muskoka and the grand opening of the newest hotel on the lakes. How they looked forward to the distinction of being counted among the first guests to register that long-ago May, and sadly, the last nearly half a century later.

Built entirely of wood, as were all summer lodgings back then, the hotel was everything the brochures claimed it to be. Spacious, elegant, and grand, with accommodations and facilities for more than 300 guests. A large wharf and boathouses, a lovely sandy beach, and bath houses. Expansive lawns and new gardens and a charming summerhouse where the girl knew she would spend countless hours alone with her journal.

And situated off the main reception foyer was a billiards room and smoking lounge with a great stone fireplace and mounted trophy heads and comfortable armchairs. Her father, and her brothers as they grew older, spent considerable time in this male domain. Opposite this foyer was a charming, light, and airy sitting room with chintz-covered wicker rockers and little writing desks tucked away in cosy corners. There were palm trees and ferns on wicker stands, and Chinese carpets on the highly polished wooden floors. Here her mother and the aunts whiled away the evening hours over endless china pots of English tea, with their ever-present fancy-work at hand.

The dining room, with its high vaulted ceiling and tall double French doors, held dozens of tables. Each was covered with snowy linen, and set with sparkling silver and monogrammed china. Every other day or so fresh bouquets of summer blooms appeared as centrepieces. The meals were nothing short of superb. Roast Muskoka lamb or chicken served with salads and fresh-baked bread. An assortment of fruits and cheeses, and great slices of moist rich cake. And on special occasions the dining room was

NO TELEVISION, NO VIDEOS, NO RADIOS, JUST COCA COLA AND A LOT OF HOMEMADE FUN.

transformed into a glittering ballroom beneath bowers of twining vines and fragrant wild blossoms; candles flickered on the tables that surrounded the ballroom floor.

The bands and orchestras were often quite renowned, as were the singers, whose stirring renditions of old and new melodies delighted guests no end. Much preparation went into these galas by staff and guests alike. The men assisted in stringing hundreds of coloured lanterns along the upper galleries and verandahs, as well as down the main driveway leading to the wharf, creating a fairy-land effect. On these occasions a light buffet of salads and sandwiches, dainty little cakes, ices and fruit in crystal bowls was served. A separate table held a selection of spirits and fruit punches. The ladies and girls spent hours collecting the flora that banked the buffet tables, taking enormous pleasure in the results.

To the girl the scenes were glorious. Her feet were clad in dainty satin slippers, and she glided over the shining floor in a kaleidoscope of colour, in the arms of some handsome youth, whose name years later she could no longer recall. But dazzling images of twinkling stars suspended like diamonds in a midnight-blue sky remained crystal clear. The gentle sounds of lapping water, laughter on a gentle breeze, and the shimmering whirl of satin and organza created a portrait frozen in time.

Social life was by no means confined to the boundaries of the family's own hotel, for much time was spent launching around the lakes and taking noonday meals with friends at their hotels. For the girl and her brothers, summertime meant freedom, though that is not to say manners or certain rituals were any the less observed.

Boys however, were allowed much greater rein than girls, a point she sorely resented. They could come and go about at will. To Monteith House for roller skating and Beaumaris for bowling. They could go barefoot too, except of course in or around the hotels. The girl was not permitted this luxury. Many of her afternoons were spent in the company of her mother and aunts and other female guests, some of whom had daughters her age. Girls were encouraged to expand their artistic abilities, and so learned the art of basket weaving and how to make picture frames and small boxes from birch bark that they gathered ourselves. In the summer of 1894 she began a new scrapbook, which she diligently filled with mementoes of the season, and she continued this tradition for many summers to come. In time, too, overcoming the strenuous protests of her aunts, she leaned how to swim and handle watercraft—more proficiently, some said, then her brothers!

The afternoon tea was a ritual observed at most hotels between four and five. Weather permitting, on the screened-in verandah off the dining room and occasionally on the stone terrace. Granted, it was less formal than at home but, in its own way, equally rigid. It meant a freshly laundered

OVER THE YEARS THOUSANDS OF POSTCARDS WERE SENT FROM MUSKOKA ALL WITH THE SAME BASIC MESSAGE: "HAVING A GREAT TIME, WISH YOU WERE HERE."

107

108

frock each day, something of cool white linen, long-sleeved, and full-skirted. And for many years until fashion dictated a change, a flower-bedecked straw hat or parasol for shade was mandatory, even on the verandah.

In fact, life on the verandah of a Muskoka resort such as this was like a stage performance. The verandah itself was a place to see and be seen, and as such it was necessary to keep up appearances. It was a gathering place for all from dawn till way past dusk. Guests played cards and board games there. Read the latest novels and the newspapers brought in daily by the steamers.

The verandah was an arena for the gentlemen too, whose spirited conversations often became quite loud. Politics, finance, and the general state of the world were discussed at great length. The girl, who couldn't resist her impulse to eavesdrop, found these assemblies much more stimulating than the afternoon teas!

From their comfortable wicker rockers, her family could watch the world unfold before them. The girl found the comings and goings of the hotel staff particularly intriguing, as she could always count on one or two romances to develop over the summer—developments she watched with lively interest, curiosity, and not a little envy. She was amused by the flurry of activity that erupted among the staff at the impending arrival of a distinguished guest, or the uproar caused when the high-spirited boys played their frequent pranks.

Summer activities were many and varied. The hotel often arranged moonlight excursions around the lake with late-night buffets and dancing. Afternoon picnics were held on nearby islands with members of the hotel staff to serve. The girl enjoyed the group nature walks into the forest—but not too far. And wild-berry socials, bazaars, costume parties, fishing derbies, and croquet and tennis and golf and baseball games. There were stimulating readings, and lectures to attend with visiting missionaries, who opened the door to exotic far-off lands.

Such were summers in Muskoka. Carefree and gay, a time when lifelong friendships were forged, old ones rekindled, and affairs of the heart blossomed. The girl's scrapbooks, long since buried in a battered old steamer trunk and yellowed with age, contain in their pages a testimony of these summers, of family and long-ago friends and events captured in sepia prints. Dance cards and programs, tinted souvenir postcards, and hotel menus. Not the least of the scrapbooks' mementoes are those that recall the annual regattas.

THE TOP PICTURE IS AN EARLY VIEW OF ROSSEAU, TAKEN FROM WHAT WOULD BECOME KAWANDAG, SIR JOHN EATON'S ESTATE. THE TWO LARGE BUILDINGS ON THE RIGHT ARE MONTEITH HOUSE, ROSSEAU'S FINEST HOTEL.

The first season the girl's family spent in Muskoka coincided with the Muskoka Lakes Association's first annual regatta, held on August 13, 1894, at Windermere. The regatta quickly became the highlight of the season, and each of the lakeside hotels vied for the honour of hosting the event. Newspaper reporters gave glittering accounts that always included the names of the socially prominent and their guests, along with the names of the individual steam launches. The Muskoka Navigation Company operated special excursions to and from the Muskoka Wharf, the various hotels, and the regatta site.

Each summer the crowds grew larger. People came from all over the surrounding lakes and towns, and up from the cities. Hotels, inns, and boardinghouses were filled to capacity. Wharfs and private docks were lined three and four deep with water conveyances of every possible description. They arrived in groups from every walk of life, if not to participate in the day's events, then to simply watch. As the great day grew nearer hotel guests watched from the verandahs with mounting interest the training and practising that took place out on the lake.

Within the hotel at which the family stayed, chaos reigned amongst guests and staff alike. Vast amounts of food and drink were brought in to fill the luncheon hampers that guests would be taking to the regatta. Special extras could be purchased from the supply boat *Constance*. The staff was run ragged, particularly the maids and laundresses who hurried up and down the long corridors between the rooms with piles of fresh linens, carefully starched shirts, immaculately pressed gowns, and yachting whites. Boots and shoes were polished to a mirror shine, and new silk flowers and streamer ribbons freshened up white straw hats. The hotel launch had to be made ready, a chore all enjoyed. While the staff saw to the gear—picnic hampers, parasols, comfortable cushions, throws, and deck chairs—the ladies helped to deck out the boat with red, white, and blue streamers and paper lanterns.

It was quite a sight. A wonderful flotilla of steam launches, sailboats, canoes, and rowboats gliding across the lake, their occupants laughing and waving and calling out to one another. The regatta, of course, was an all-day event, colourful and exciting with great crowds lining the shores and spread out along the hillside. On board the larger hotel launches, concerts and lively tea parties were often held.

The events were many, and canoeing and rowing were great favourites among spectators and participants alike. Later in the evening, weary but jubilant, everyone packed up and joined the throngs at the wharfs, waiting to board boats that would take them back to their respective hotels and cottages.

Almost all the hotels hosted a ball and supper. Linking

Royal Muskoka

Hotel. When you come to the Royal Muskoka you have the satisfaction of knowing that none of Muskoka's beauties——none of her recreations——can escape you. All are focussed for you here at what is admitted to be the most comfortable hotel in Canada. Location, the most healthful on the Lakes—deep in the craggy heart of Lake Rosseau. Absolute comfort studied in equipment. Running water in bedrooms—splendid table—orchestra—wide, cool piazzas inviting rest and meditation. Miles of beautiful and restful forests, lake and island scenery visible from every room and verandah.

The atmosphere of the Royal Muskoka is one of courteous welcome—so genuine that it cannot be classed as a mere hotel. One never leaves it with the impression that he has been stopping at a hotel, but rather that he has been a welcome guest at a most beautiful home.

Its visitors are members of a great family of congenial people, who find here the ideal conditions and the home in the woods which they seek. It is a rendezvous for lovers of outdoor life and spontaneity of thought and action is apparent in the lives and doings of the great number of young people who visit the Royal Muskoka. Tournaments in golf, tennis, bathing, boating, regattas, pilgramages to forest retreats and to mountain tops; excursions by water and by land; dancing, musicales, and entertainments.

But the new attraction is the newly improved golf course—opened by His Excellency the Duke of Devonshire, in 1918—the last word in a nine-hole watered course. Several hundred yards have been added to the old course and you now begin and finish your play in front of the hotel.

For Booklets, reservations, and further information, address the Manager, Royal Muskoka Hotel

Until June 10th : 347 Adelaide St. West, Toronto.   After June 10th : Royal Muskoka P.O., Lake Rosseau, Ont., Can.

90

THE ROYAL MUSKOKA HOTEL, BUILT IN 1901 BY THE MUSKOKA LAKES NAVIGATION AND HOTEL COMPANY, WAS ONE OF THE FINEST OF MUSKOKA RESORTS. IT BURNED DOWN IN 1952.

MUSKOKA LAKES MUSEUM

arms, laughing and cheering, guests would make their way up the gaily lit paths to the front verandah as the band struck up a lively tune. They would toast their winners and dance the night away as the band played on.

With the death of Queen Victoria in 1901 came the end of a glorious era. The Edwardian years, between 1901 and the First World War, were confident, no-nonsense, and full of changes. Muskoka by then had entered its heyday. The resort trade grew in leaps and bounds, and every summer one could expect to find at least one or more new hotels along the forested shorelines.

All the larger resorts now advertised farther afield, and their brochures touted Muskoka as a haven for those seeking relief from hay fever. The Grand Trunk Railway pamphlets and posters and the social columns in the Toronto newspapers helped to promote Muskoka as a "Wealthy Man's Paradise," and indeed it was. Existing hotels seemed always to be adding a new wing, a larger ballroom, a boathouse, or simply extending their verandahs. By now most hotels had tennis courts and bowling greens, and some of the larger resorts even had golf courses. Amenities such as gas lighting and private bathing facilities, which included hot running water and gleaming porcelain tubs and sinks, were further enticements. By 1913 there were hotel and boardinghouse accommodations for more than 5500 tourists, catering not only to the wealthy but to those with limited budgets.

The revelry came to an abrupt halt on August 1, 1914. Germany declared war on Russia, and soon thousands of Canadian men marched off for the battlefields of France, many never to return. Those left behind still ventured north each summer, but the spark was gone. Everyone had a husband, a son, or a brother off fighting for our country, and because of this special bonds were forged. Those on the homefront sat on the shady hotel verandahs and shared the latest news and letters sent from the trenches of Europe. The women knitted caps and socks and made up parcels to be sent overseas. They prayed together and consoled one another and the summers passed more solemnly than in any year gone by.

In the wake of the war was depression and much labour unrest. No new hotels sprang up on the lakes, perhaps in part because there were fewer men to build them. By the mid-1920s, however, things gradually returned to normal— and then beyond. An era of reckless abandon began, and the Roaring Twenties were here.

Frivolity and high jinks were the order of the day. Ladies considered themselves thoroughly "modern" now and took to smoking in public, bobbed their hair, and raised their hemlines to shocking levels. Taste in music changed. Ragtime and rhythm and blues were all the rage, and the Charleston was the latest dance craze. Muskoka hotels

ONLY A HANDFUL OF RESORTS FROM MUSKOKA'S "GOLDEN ERA" LIVE ON. WINDERMERE IS ONE OF THE PRETTIEST.

111

changed, too. The genteel formality of earlier decades all but vanished, as the good times rolled on.

Then, on October 26, 1929, disaster struck again. Suddenly, and for most without warning, the Great Depression began. Old established businesses went bankrupt, banks failed, and money became scarce. Lives changed overnight. No longer could many families afford the luxury of the season in Muskoka. They counted themselves fortunate if they could stay for a week or two at the most. The resort

industry felt the strain. Some hotels and boardinghouses were forced to close, and those that remained open did so on a shoestring.

As the depression began to lift, many longtime tourists who'd once found their pleasures as hotel guests were now becoming cottagers. This was partly due to the fact that roads were upgraded and Highway 11 was now paved. Whether simply out of habit or sentiment, many chose to build their new summer residences near their old haunts. The number of private cottages that sprang up was staggering, and by the late 1930s cottagers outnumbered resort visitors.

CLEVELANDS HOUSE, THE BRAINCHILD OF CHARLES MINETT AND HIS WIFE, FANNY, BEGAN AS SO MANY OF MUSKOKA'S RESORTS BEGAN—AS A FARMHOUSE WITH A VIEW.

113

CLEVELANDS HOUSE, WATERCOLOUR, LYNN HAGEY.

HOTELS AND BOARDING HOUSES AT MUSKOKA

(The name of the lake is shown in brackets after each name. The railway station, unless otherwise mentioned, is Bala.)

Town	Proprietor or Manager	Plan	No. of Rooms	Rate Per Day	Rate Per Week	Distance from Bala
BALA						
Birch Haven House	Mrs. W. Gray	AS	17	2.50	12.00 up	1¼ miles
Fairview Lodge	Mrs. E. Wright	AS	10	3.00	14.00 up	¼ mile
Grassmere House	Patterson Bros.	ABS	9	2.50	15.00	2½ miles
Moon Chute House	T. A. Edwards	AS	14	3.00	18.00	4 miles
Musquash Lodge	Mrs. E. M. Allen	ABS	10	2.50	15.00	3 miles
Windsor	Capt. J. Malcolmson	A	60	4.00 up	22.50 up	½ mile
Pine Grove Lodge	Mrs. Brush	AS	10	2.00	14.00	500 yards
Swastika	F. W. Sutton	ABS	54	3.50	18.00 up	¼ mile
Tree Lawn	Mrs. C. H. Pike	AS	12	2.00	12.50 up	¼ mile
BALA PARK (Station, Bala)						
Bala Park House	W. E. Ham	AS	10	2.00	14.00 up	2½ miles
Clovelly Inn	W. E. F. Colwill	ABCS	25	2.50 up	14.00 up	2½ miles
BEAUMARIS (Station, Bala)						
Beaumaris	J. E. McDonald	ABS	115	5.00 up	35.00 up	10 miles
Roseneath	Mrs. T. Mears	ABS	20	3.00	15.00 up	10 miles
BRACEBRIDGE (Station, Bala)						
Albion	R. Craig	A	30	3.00 up		25 miles
Bracebridge Inn	Mrs. W. B. Moore	A	40	2.00 up	10.00	25 miles
Queens	J. Thomson	A	30	3.50 up		25 miles
CRAIGIE LEA (Station, Barnesdale)						
Carlingford House	F. J. Ames	ABS	20	3.00	14.00 up	25 miles
Ma-Le-Ha-La-Lodge	Mrs. C. Campbell	AS	8	2.50	15.00	25 miles
DUDLEY (Station, Bala)						
Dudley House	C. Keeley	AS	15	2.50	12.00	2½ miles
ELGIN HOUSE (Station, Bala)						
Elgin House	L. E. Love	ABCS	200	5.00 up	24.50 up	20 miles
FERNDALE (Station, Bala)						
Ferndale House		ABS	56	3.50	16.00 up	13 miles
GORDON BAY						
Gordon House	Mrs. A. J. Clegg	AS	20	2.50 up	14.00 up	¼ mile
Island View	H. G. Ball	ABS	33	3.00 up	18.00 up	1 mile
GRAVENHURST (Station, Bala)						
Albion	M. Wasley	A	30	3.50 up	20.00 up	25 miles
Fern Glen	Mrs. M. F. Baillie	ACS	10	3.00	15.00	25 miles
Gilmour House	J. F. Gilmour	A	28	3.00	12.00 up	25 miles
Glen Ridge Lodge	C. B. Pitcher	AS	12	2.75 up	16.50	9 miles
Pine Dale	J. D. Brown	ABCS	75	3.00 up	18.00 up	25 miles
GREGORY (Station, Bala)						
Nepahwin-Gregory	Graham-Bell	ABCS	40	4.00 up	18.00 up	7 miles
HAMILL'S POINT (Station, MacTier)						
The Highlands	Bremner & McKeig	ABCS	50	Apply	18.00	6 miles
HUTTON HOUSE (Station, Bala)						
Hutton House	Mrs. J. Hutton	ABS	21	3.50 up	14.00 up	10 miles
Scarcliff	C. W. Riley	ABS	16	2.50 up	14.00 up	8 miles
JUDDHAVEN (Station, Bala)						
Ernescliffe	A. Judd	ABS	50	3.00 up	21.00 up	8 miles
Rest Harbor	R. Judd	AS	14	2.50	14.00 up	7 miles
The Bluff	T. L. Snow	ABCS	40	3.00	17.00 up	7 miles
LAKE STEWART (Station and P.O. MacTier)						
Buckeye Inn	H. O. Clinch	AS	13	2.50	14.00	1 mile
MILFORD BAY (Station, Bala)						
Cedar Wild	H. J. Sawyer	ABS	110	4.50 up	15.00 up	11 miles
Inglewood Cottage	Misses Riley	AS	16	3.00 up	11.00 up	11 miles
Milford Bay House	R. J. Stroud	ABCS	42	3.00	16.00 up	11 miles
MINETT (Station, Bala)						
Balmoral House	Mrs. H. Wallace	AS	10	2.50	15.00 up	18 miles
Cheltonia	Mrs. W. E. Fraling	AS	14	3.50	20.00	17 miles
Cleveland House	S. A. Minett	AS	100	4.00 up	25.00 up	17 miles
Leefholme	E. C. Leef	ACS	18	3.00	18.00 up	18 miles
Paignton	R. D. Pain	AS	30	3.00	17.50	17 miles
MORINUS (Station, Bala)						
Morinus House	E. Jacques	AB	27	3.00 up	15.00 up	20 miles
MORTIMER'S POINT (Station, Bala)						
Pleasant View	A. H. Bickmore	ABCS	40	3.00	14.00 up	7 miles
MUSKOKA ASSEMBLY (Station, Bala)						
Chautauqua Inn	W. E. Telfer	ABCS	65	3.50 up	18.00 up	15 miles
PINELANDS (Station, Bala)						
Belmont House	W. H. Fairhall	ABS	80	3.00	18.00 up	9 miles
Pinelands House	E. H. Jones	ABS	45	3.50 up	18.00 up	9 miles
PORT CARLING (Station, Bala)						
Havington Farm	W. K. Foreman & Son	ABS	35	2.50	14.00 up	12 miles
Oak Crest House	Mr. and Mrs. W. Wroe	ABS	15	2.50	14.00 up	12 miles
Port Carling House	G. Cannell	AB	50	3.00 up	16.00 up	12 miles
Riverdale Lodge	Mrs. J. Seehaver	A	10		12.50 up	12 miles
PORT SANDFIELD (Station, Bala)						
Edgewood Cottage (P.O., Elgin House)	Miss James	AS	12	2.00		6 miles
Elgin Lodge	L. M. Hall	AS	12	3.00	18.00 up	7 miles
Gleniffer Braes	Mrs. J. E. Hurrell	AS	14	2.00		6 miles
Hillview	W. Hall	AS	6	2.50	14.00	10 miles
ROSSCLAIR (Station, Bala)						
Rossclair	F. W. Foreman	A	12	2.50	12.00 up	8 miles
ROSSEAU (Station, Bala)						
Bay View	Mrs. M. E. Morris	AS	15	2.50	12.00 up	26 miles
Bide-A-Wee	Mrs. V. Einarson	AB	14	2.50	15.00	26 miles
Canadian Inn	W. R. Meads	AS	20	3.00	15.00 up	25 miles
Glenburnie	Mrs. J. K. Brown	S	10	Apply	Apply	26 miles
Maplehurst	Mrs. J. P. Brown	ABS	20	3.50 up	22.00 up	25 miles
Monteith Inn	R. J. Abbs	ABS	100	4.00 up	28.00 up	26 miles
Rossmoyne	J. Ariss	ABCS	30	3.00 up	14.00 up	26 miles
ROSTREVOR (Station, Bala)						
Rostrevor	Major E. Trump	ACS	50	5.00 up	25.00 up	8 miles
ROYAL MUSKOKA (Station, Bala)						
Royal Muskoka	C. B. Creighton	ABS	150	7.00 up		18 miles
STANLEY HOUSE (Station, Gordon Bay)						
Stanley House	Mrs. W. Bissonette	ABS	30	3.50 up	16.50 up	3½ miles
THOREL HOUSE (Station, Bala)						
Thorel House	G. Thorel	AS	45	2.50 up	14.00 up	16 miles
TORRANCE (Station, Bala)						
Camp Pine Crest (Boys)	Y.M.C.A.	ABS		Apply	12.50	4 miles
East Bay House	Mrs. S. Packer	AS	15	2.50	12.00 up	6 miles
Fairview House	W. G. Jeslin	AS	8	2.00	12.00	3 miles
Muskoka Springs Resort	W. O. Whiting	AC	11	2.50	15.00	2 miles
Torrance Pavilion	J. S. Davidson	AS				2½ miles
White House Farm	Mrs. T. Jeffrey	A	16	2.50	15.00	4 miles
WALKER'S POINT (Station, Bala)						
Montcalm	J. H. C. Willis	ABCS	9	3.00	16.00 up	14 miles
Walker House	H. Walker	ABS	19	....	12.00 up	9 miles
WHITESIDE (Station, Bala)						
American House	T. F. Walker	ABS	20	3.50 up	15.00 up	5 miles
WINDERMERE (Station, Bala)						
Fife House	A. W. Fife	ABS	31	4.00 up	23.00 up	15 miles
Ingleside	W. W. Brooks	ABS	28		10.00 up	16 miles
King's Park	Miss B. E. King	ABCS	40	2.50 up	14.00 up	11 miles
Maple Leaf House	I. Hough	ABS	24	3.00	16.00 up	16 miles
Newtonia Inn	F. W. Newton	ACS	20	5.00	30.00 up	17 miles
Windermere House	L. Aitken	ABS	100	4.00 up	25.00 up	26 miles
WOODINGTON (Station, Bala)						
Woodington House	M. Anderson	ABS	62	3.00 up	20.00 up	20 miles

A—American Plan
B—Sends its own booklet
S—Open in summer only
E—European Plan
C—Cottages to rent
Rates not guaranteed by Canadian Pacific

114

The winds of change blew again in 1939. For Muskoka resorts the Second World War meant a time of constraint. Everyone seemed to have money to spend, but precious little to spend it on, for nearly every material item was hard, if not impossible, to come by—gasoline in particular. As a result motoring north was out of the question so tourists soon began to come again by train and steamer in record numbers. This of course was a boon for the resorts and the surrounding communities. Locals were employed as maids, cooks, clerks, bellhops, and grounds-

1930 CANADIAN PACIFIC BROCHURE "MUSKOKA LAKES."

keepers, and their livestock and produce were needed to feed the guests.

After the war, life began to change dramatically as progress reared its ugly head. By the end of the 1950s both trains and steamers, once the only modes of transport to the resorts, were things of the past, and hotels, now fewer in number, again suffered. Trailer parks, motels, and cabin rentals began to appear rapidly. The number of privately

BY THE TIME THESE PICTURES WERE TAKEN, WIGWASSAN LODGE, AT THE NORTHERN END OF TOBIN ISLAND, HAD BEEN TAKEN OVER BY THE AFFABLE MR. GEORGE MARTIN. AFTER HIS DEATH IT FELL INTO DISREPAIR AND WAS TORN DOWN. ABOVE, WIGWASSAN SUMMER STAFF, 1941. HAD ALL THE BOYS GONE OFF TO WAR?

fire. The young girl who thrilled to her first summer at one of these would have been saddened at the passing, some of which happened in her time.

FIRE STRUCK THE DEATH KNELL FOR MANY OF MUSKOKA'S GRAND HOTELS:

Oaklands Park, Lake Rosseau,	1887–1900;
The Windsor Hotel, Bala,	1890–1909;
Bala Falls Hotel, Lake Rosseau,	1887–1913;
Summit House, Lake Joseph,	c1885–1915;
Prospect House, Port Sandfield,	1882–1916;
Brighton Beach Hotel, Lake Muskoka,	1895–1917;
The Bluffs, Lake Rosseau,	1902–1934;
The Beaumaris Hotel, Lake Muskoka,	c1870–1945;
Monteith House, Lake Rosseau,	1887–1950;
The Royal Muskoka Hotel, Lake Rosseau,	1901–1952;
and Ernescliffe, Lake Rosseau,	c1890–1968.

owned cottages increased greatly, and the last of the Muskoka supply boats were laid up forever as the lakeside marinas took their place. All of these changes no doubt helped to bring about the demise of many of the once grand old hotels. A good number were also destroyed by

All those many years ago . . . all those memories ago. And all that remains are the roads that bear their names. Muskoka's old resort hotels both past and present are as unique and diverse as the men and women who founded them, and each represents a special place in history and in the continuing story of Muskoka. ▷

SEGWUN SPRING, ACRYLIC, JANICE BARNES.

9
MEMORIES

Cottage Life at the Turn of the Century

BY BRENDAN O'BRIEN

IN SOME RESPECTS SUMMERS at the cottage have changed little in the past 100 years. The early morning, when the lake is calm and shrouded in mist, is still the best time to enjoy canoeing. The cry of the loon can still be heard echoing across the water. The upside-down tree on Hawk's Nest Rock near Port Cockburn, which was sketched by Edward Roper in 1883, yet remains. When the *Segwun* emerges from behind a distant island, it is easy to imagine the old *Kenozha* or *Islander*.

But differences, of course, abound. In the past there was almost no electric power, which meant no electric lights, no refrigerators or stoves, no radios or televisions or electric water pumps. Instead cottagers relied on oil lamps, ice-boxes, and wood stoves; some had gramophones, whose spring motors had to be cranked by hand. A few cottages were equipped with acetylene gas plants to provide light, and some had the Ericsson hot-air engine for pumping water. (One of these curious machines can be seen in the Port Carling Museum).

By the turn of the century the gasoline engine had been invented, but it was quite impractical for such domestic things as pumping water or propelling a small boat. The early engines were veritable monsters with huge heavy fly-wheels. They were hard to start—much laborious hand-cranking was in order—and once started made tremendous noise and emitted foul-smelling fumes. An inexperienced operator trying to crank one of these engines ran the risk of ending up with a broken arm. The 1906 MLA yearbook listed only four gasolines launches in all three lakes, but 52 steam yachts.

In the second decade of the century the gasoline engine saw two important improvements. The first, in 1912, was the invention of the electric self-starter, and about the same time, much smaller gasoline engines began to be produced. These engines, used in the first disappearing-propeller boats in 1917, did not need the self-starter, and even a child could start one by spinning the small flywheel. Some later models had a kick-starter and others a pull-cable. In John Rogers' *Muskoka Lakes Blue Book and Directory* of 1915 an advertisement appears for an Evinrude motor, describing it as a "portable detachable row-boat motor."

Gasoline boats in the early days did come with one major problem—the difficulty of getting gas. Even as late as 1918 one of the few suppliers was Charles Woodroffe on upper Lake Joseph. He operated a boat livery service near Foots Bay and sold gasoline in 45-gallon drums. At least two strong people were needed to heft one of these into or out of a boat.

But most cottagers in those days were happy with their canoes, rowboats, and sailboats, and enjoyed competing in regattas. Similarly, picnics and camp-fire cookouts, with everyone gathered round for a singsong after the food was consumed, were just as much fun as sitting on a deck with a gas barbecue—and unquestionably more romantic. As well, there was no worry about running out of propane with the meat half-cooked.

Another great difference between then and now lay in communication. At the turn of the century no one had a telephone, and there were few telegraph offices. What cottagers did have, however, was excellent mail service and lots of post offices. At the north end of Lake Joseph, within a radius of three miles, were six post offices—at Port Cockburn, Stanley House, Craigie Lea, Yoho, Barnesdale, and Gordon Bay. A 1906 advertisement of the Hanna store in Port Carling read "Letter Orders Promptly Filled," and such promises were always kept.

Cottagers were also presented with the problem of obtaining supplies. There were no automobiles, and even when they began to appear in the 1920s, the roads were something of a challenge. At the turn of the century the expression "year round road access" would have been quite meaningless. What was important was proximity to a steamboat wharf where the passenger steamboats and supply boats could make calls, which they did, frequently.

John Denison's *Micklethwaite's Muskoka* reports that the first automobile was seen in Bracebridge in 1903, and according to Geraldine Coombe's *Muskoka Past and Present*, one of the earliest automobiles to reach Muskoka was a white steam-powered vehicle from Pennsylvania that made it to Beaumaris in 1905. The first automobile to reach Port Cockburn, at the top of Lake Joseph, was in 1909. A chauffeur-driven, gasoline-powered Stearns-Knight

touring car, it was owned by William W. Harker of East Liverpool, Ohio, who was a regular guest at the Summit House Hotel. The arrival of this vehicle created quite a sensation, and the hotel proprietor, Alex Fraser, and his family posed in it for a photograph. It wasn't long before the photo appeared in colour on a postcard with the message "U auto come to Summit House, Port Cockburn, Muskoka, Canada." No doubt Alex Fraser, notorious for his bad puns, was the author of this bit of advice. Another photo taken a short time later, which did not find its way onto a postcard, showed the same automobile being loaded onto the *Sagamo* and making a most ignominious departure from Port Cockburn. A recent rainstorm was the culprit, for when wet, the clay on Skeleton Hill, just east of Rosseau, made the road impassable.

The first automobile trip the O'Brien family made to Muskoka was much later, in 1923, when I was 14. It was a McLaughlin Light-Six touring car, and I well remember our getting struck in the mud at a swampy section of the road between Foots Bay and Gordon Bay. We were there for what seemed like an eternity, up to our knees in mud and pushing the car with everything we had, all the while being attacked by swarms of mosquitoes and blackflies. On the trip home the car had trouble climbing the steep winding hill just south of Gravenhurst. With the continuous use of low gear and much pushing we finally reached the top, only to find the radiator boiling over violently, which of course necessitated a search for water. This trip to Muskoka, via Beaverton, took us almost a day in each direction!

Our cottage, named Kinkora, was built in 1905 not far from the Summit House Hotel at Port Cockburn. (The Summit House, sadly, was destroyed by fire in 1915.) We did not then own an automobile, but by horse and buggy we used to travel over reasonably good roads to Maple Lake and Rosseau where good stores could be found—and more importantly, at Rosseau, a barber, for children's hair seemed to grow awfully quickly in the healthy Muskoka climate. Because we were close to the hotel we had the advantage of being near a post office and a telegraph office; in addition we were able to get running water by connecting a pipe to the hotel water tank, which was supplied from the lake by a large steam-driven pump tended by an engineer. We could also get ice from the hotel icehouse for our icebox.

One hundred years ago, when the Muskoka Lakes Association was founded, nearly all travel to and from Muskoka was via the Grand Trunk Railway to Muskoka

Wharf at Gravenhurst and from there by steamboat up the lakes. My father was one of a very few travellers who reached the Muskoka Lakes via Georgian Bay and Parry Sound. Around 1890 he and a handful of other young men sailed up Georgian Bay from Penetang to Parry Sound in a Mackinaw sailboat. From there they went by stage to Port Cockburn where they stayed for several days at the Summit House, returning home by steamboat to Muskoka Wharf and then by rail to Toronto. Others sometimes made this round trip by taking a steamboat from Collingwood or Penetang to Parry Sound. The trip could also be made in the reverse direction.

In 1897 rail service to Muskoka improved, especially from Ottawa and points east. In that year J. R. Booth's Ottawa Arnprior and Parry Sound Railways began service from Ottawa to Depot Harbour on Parry Island, crossing the Grand Trunk line at Scotia Junction about 15 miles north of Huntsville. The new line provided a stage connection to Port Cockburn from Maple Lake Station, which was over a shorter and better road than the previous stage connection to and from Parry Sound.

Ten years later rail service to Muskoka saw a great improvement. MacKenzie and Mann had opened the new Canadian Northern line from Toronto to Parry Sound and beyond. Muskoka travellers had the convenience of no less than 10 stations, the most important of which were Bala Park and one at Lake Joseph Wharf, where direct steamboat connections could be made. A few months later the Canadian Pacific opened a parallel line that provided service to the village of Bala, which had steamboat connections, as well as service to Gordon Bay on Lake Joseph. But the CP station was farther from the lake than the Canadian Northern station, and consequently was little used for Lake Joseph travel.

The brochures the Canadian Northern Railway published, in describing the new Muskoka service, were not given to understatement or undue modesty. In one publication it was confidently asserted that the islands at the north end of Lake Joseph "are all within a short row of Lake Joseph Wharf," yet some of the islands mentioned were as much as seven miles away. Another brochure read:

From Long Lake Station on the Canadian Northern Railway a coach road has been constructed to Port Cockburn. The road winds through the quiet shadow of the woods and affords a pleasant driveway mightily convenient for visitors to the head of Lake Joseph.

These words caused much merriment at the Summit House and Kinkora. There was good reason that the four-mile road to Long Lake was known locally as the Rocky Road to Dublin. It is now Clear Lake Road.

"THE PRETTIEST SPOT IN MUSKOKA."

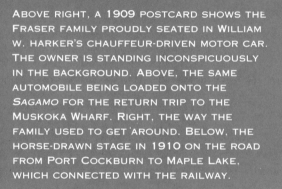

ABOVE RIGHT, A 1909 POSTCARD SHOWS THE FRASER FAMILY PROUDLY SEATED IN WILLIAM W. HARKER'S CHAUFFEUR-DRIVEN MOTOR CAR. THE OWNER IS STANDING INCONSPICUOUSLY IN THE BACKGROUND. ABOVE, THE SAME AUTOMOBILE BEING LOADED ONTO THE *Sagamo* FOR THE RETURN TRIP TO THE MUSKOKA WHARF. RIGHT, THE WAY THE FAMILY USED TO GET 'AROUND. BELOW, THE HORSE-DRAWN STAGE IN 1910 ON THE ROAD FROM PORT COCKBURN TO MAPLE LAKE, WHICH CONNECTED WITH THE RAILWAY.

BRENDAN O'BRIEN

LEFT, THIS ADVERTISEMENT FOR A MACHINE TO MAKE ACETYLENE GAS FOR HOME LIGHTING APPEARED IN THE 1906 MLA YEARBOOK. FEW COTTAGES USED GAS AT THE TIME, RELYING ON KEROSENE LAMPS OR CANDLES. ABOVE RIGHT, IN 1908, ON HIS WAY TO THE TENNIS COURT, MILEY O'BRIEN PAUSES TO ENJOY THE LATEST RAGTIME ON THE PHONOGRAPH.

IN 1911 SOME OF THE O'BRIEN FAMILY ARE ABOUT TO LEAVE PORT COCKBURN FOR THE CANADIAN NORTHERN STATION AT LAKE JOSEPH WHARF. THE STEAMBOAT IS THE *DREADNOUGHT*, OWNED BY JOHN HAMER, STANDING BY THE WHEELHOUSE.

The same brochure gave further assurances:

A mile from the Toronto Union the railway begins to skirt the River Don and soon afterwards ascends the exquisite valley which gives peculiar zest to the first dozen miles of the journey away from the Lake Ontario metropolis . . . An American traveller said recently, "I had no idea there was anything like it on this continent."

How could anyone resist the lure of a trip on this marvellous new railway?

Perhaps encouraged by the bit about the short row from Lake Joseph Wharf to nearby islands, my father, planning to come from Toronto on the night train, arranged to have a rowboat waiting for him at Lake Joseph Station. But the night was very dark and he mistook Emerald Island for Round Island. Not until he found himself near the head of Dixon's Bay (now Hamer's Bay) did he realize his error. The short row turned out to be closer to nine miles than six.

My father also had his problems with the Ottawa–Scotia Junction route to Port Cockburn. On one occasion he took the afternoon Grand Trunk train from Toronto to Scotia Junction, where he learned that a wreck in Algonquin Park meant no connecting train to Maple Lake. Faced with the prospect of spending the weekend at Scotia Junction, he managed to persuade a section worker to locate a handcar, which the two of them pumped by hand the 32 miles to Maple Lake. There he roused Percy Sword, the proprietor of the stage line—it was the middle of the night, don't forget—and got him to dispatch a special stage to Port Cockburn, finally arriving there toward dawn. In recounting this trip many years later, my father recalled that it was a beautiful moonlit night and that the occasional long upgrades the handcart had to climb were more than compensated by the exhilaration of cresting the rise and coasting for a great distance, seeing the silvery rails far ahead glinting in the moonlight.

A trip to Muskoka by rail, no matter what the connecting mode, was usually a challenging experience that bore no resemblance to the boring two-hour drive from Toronto afforded by fast cars and super highways today. I remember as a child eagerly anticipating the glorious adventure of a railway trip to Muskoka.

Planning a trip always began with packing the trunks, usually at least three for our family—six children made quite a crew—followed by organizing our hand luggage, of which there was all kinds. One item in particular I remember was the carryall, which consisted of an arrangement of straps and a handle by which a steamer rug could be converted into a large carrying device. All sorts of things could be packed in that.

THERE WERE TWO STATIONS AT BARNESDALE FOR THE SIMPLE REASON THAT THERE WERE TWO RAILWAYS RUNNING UP THE WEST SIDE OF LAKES MUSKOKA AND JOSEPH—THE CANADIAN PACIFIC AND THE CANADIAN NORTHERN. PICTURED HERE IS THE CP STATION.

For Muskoka travellers living in Toronto or any other large centre, the next step after the packing was to telephone a transfer agent to pick up the trunks and any other bulky items and take them to the station to be checked. Then arrangements had to be made to get to the station either by streetcar or horse-drawn cab; by 1905 taxicabs began to appear. American travellers had the additional problem of clearing customs, but this became easier and long delays were eliminated when customs officers began to ride the train between the border points and Toronto. There were through sleeping cars from Buffalo and Pittsburgh to Muskoka Wharf, as well as, by special arrangements, from Cleveland, where many cottagers lived. Some Americans preferred not to use the through sleeping cars and would plan a stopover in Toronto. They would probably stay at the Queen's Hotel on Front Street (at the site of today's Royal York Hotel) and visit Michies store at 5 King St. West. Michies supplied almost everything a cottager needed, from quality perishables, packed in sawdust in wooden boxes, to live dew worms, also packed in wooden boxes with moist sphagnum moss. Michies was internationally known for its fine foods and

123

fine service—once an order was placed all the shipping arrangements were seen to.

Cottagers obtained food supplies from many sources. Canned goods and such staples as flour, sugar, and tea might be shipped in bulk from Toronto, along with a ham or a side of bacon.

Before the First World War there were very few packaged foods. Some of the earliest were Quaker Oats, Cornflakes, and Shredded Wheat; Christies Soda Crackers came in large tin boxes with hinged lids. Cottagers could obtain fresh meat and dairy supplies from local farmers or the supply boats. One specialty was Muskoka spring lamb, and its fame spread far beyond Muskoka. And, of course, in season, strawberries, raspberries, and blueberries were plentiful; usually the fishing was good all summer. In the fall there were ducks and partridge and, later still, venison.

The summer supply of provisions for the O'Brien family was complicated by certain of my mother's strongly held beliefs. That they lacked scientific proof didn't trouble her in the slightest. For one, she knew that eating tinned food was extremely risky. Not only did you have an excellent chance of getting ptomaine poisoning from the contents, but you ran the danger of receiving an ugly cut from opening the tin with the primitive can openers of the time. Worse still, if the cut should be in the web between the thumb and first finger, the dreaded lockjaw was sure to follow. There was one exception to this rule about canned goods, and that was sardines. My mother believed that because they were packed in oil, sardines had certain medicinal and therapeutic properties, *and* they could be safely opened by the key that came with the tin. We had lots of sardines at Kinkora, but no Heinz pork and beans or Campbell's alphabet soup.

I wish my mother could have lived long enough to read about the recent scientific theory regarding the Franklin expedition to the Arctic—that the members succumbed to poisoning from eating tinned food.

Much of my memory of life in Muskoka before the First World War is fragmentary, but I do have one distinct continuous memory, and it's of our trip to Muskoka in the early summer of the year I turned five. Because we lived on a small farm in Dixie, about 12 miles west of Toronto, the journey was more difficult than the one from the city, where we'd lived until 1911. There was no baggage-transfer agent in Dixie, and our shipping problems were complicated by the fact that we not only had to get the trunks to the station ourselves, but also that Beauty, our Jersey cow, had to be taken to the Grand Trunk freight office at Port

THIS MICKLETHWAITE POSTCARD SHOWS THE VIEW FROM KINKORA WITH ROUND ISLAND IN THE DISTANCE. THE *KENOZHA* HAS JUST LEFT THE WHARF TO START ON ITS LONG TRIP DOWN THE LAKE.

125

LEFT, THERE'S NOTHING LIKE A PICTURE OF AN OUTHOUSE TO CONJURE UP IMAGES OF BLACK NIGHTS, FROSTY MORNINGS, WASP NESTS AND MAIL-ORDER CATALOGUES.

Dry Goods		Post Office
Groceries	**W. HANNA & CO.**	
Provisions		—
Boots and Shoes	**General Merchants**	Great North
Hardware		Western Tele-
Paints and Oi s	**PORT CARLING**	graph Co.
Tinware		
Crockery	*The Hub of Muskoka Lakes*	Canadian
Stoves		Express Co.
Furniture		

For over twenty years we have been catering to the tourist trade in Muskoka, and we feel confident we can supply all the wants of cottager, camper or traveller.

Our stock will be found larger and better assorted than ever. Our supply boat "MINK" will, as usual, make daily trips, calling at all points on Lakes Rosseau and Joseph. A fully assorted st ck of provisions, fruit, confectionery, fresh meat and bread on board.

Letter Orders promptly filled

FIRST STORE FROM BOAT LANDING

HANNA'S STORE WAS THE LARGEST IN PORT CARLING. AS WELL AS THE TOWN TRADE, MR. HANNA SERVED HIS COTTAGE CUSTOMERS BY RUNNING SUPPLY BOATS IN THE SUMMER.
THIS ADVERTISEMENT IS FROM THE 1906 MLA YEARBOOK. THE FACT THAT THE GROCERIES COULD BE ORDERED BY LETTER ATTESTS TO THE EFFICIENCY OF THE POST OFFICE.

Credit to be loaded on a freight car. I should tell you that my mother also believed that milk from Muskoka cows lacked the nutritional qualities growing children needed. Beauty's milk, on the other hand, was rich and plentiful.

Getting the cow to the freight office was done a couple of days in advance of the family's departure. We had to take an early-morning Grand Trunk local train from Golflinks station on the Dixie Road, to which point we had previously hauled our trunks by wagon. Since there was no station agent at Golflinks, when the train arrived we had to help load the trunks into the baggage car. The train pulled out and half an hour later we were at Toronto Union. With the co-operation of the conductor on the local train our trunks were checked through to Port Cockburn. After a short wait in Union Station we boarded Grand Trunk's famous Muskoka Express and we were on our way.

The train was complete with standard coaches, parlour cars, sleepers, dining cars, and an observation platform at the rear, and provided the very finest in railway accommodation. This was the trip we had looked forward to all spring. My three older siblings were already familiar with the significant landmarks along the route, and they pointed them out to me as we went.

The first sign of lake country was Kempenfeldt Bay at Barrie, which the railway tracks skirted for some distance. Then there were the Narrows at Atherley, where Lake Simcoe flows into Lake Couchiching. Next came the Indian reserve at Rama, followed by the level crossing of the Canadian Northern line at Washago. If a train was spotted on the other line, there was much speculation and rivalry among the O'Brien children as to which train would be the first to go over the crossing. I rooted for the Canadian Northern train. For young as I was, I had already become a firm supporter of that railway.

The reason was somewhat complicated. My younger sister and I were looked after by a nursemaid named Margaret Morrison. She was from Kirkfield, Ontario, which was also the home of Sir William MacKenzie, one of the owners of the Canadian Northern. Her father was the gardener at the MacKenzie estate, and before working for our family she was an employee in the MacKenzie household. I adored Margaret. Hence my undying loyalty to the Canadian Northern.

The indisputable highlight of a trip on the Muskoka Express was the visit to the dining car with its linen-covered tables, sparkling silverware, uniformed waiters, and tantalizing aromas from the galley. For a child nothing could equal the delight of dining on the exotic fare as the scenery slipped by the wide dining-car windows—except perhaps seeing all the envious train-watchers standing on the platform if we stopped at a station. No child could have asked for more.

Soon after leaving Washago we reached Muskoka Wharf, where we were reunited with Beauty. After much bustle and movement of people and baggage, we boarded the waiting *Medora* with Beauty and our trunks. After a warning blast of the whistle, we children watched over the stern rail as the water boiled up around the propeller and the steamer began to inch away from the wharf. Within minutes we were threading our way through the narrows into the broad and sparkling expanse of Lake Muskoka. Then began the long run to Beaumaris, where connections could be made for Bala and Bracebridge. One thing I clearly remember about the ride on the *Medora* was watching a deckhand lower a bucket overboard to get water for Beauty. I also recall a visit to the engine room with its distinctive smell of steam and hot oil; the powerful surging movement of the enormous piston rods, which caused the propeller shaft to revolve, was a sight not easily forgotten. Afterward we visited the dining room, on the main deck at the stern. I can still remember the taste of the Muskoka blueberry pie.

Eventually we arrived at Port Carling where we disembarked to board the *Kenozha*. Again a great bustle of activity, and soon our family, our baggage, and one no doubt bemused cow were on the last leg of the journey. But it was still far from over. Not only were there all the regular calls to make, such as Ferndale, Clevelands, Woodington, Gregory, and Port Sandfield, but also many calls at private docks. In Lake Joseph we stopped at Pinelands, Elgin House, Redwood, and Hamill's Point. By this time it was quite dark, and because the *Kenozha*'s boilers were fired by great billets of cordwood, from time to time we would see a glorious burst of sparks from the smokestack, accompanied by the unmistakable smell of burning hardwood. I remember being told that the next stop would be Craigie Lea, but I must have fallen asleep about this time, because the next thing I remember was waking up as I was being carried up the hill at Port Cockburn. Behind me at the wharf the lights of the *Kenozha* were still visible. It was almost midnight, and an unforgettable day was drawing to a close.

Soon I was in bed, lulled to sleep by the call of the whippoorwill and the distant tinkle of cow bells. The endless summer lay ahead. No one could have foreseen the horrors of a distant war, which August would bring. ▷

128

Summer Retreat, bronze & sodalite sculpture, Brenda Wainman Goulet.

10
ROOM WITH A VIEW

Cottage Architects & Builders

BY GRAHAM SMITH

A COTTAGE MAKES PARTICULAR demands on its architect and builder because the relationship of the architectural space to the landscape determines our experience of the setting. We experience space by the way we inhabit it, and we inhabit space by the way we wish to experience it. The arrangement of physical space, whether natural or man-made, greatly influences the conduct of our daily lives. The presence of an object or group of objects not only provides a view, but creates a distinctive atmosphere. We need not debate whether or not the falling tree makes a sound if no one is there to hear it, but stopping every once in a while to take a look around can be quite enlightening, for we will see that things we build define our experience. Although we cannot control the weather, the changing light of day, or the passing seasons, we react to such phenomena instinctively by building shelter.

The automobile is not often considered a shelter device; squealing tires and rapid acceleration do not have much in common with architecture. What automobiles and architecture do have in common is doors and windows. In his novel *Zen and the Art of Motorcycle Maintenance* Robert Purcig writes: "In a car you're always in a compartment, and because you're used to it you don't realize that through that car window everything you see is just more TV. You're a passive observer and it is all moving by you boringly in a frame." Similarly, architecture provides isolation from the surrounding environment. While this is often a desired effect in urban homes, such is not the case in Muskoka. The cottage architect seeks to fuse interior and exterior environments so that the transition from one to the other is not as jolting as opening the car door in the middle of the highway. Purcig continues: "On a cycle the frame is gone. You're completely in contact with it all. You're in the scene, not just watching anymore, and the sense of presence is overwhelming."

The precedent for the cottage goes back to classical times; for all intents and purposes the cottages of Muskoka are no different than the seaside villas of Pompeii, the chateaux of the Loire Valley, or, most notably, the country retreats of nineteenth-century England. The unsanitary and unhealthy conditions of Rome, Paris, London, Pittsburgh, or Toronto, in their respective eras, was more than enough to drive away those of our ancestors who could afford to leave.

William Hamilton commented on city dwellers in the 1879 publication of the *Guide Book and Atlas of Muskoka and Parry Sound Districts*: "In addition to what may be called the emigrating class (embracing all ranks and grades of society, from the richest to the poorest, and from the most highly cultivated down to the illiterate peasant) another very important and increasing multitude make Muskoka their temporary home—we mean the tourists, those birds of passage, who, like swallows, annually cool themselves by a migration to our northern fastnesses, and depart refreshed."

Attracted by the free land grants of the 1860s, the "emigrating class" came to Muskoka with expectations of farming the land. Hamilton notes that population of the free grant districts in 1879 numbered between 26,000 and 30,000. "We have pioneers from almost every country in Europe, except Turkey, the British Isles being our main feeders, though we have a respectable German and Scandinavian contingent. . . . Until lately, take of English, Irish, Scotch equal parts, sift thoroughly and add a dose of Canadian equal to the whole, would have been a good recipe to get at our Muskoka mixture. . . . We have also a sprinkling of intelligent Americans and would like more."

The census of 1871 for the townships of Wood and Medora, District of Muskoka, lists one Samuel W. Tracy, 42, of English origin; his occupation is shown as "architect, civil engineer & surveyor." Formerly a resident in Craven Road, Hyde Park West, London, and an associate of the Royal Institute of British Architects since 1854, he advised the institute of a change of address to "Gravenhurst P.O.," in 1870, just before disappearing from its list of members. Appearing in the census above Samuel Tracy's name is one Joseph Tracy, a farmer some 13 years younger than the architect who was probably his brother.

It is uncertain where in Muskoka Samuel Tracy resided or if he remained in the area for long. Joseph Tracy, however, married one of George Parlett's daughters and moved to

LAURALEA, LAKE ROSSEAU, WATERCOLOUR, MARION STEVENSON.

'THE BRACKENS'
LAKE ROSSEAU MUSKOKA
FOR HON. C.R. BRECKINRIDGE
BURKE & HORWOOD ARCHITECTS
28 TORONTO ST TORONTO ONT.
OCT 21 1904
SCALE 1/8 INCH 1 FOOT

NORTH ELEVATION

SOUTH ELEVATION

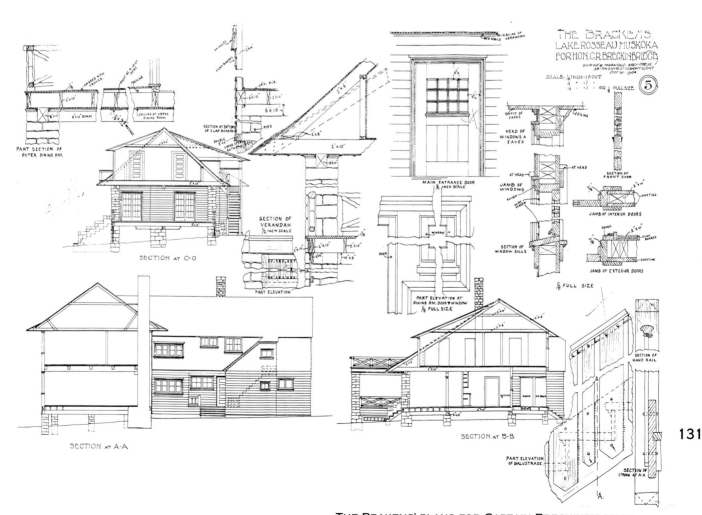

131

THE BRAKENS' PLANS FOR CAPTAIN BRECKINRIDGE BY
BURKE & HORWORD, ARCHITECTS. OCT. 21, 1904.

Walker's Point in 1874. According to Mrs. Joyce Schell of Walker's Point, he established a school that her father attended, and Joseph's sister-in-law built a home on the island opposite the Parletts' mainland property that "was impressive—far different from the customary log cabins of the day."

Let us assume for a moment that the cottage was indeed designed by Samuel Tracy. What might it have been like? Probably heavily influenced by the English design tradition known as the Picturesque and distinctly different from "the plain and homely barn with an added verandah" that Ann Hathaway described in *Muskoka Memories*, published in 1904. The Picturesque was a philosophy of design that extended well beyond providing mere shelter. It embodied the idea that architecture should allow the individual to see the landscape from the building, and see the building from the landscape, and that neither should be the lesser experience.

This idea was of little importance to the first settlers in Muskoka. Whether educated or illiterate, rich or poor, their need was for architecture that provided shelter from the harsh Canadian winter. Commonly they built houses that were one or two storeys and compact in form to minimize the external surface area. They had high-pitched roofs to avoid snow build-up, and small windows to conserve heat. Typical of farmhouses found throughout North America, many of these structures can still be seen on the lakes today, looking slightly out of place to modern eyes.

An excellent example of a very primitive Muskoka residence stood on the shore of the Moon River near Bala. This rustic log cabin, belonging to Thomas Renshaw, was photographed by John Boyd in 1888, although probably built some 20 years earlier. It forced on its inhabitants a rustic lifestyle for which an adventurous pioneering spirit was necessary. Yet, as with the automobile, the interior of the house is isolated from the external environment. Similar to, although considerably less comfortable than, a Victorian rowhouse, its small, dark, and poorly ventilated rooms probably gave rise to strong feelings of isolation.

Although a few adventurous tourists began to explore Muskoka in the 1860s, the first large wave of them came with the arrival of the railroad at Gravenhurst in 1875. Apart from Torontonians and other residents of southern Ontario, a great number of Americans travelled northward from Virginia, Ohio, Pennsylvania, and New York. There

were even some English families who crossed the Atlantic each year to summer in Muskoka. They built small cottages in a variety of styles on islands not far from the wharves where the steamers stopped. Proximity to the wharves was essential for transportation and supplies, since for individuals, rowboats were practically the only means of getting about. An island site, apart from its romantic isolation and variety of views, was also a pragmatic choice: its steady cool breezes tended to keep the bugs at bay, and perhaps most importantly, an island was separate from the mainland, which had a bad habit of catching fire.

Because the tourists required seasonal shelters rather than year-round homes, they introduced a new type of architecture to Muskoka. The fundamental difference was that, instead of keeping the heat in, as traditional residences needed to do, the object of seasonal architecture was keeping the heat from the hot summer sun out. Design restrictions imposed by the cold Canadian winter could be ignored because the buildings were for summer use only. Thus the size and shape of the building envelope was limited only by the owner's pocketbook rather than the architect's ability to insulate and heat the structure. Light, ventilation, and views of the landscape became primary concerns, along with the appearance of these pleasure homes. As the quality of the architectural space was brought into question, owners turned to architects and builders for answers.

On Evangeline Island, not far from Beaumaris, is an unpretentious little dwelling hidden in the woods. One of about a dozen cottages that make up the Fairhaven Island Association, it is quite different from the Gatsby-esque summer residences, some measuring up to 10,000 square feet, for which Beaumaris is famous. The outer dimensions of Evangeline (the cottage was named after the island) are 22 by 26 feet, excluding the verandah, and it has a very compact second floor. However, this cottage provides valuable insight into how architects and builders worked in Muskoka.

The story begins with the Ross family who built a summer residence on Keewaydin Island in 1880. Rev. William Wilson Ross was a Methodist minister who a short while later moved from Hamilton to Ingersoll where he became friends with Rev. William Kettlewell. After Ross died in 1884 his widow rented the cottage to the Kettlewell family. The following summer Kettlewell invited Rev. J. E. Hunter and Dr. H. T. Crossley (both men were known by their initials) to visit Keewaydin, and it was during this visit that the three men decided to look for an island to purchase. They ended up by buying both Fairhaven and Evangeline for $43 in 1886.

The first cottage was built on Fairhaven. Designed by

133

THOMAS RENSHAW'S LOG HOUSE ON THE MOON RIVER NEAR BALA, TOP, AND EILEEN GOWAN COTTAGE. BOTTOM, ON GOWAN'S OR HOG ISLAND, LAKE MUSKOKA. IT WAS BUILT BY NEIL LIVINGSTON IN 1878–9 FOR JUDGE J. R. GOWAN OF BARRIE.

134

GAZEBO, SOFT PASTEL, DAVE BECKETT.

Kettlewell and built by the clerical trio in 1888, it was intended to accommodate all three families, but turned out to be too large for the ladies of the household to manage. Two years later it was sold to the Tillson family of Tillsonburg. In a letter, dated August 1, 1947, E. V. Tillson recalled his father's purchase:

When he saw it—and examined it he had a hearty fit of laughter because it was a pretty crude affair as houses go. However no complaint was made—in fact father gave Mr. Crossley a great deal of credit as a "ministerial carpenter." It is quite evident from the cottages on Evangeline and Fairhaven that Mr. Crossley and Mr. Kettlewell advanced greatly in design and skill in their later efforts.

In reality, Crossley, Kettlewell, and Hunter could take even less credit for the "design and skill" of their subsequent projects. When Kettlewell built a new cottage on Fairhaven in 1898, the construction contract was awarded to the Brown Brothers of Bracebridge. And in the following year Crossley, the "ministerial carpenter," had Evangeline built. Perhaps realizing the limits of his own talents or being unwilling to give Kettlewell another chance at the drawing board, he commissioned the architect Sidney R. Badgley to provide the plans, which survive. Once again, the Brown Brothers were the builders. Left to their own devices, skilled builders like the Browns could also produce plans, although their designs lacked the sophistication that an architect could bring to the job.

In hiring Badgley it appears Crossley was acting on Hunter's behalf, since upon its completion the cottage was occupied by the Hunter family, who continue to summer there today. Crossley's own cottage, Coyne Crest (now Rock Holme) was erected on Fairhaven at the same time. Although no plans for it survive, the building is so similar to Evangeline in its layout and Queen Anne style there can be no doubt that Badgley was its architect, too. The same can be said for two other cottages built in 1902: Westholme, which is beside Rock Holme; and Seldoncliffe, which was identical to Evangeline right down to the last detail. Seldoncliffe, erected on Ross Point, Keewaydin Island, was built by Thomas Seldon, a close friend of Crossley and Hunter. It was demolished in 1974.

Crossley and Hunter were not only good friends but partners in conducting religious revival meetings across Canada and the United States. It may have been their tours that brought them into contact with Badgley, a Canadian

DAVE GIBSON

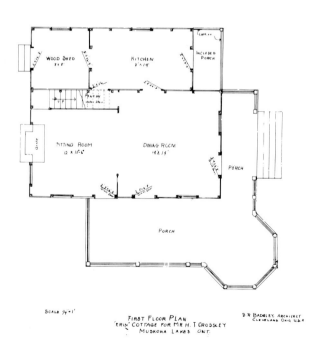

UPPER RIGHT, THIS PHOTOGRAPH OF SELDONCLIFFE, ROSS POINT, KEEWAYDIN ISLAND, WAS TAKEN BY ANOTHER KEEWAYDIN RESIDENT, PROFESSIONAL PHOTOGRAPHER EDGAR HUGILL. RIGHT, FIRST FLOOR PLAN FOR EVANGELINE.

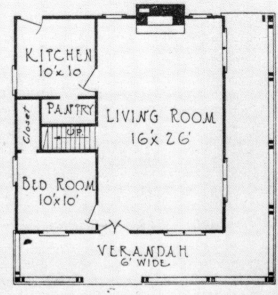

FIRST FLOOR PLAN

THE PARRY

AN all-summer home for a large family and their guests. If you can get the mate to it, you will care little whether the fish bite throughout the summer or not. Boating, bathing and fishing, long rambles in the woods and a summer home like this to return to at night and the troubles of life will be forgotten.

With the verandah screened against uninvited guests, the capacity of the first floor is nearly doubled. The second floor rooms are all open to the roof.

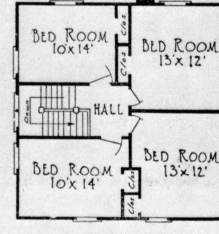

SECOND FLOOR PLAN

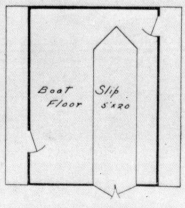

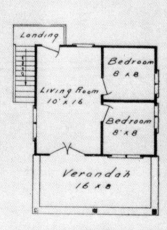

THE CARLING

FIRST FLOOR PLAN   SECOND FLOOR PLAN

HALF the pleasure in life is in variety. When city life palls, when the professional man's clients or patients get on his nerves, or the business man is tired in the morning, a location where he can tramp the woods and be on and in the waters of lake or river, gives the needed change.

Many, however, do not feel they can invest largely in a play home for two or three months of the year.

This combination of cottage and boat house, will offer a long needed solution at a price within the reach of all.

See terms on page 5 and specifications on page 77.

Eighty-seven

136

who had left St. Catharines, Ontario, to establish a practice in Cleveland, Ohio, in 1887. His projects included more than 100 churches throughout Canada and the American Midwest. He was noted particularly for his expertise in acoustics, which led to his being commissioned by Hart Massey in 1893 to design Toronto's Massey Hall.

Just as Evangeline and Seldoncliffe were built from the same plans, some cottages on the lakes resemble others because builders borrowed elements from drawings still in their possession from previous jobs. Another source of similarities was the use of pattern books, a popular Victorian practice that continues to this day. As early as 1889, catalogues of architectural plans were advertised in the *Bracebridge Gazette* by companies in Ontario, Pennsylvania, and as far away as England. Pattern books tended to feature year-round residences, but as the demand for summer houses by the growing middle class increased toward the turn of the century, companies began to provide small cottage designs in a variety of styles. Aladdin Homes of Toronto was one such company; it dedicated an entire section of its catalogue to prefabricated summer residences, attaching names like The Carling and The Parry to the designs.

By 1890 small cottages dominated the lakes. There were some notable exceptions, but few really large summer residences were built in Muskoka before the mid-1890s. Rather than cottage life, wealthy tourists preferred either the comfort of the numerous grand hotels or the minimal amenities of hunting and fishing camps. All this changed, however, between 1895 and 1915 when Muskoka was the focus of an enormous building boom fuelled by the availability of inexpensive land and the desire of rich city dwellers to escape the polluted air of industry. During this period no fewer than 300 cottages were built, a majority of them large, compared to only 100 or so in the previous two decades.

The boom in cottage building transformed the local economy, as lumberjacks became carpenters and cabinetmakers, farmers became builders and masons, and other year-round residents opened hotels and general stores to serve the growing number of tourists. Of the 30 or so local builders who competed for the larger contracts, several were particularly popular—the Brown Brothers, J. J. Knight, Harry Sawyer, C. A. Young, Alex Cameron, Robert Rogers, Norman Kaye, and George Leask. Yet none were as sought after as Peter Curtis.

Peter Curtis was not originally a Muskoka resident; he was a builder from New Castle, Pennsylvania. In 1895 J. P. H. Cunningham, also of New Castle, hired Curtis to

build a cottage in Muskoka that had been designed by a third New Castle resident, the architect Sydney Foulk. Blarney House, as it is known, still stands just south of Beaumaris, and while not the best example of Curtis's work, it illustrates the role a skilled builder could play. The original blueprints show a very different design from that built by Curtis. He rearranged the plan, moved the stairs and windows about and redesigned the foundations. The reason for these changes is that Foulk, like many American architects who designed cottages for the lakes, probably never came to Muskoka. As a result, while their drawings might have reflected highly accomplished designs, they assumed the sites were flat and grassy. In actual fact most cottages were constructed on slopes of jagged rock, so it was left to the builder to make adjustments for terrain or to alter the layout and fenestration to take advantage of a view while not jeopardizing the integrity of the design.

It appears that after completing Blarney House, Curtis continued to live in Pennsylvania and did not move to Milford Bay on a permanent basis until 1905. From this point onward the commissions poured in as wealthy Americans and Canadians bid for his services. Although he worked under a number of architects, notably Brandon Smith of Pittsburgh and Charles Gibson of Toronto, it is easy to distinguish Curtis's hand. His work is characterized by a phenomenal attention to detail and craftsmanship. For example, he required his carpenters to wear gloves when working on the interiors so that the acid from their skin wouldn't stain the wood. He also insisted that the tongue-and-groove walls be seamless, that is, every board had to extend from baseboard to ceiling or from beam to beam; never could two boards be used in a single course. He was also very particular about the types of wood used: maple or pine for the floor, basswood or birch for the walls, basswood for the ceiling, and ash for the beams and mouldings. Curtis's commitment didn't stop there; as well as outdoor furniture, he designed and built furniture specific to each room. The pieces are very masculine and geometric in design, inspired by the arts-and-crafts movement, particularly the work of Stickley and Morris. Some of this furniture can still be found in its original location, although many pieces have become scattered throughout Muskoka, but like his cottages, they are easily recognizable. His furniture was made exclusively of oak and finished with a variety of stains, but rarely painted.

The activities of local builders throughout the history of Muskoka are relatively well documented by local papers, and also recalled by their families, many of whom still live in Muskoka. However, because the cottagers tended to hire designers who lived in their hometowns, tracking the activities of architects has been difficult. While some cottagers are fortunate to have signed plans in their possession, these

KEWEKIJIK WAS DESIGNED FOR WILLIAM J. CASSIDY OF PITTSBURGH BY CHARLES J. GIBSON OF TORONTO IN 1902 AND BUILT BY PETER CURTIS.

account for only a dozen or so of the hundreds of cottages built before the First World War. In other cases, such as the Fairhaven cottages, it is possible to make attributions on the basis of style. But by far the richest sources of information have been the architectural press, the architect's families, and various archives.

An example of this is found in the work of the Toronto architect Charles J. Gibson. Born in Quebec City in 1862, Gibson received his architectural training in New York and came to Toronto in 1885, where he worked under Henry Simpson. Five years later he founded his own practice. His first recorded commission in Muskoka, reported in the *Canadian Contract Record*, was for additions to Prowse's Hotel at Beaumaris in 1902, which included doubling the north wing of the hotel, and adding one bay to the south and the very distinctive cupola with bell-cast roof and double columns to the top of the central tower. This account also mentioned that Gibson had prepared plans for a summer residence for a Pittsburgh gentleman on a 40-acre island about a mile from Beaumaris. That commission included designs for a main house, wharves, icehouse, and boathouse; as well, the architect was responsible for purchasing a steam yacht for his client. The total cost for the cottage was estimated to be $80,000, a considerable sum. The article went on to state that "Mr. Gibson has commissions to build several costly summer residences near this place [Beaumaris] for American summer residents."

The architect's descendants were able to provide supplementary evidence: a photograph of a cottage interior and a watercolour of an exterior that was signed by Gibson and dated 1902. The watercolour depicted Kewekijik on Tondern (Beaumaris) Island built for Pittsburgher William Henry Cassidy; it was demolished in 1964. The photograph was identified as showing the living room in the main house on Belle Island built for Pittsburger James Kuhn. Belle Island and Kewekijik are similar in style and in many specific details. A comparison with the report in the *Canadian Contract Record* reveals that Belle Island is without doubt the cottage described. The steam yacht *Ella Mary* serviced the cottage until 1925, when it was transported to Lake of Bays to become the infamous *Bigwin* ferry.

In 1905 Gibson designed another cottage on nearby Idlewylde Island for Canadian publisher Sir William Gage. In this case a clear comparison with the Cassidy and Kuhn cottages cannot be made, as they are very different in appearance. However, Gage had commissioned Gibson to design two warehouses in Toronto in 1904 and 1905. As people usually do with lawyers and doctors, clients tended to display a certain amount of loyalty to their architects; the architect responsible for a client's home or office more often than not was the one who designed his cottage. A close look at the cottage reveals some of Gibson's

MANY FAMOUS FAMILIES HAVE SPENT THEIR SUMMERS IN MUSKOKA. SIR JOHN EATON AND HIS WIFE FLORA BUILT KAWANDAG AT ROSSEAU, TOP, WHILE HIS FATHER TIMOTHY EATON, HAD HIS PLACE, RAVENSCRAG, NEAR WINDERMERE. THE MELLON FAMILY OF PITTSBURGH HAVE BEEN COMING TO SQUIRREL ISLAND, BOTTOM, NEAR BEAUMARIS FOR GENERATIONS.

139

CANON BLAND'S REEF ISLAND COTTAGE. LAKE JOSEPH. MUSKOKA LAKES. CANADA.

MICKLETHWAITE 943.

calling cards, particularly the single-diamond-patterned windows and turned columns, as opposed to the more common square post.

Also prolific in Muskoka was the Toronto firm of Burke & Horwood, whose drawings are preserved in the Ontario Archives. Edmund Burke was born in Toronto in 1850, and upon graduating from Upper Canada College, he entered the firm of Thomas Gundry and Henry Langley. He rose to junior partner, then in 1869, became a full partner. Burke then took over the prominent practice of William Storm following the architect's death in 1892. John Horwood, who had previously been Burke's employee, was admitted into partnership.

It is documented that between 1899 and 1912 Burke & Horwood designed no less than 14 large cottages on lakes Rosseau and Joseph. They also did numerous designs for buildings at the Muskoka Sanatorium at Gravenhurst and for Lambert Love's Elgin House, including the chapel. Their clients were such Muskoka personalities as Rev. Elmore Harris, Sir Wilfred Hepton, and Captain Breckinridge; however, it is the cottages themselves that attract our attention. Burke & Horwood's designs are as distinctive as the work of Peter Curtis. Where Curtis was a master of materials, Burke & Horwood displayed exceptional perception in design.

They recognized the unique character of the Muskoka landscape and were aware that architecture had to be derived from that character; foreign styles could not be imported without looking out of place, as the local farmhouses did. They developed an eclectic "language" derived from Dutch Colonial, California Bungalow, and traditional English Tudor forms, among other styles. The result is an architecture that competes with and relates to the landscape. The cottages are not overpowered by rustic Muskoka; instead, they stand firmly on their sites, asserting their presence by means of a clever "dialogue" with their surroundings. The viewer is presented with an enormous hipped-roof-line typically accounting for more than half the area of the main facade. Pierced by windows and occasionally a balcony, the roof hovers over a wraparound verandah fronted by a wide course of stairs. The visual effect is solidity; a strong relationship with the ground is emphatically stated. The effect is strengthened by the architects' bold use of materials; clapboard, wood-shingle,

natural timber, stone, and lattice come together to create an interplay of texture as rich as the environment in which the cottage stands, and the two are harmoniously blended. The interplay is not lost in the interior. Giant stone fireplaces rise from the earth, railings and posts are made with cedar trunks and branches, and like the forest, the cottage's essential structure becomes its ornament. The composition is so strong one is left feeling that nothing could be added or taken away except for the worse.

Every cottage in Muskoka has a history, and thus holds the potential for us to better understand this place we have made so special. Cottages serve as timeless interpreters of the ever-changing landscape in an increasingly complex world. And every summer, with thanks and admiration, we celebrate the achievements of their architects and builders. ▷

ACKNOWLEDGMENTS

I wish to thank the Muskoka Heritage Foundation whose initiative and support have made research into Muskoka's architectural history possible. Special thanks to Stephen Otto for his expertise and motivation and to the cottagers of the Fairhaven Island Association for making the effort to record and preserve their cottage history. To the many historians and chroniclers of Muskoka, both past and present, and to all of those who welcomed me into their summer homes, I give my thanks.

– G. S.

141

TOP, THIS IS THE INTERIOR OF SIR WILFRED HEPTON'S COTTAGE ON LOON ISLAND, DESIGNED BY THE TORONTO FIRM OF BURKE & HORWOOD. BOTTOM, NOT ALL THE COTTAGES IN MUSKOKA WERE ELABORATE AFFAIRS. THE FIRST PRESIDENT OF THE MLA, REVEREND E. MICHAEL BLAND, ENJOYED A MODEST HOME AWAY FROM HOME ON REEF ISLAND, LAKE JOSEPH.

11
GETTING THERE IS HALF THE FUN

Transportation In and Around Muskoka

BY RICHARD TATLEY

IN MANY WAYS, Muskoka's transportation history is more typical of various portions of southern Ontario than other parts of the Canadian shield. Geographically, the district lies wholly within the shield, but in several respects it has more in common with such regions as northern Simcoe County and the Kawartha Lakes than, for example, the Almaguin Highlands or Algonquin Park.

Three important factors help to make Muskoka distinct. One is its reasonably close proximity to various metropolitan centres such as Toronto, Hamilton, and Oshawa, and its position directly straddling all overland routes from these centres to northern Ontario. The second is Muskoka's fair allotment, compared to most other parts of the shield, of tolerably good farmland, consisting entirely of small clay belts laid down thousands of years ago by meltwater glacial lakes. The third factor, of course, is the abundance of navigable waterways, all of which flow into Georgian Bay, and which provide convenient local access to or throughout 19 of Muskoka's 22 original townships, plus two more in the Parry Sound District. Extensive though they are, however, the Muskoka waterways (not counting the Severn River, which has always been peripheral) form three distinctly localized systems—the Muskoka Lakes proper, the Huntsville lakes, and Lake of Bays—none of which offers convenient access to outside regions, though all have, at various times, been exploited as corridors of commerce.

As far as we know, the earliest visitors to the Muskoka District were small bands of primitive Amerindian hunters and gatherers, looking for fish, fruit, and game. Some of these people may have set foot in the area as early as 8000 years ago, when the climate was still sub-Arctic, and probably continued to do so for centuries afterward, but relentless Time and his allies—frost, vegetation, and erosion—have erased almost all trace of their presence. No doubt all the travelling was on foot or by dugout canoe, but dugouts are awkward and heavy out of water and were seldom carried great distances overland; this may have discouraged trips into central Muskoka for a long time. Perhaps the early

Indians began to appear more frequently after the birch-bark canoe was invented, but there is no reason to suppose that any of them ever lived in the area year-round until comparatively recent times.

The first Europeans to come anywhere near Muskoka were the French in the early seventeenth century, following the establishment of Champlain's Habitation at Quebec in 1608. The French, in the main, were interested in three things: furs, mission-work among the Indians, and a route to the Pacific. Of these, only the first was likely to entice them into Muskoka, and even that was improbable, since the French usually relied on the Indians to provide the actual furs. Hence it is not surprising that records from the French period, while providing interesting detail about Lake Nipissing, Georgian Bay, the Kawartha lakes, and Huronia, have almost nothing to say about the mysterious, forbidding lands north of the Severn. Perhaps the Nipissings, an Algonkian people, used to paddle across the Muskoka lakes looking for furs they could then barter with the Hurons, who in turn bartered with the French; indeed, there are reports that seventeenth-century axe-heads and other relics of French origin have been discovered amid rapids of the Moon River, but whether these items were carried by Indians or some nameless fur trader, we will never know.

The early fur-trade economy was almost completely disrupted in 1649, when a thousand Iroquois warriors from what is now New York state invaded Ontario, paddled up the Trent River system—probably in elm-bark war canoes—and practically wiped out their enemies, the Hurons. As a result, all of Ontario as far north of Lake Nipissing was abandoned to the Iroquois for more than a century, but again, there is no sign they had ever used Muskoka for anything more than a seasonal hunting ground.

During the eighteenth century, the Iroquois were gradually displaced by the Ojibwa, who thus fell heir to the Muskoka fur-lands. The occasional French or English fur trader may also have paddled through the Muskoka lakes during this period, but none left any record of his activities—although some early maps show lakes and rivers that vaguely resemble those of Muskoka.

143

THE BEST WAY TO SEE THE WONDERS OF MUSKOKA IS BY BOAT, AND WHILE A SLOW CANOE MAY LIMIT HOW MUCH YOU CAN SEE IN A DAY, THE GRACE AND SILENCE MORE THAN MAKE UP FOR THE LOSS OF SPEED.

Things changed little after the British conquest in 1760, or even after the Loyalist immigrations from the United States in 1784. Except for a few rugged individualists like George Cowan who established a fur-trading post on Beausoleil Island on Georgian Bay before 1793, Muskoka remained—to the Europeans—a backwater. Nonetheless, activity increased around the Severn River, prompted partly by fears of a possible American invasion, a threat that became a reality during the War of 1812. After the war the British authorities sent several expeditions—mostly military—to explore and map the waterways between Georgian Bay and the Ottawa River, but since none of them could find a convenient route for transporting troops or provisions, nothing came of these explorations. It is interesting to note, however, that at least one of these expeditions, that of Captain Baddeley in 1835, used "tin canoes."

Muskoka's long isolation from the outside world suddenly began to change during the 1850s. Sawmills were being opened at Washago and Parry Sound, and gradually gangs of lumbermen began cutting white pine along the Severn, Moon, and Seguin rivers. To move provisions, at first the lumbermen simply made do with punts and rafts on the waterways, or teams of horses or oxen on land; later, as their operations extended farther into the bush,

they had to build "tote roads" to supply their camps and depots. The Great North Road from Parry Sound, which now approximates Highway 124, and the Nipissing Road, which ran north from Rosseau village eventually to Lake Nipissing, both began in this manner.

By 1859, settlement was also under way, largely at the prompting of the government, which was disturbed to find people deserting Canada for the United States just as rapidly as they were coming in. Anxious to find more land for immigrants, the government decided to open up the Ottawa-Huron Tract, which lay north of the Trent-Severn system, east of Georgian Bay and west of the Ottawa River—thus including Muskoka. This entailed the construction of a network of colonization roads, each running inland from an existing settlement. One of these, the famous Muskoka Road—which roughly approximated the modern Highway 11—was started north from Washago, the terminus of steamboat navigation on Lake Couchiching, in 1859. By 1860 it had reached the vicinity of Muskoka Bay, where Gravenhurst was soon to arise, and by 1861 it had been extended to South, or Muskoka, Falls. By 1863 it reached North Falls (Bracebridge) and slowly crept northward to Falkenburg, Wingfield's Corners (Utterson), and beyond, though it did not actually extend to the site of Huntsville until 1869. Eventually it reached Lake Nipissing.

Meanwhile, another road, the Bobcaygeon, was being extended north from Bobcaygeon to Kinmount, Minden, and Cedar Narrows (Dorset). Originally it was supposed to continue right up to Callander, but instead by popular demand it was deflected westward, north of Lake of Bays, to link up with the Muskoka Road at Huntsville. At the same time other roads were branching off from the Muskoka Road, including: the Peterson Road, which started at Muskoka Falls and was soon opened as far as the Ottawa; the Parry Sound Road, which was first completed from Falkenburg to Parry Sound in 1864; and the Joseph Road, which ran from Falkenburg to Bardsville, Indian Village (Port Carling), and beyond by 1868. Others were soon to follow, such as the Maclean Road to Baysville, and the Brunel Road from Utterson to the future Port Sydney.

The early roads were a far cry from those of today. Even the lowliest modern gravel concession road would have been considered marvellous by nineteenth-century folk, who were used to roads that were narrow, muddy, bumpy, and full of ruts and potholes. In Muskoka they were even worse; the contractors were usually content just to slash pathways through the bush, leaving the stumps in place and perhaps throwing logs over the swampy sections. If these "roads" attracted little traffic, such as the Peterson, they soon reverted to the bush. If, on the other hand, they did attract traffic, they only deteriorated faster. In those days, governments were not in the habit of spending money on roads—the local people were expected to do that. But in Muskoka the local population was sparse, and much too preoccupied with clearing the land and getting established to devote much attention to the roads. As a result, the Ontario government was forced to allocate funds for road repairs, starting in 1870, when the Muskoka Road was planked from Severn Bridge to a point a few miles south of Gravenhurst. The planks, we are told, held up for about three years! Even so, it usually took three or four hours to move a loaded wagon over the 15-mile divide between Washago and Gravenhurst, while paying passengers frequently found it preferable to get out and walk rather than be jolted and jarred on a Muskoka stage.

With roads in this sort of condition, it is not surprising that travellers were anxious to avoid them as much as possible—except in winter, when they could get about in sleighs. Consequently, everyone looked to the waterways. Few settlers were initially inclined to try canoes, since birchbarks looked far too frail and prone to capsize. (The canvas-covered cedar-strip canoe was not invented until 1877 on Rice Lake.) In 1861 a survey party headed by John Dennis imported a large sloop to lakes Muskoka and Rosseau; it seems to have lasted for more than 20 years, and was probably the first sailboat on the lakes. By 1861 James "Micky" McCabe, who built Muskoka's first tavern at Gravenhurst, also constructed a punt on Muskoka Bay, but this craft

NO MAN DID MORE THAN ALEXANDER PETER COCKBURN TO OPEN MUSKOKA FOR ALL TO ENJOY. (MARCH 1879)

proved so leaky that it was all anyone could do to coax it as far as the Gravenhurst Narrows in a day. In 1862 Thomas Robinson, an English sailor who had settled on the bluffs overlooking Muskoka Bay two years earlier, advised a group of incoming campers to bring their own boat, preferably one with sails, while remarking that "boats are in great demand here at this time." Robinson imported his own sailboat, the *Breeze*, in 1863, and sometimes used it to transport passengers and freight up the lake. The following year, the Bradley brothers of Gravenhurst brought in an expensive sloop for the same purpose, but as freight carriers those boats proved inadequate. As late as 1869, when the first regatta was held off Browning Island, there were only two sailboats in the race: the *Breeze* and the *Wave*, which was owned by Paul Dane, the first settler at Beaumaris. The *Breeze* won.

Around 1864, a Bracebridge settler named William Holditch, frustrated by the endless delays in trying to import commodities of all kinds—and probably anxious to help export flour from Alexander Bailey's new gristmill—built a large, flat-bottomed horse-boat, propelled by paddlewheels worked by horses walking on a treadmill. Assisted by the current in the Muskoka River, the scow-like craft managed to reach Muskoka Bay in 12 hours, but it never returned to Bracebridge. Evidently a more efficient form of horsepower was needed on the Muskoka lakes.

Improvements came by the spring of 1866. A venturesome young merchant from Victoria County, A. P. Cockburn, had taken a trip all through Muskoka in the previous fall and immediately grasped the region's potential. He resolved to devote the rest of his life to promoting Muskoka's interests. Realizing that transportation was one of the district's main concerns, he borrowed some money and inaugurated the first regular stage service up the Muskoka Road from Washago to Gravenhurst. (In 1867 he relinquished the business to the Harvie brothers of Orillia, who were soon running up to 100 teams a day.) He also built an 80-foot sidewheel steamboat on Muskoka Bay, fitted her out with a 33-horsepower low-pressure engine, and launched her by June of 1866. Soon she was sailing daily to Bracebridge, Tondern Island (Beaumaris), Indian Village, and other points on Lake Muskoka, although her superstructure cabins were still unfinished.

The benefits were immediately apparent. Freight rates dropped to less than half what they had been before, and settlers were now favoured with a daily mail service. But problems persisted. Cargoes had to be unloaded from steamers to stages at Washago, and from stages to the steamer at Gravenhurst. The roads were so rough that goods often got broken in transit; in 1869 a Bracebridge merchant lamented that every single pane of glass in a shipment from the "front"—older existing settlements—arrived shattered.

Stumps and potholes often disabled a stage—in which case the passengers were expected to get out and help get it moving again—and forest fires occasionally endangered travellers or burned out bridges and causeways. The dreadful state of the roads made it very difficult for settlers to export any surplus grain or potash.

Things were more pleasant on the lake. The steamboat *Wenonah*, which means "first born," was a far cry from her distant successors, such as the *Sagamo* or the *Segwun*, having been built of whip-sawn planks and designed to carry freight as much as passengers. Her main deck was always liable to be packed to the rafters with hay, lumber, crates, barrels, tools, and provisions, perhaps a few horses, cattle, or oxen; passengers travelled on the upper deck or in the dining saloon. Her furnishings were spartan, with only coal-oil lanterns for use at night; on a cold day the only place to get warm was near the boiler room. Her noisy engine could not deliver speeds of more than 10 miles an hour—considered not bad at the time—and she frequently had to stop to "wood up" with fresh cordwood to stoke the fireboxes. Nonetheless, the *Wenonah* was a welcome sight for weary travellers who had just endured a bone-breaking trip overland on a Muskoka stage. There was always a good meal or a pleasant hot tea to be had, the scenery was delightful—at least until the lumbermen arrived!—and the officers were courteous and friendly.

Crewing on the vessel was not always so pleasant. The hands were sometimes obliged to work 16 hours a day or more, depending on conditions. Officers often spent long

146

A. P. COCKBURN WAS INSTRUMENTAL IN HAVING LOCKS BUILT IN PORT CARLING IN THE EARLY 1870S. THIS OPENED UP LAKE ROSSEAU AND, WITH THE CUT AT PORT SANDFIELD, LAKE JOSEPH AS WELL. SINCE THEN THE LOCKS HAVE HAD NUMEROUS FACELIFTS INCLUDING A WIDENING IN 1902-3, WHICH ALLOWED FOR THE BUILDING OF LARGER STEAMERS, SUCH AS THE *SAGAMO*.

hours at the wheel, navigating through fog or pitch-black nights without a single light in sight, dodging logs and deadheads, bucking ice and snowstorms in the late season, and constantly dreading a pile-up on some previously undetected shoal. Not only were there no charts of the lakes in the early days, but new rocks and small islands kept appearing in the channels as the lake levels dropped every season. It was not until 1873 that the provincial Ministry of Public Works got around to building a control dam at Bala.

Of course the *Wenonah*'s arrival and departure times could not be guaranteed, since she could easily be delayed by a late-arriving stage or bad weather. Furthermore, she was initially confined to Lake Muskoka, since the rapids on the Indian River at the modern site of Port Carling precluded her from continuing on to Lake Rosseau; for the first few seasons, only a skiff, occasionally supplemented by sails, was available to make triweekly trips from Port Carling to Ashdowne village, near Rosseau. Sometimes the steamer could not even reach Port Carling on account of boulders and sandbars in the river, which meant running a gangplank ashore about half a mile downstream. The

Rosseau for $1.75, and a twice-daily service to Bracebridge for $1.25. Even for the times, the rates were cheap.

The next major advance in Muskoka transportation was, of course, the railway. Nowhere else in Ontario was a railway so badly needed during the 1870s. Thanks largely to the Free Grant and Homesteads Act of 1868, which promised free land to bona fide settlers, and an extensive advertising campaign in Britain and Europe, immigration to the district had become fairly brisk, while at the same time the forests in the Lake Simcoe watershed were being logged out. Without a railway, it was difficult to entice people to Muskoka—either as colonists or campers—or to export any surplus crops; worse, it was hopelessly impractical to conduct lumbering operations on a big scale without some efficient economical way of exporting the lumber. Hauling it over the Muskoka Road simply made no sense, and the only other way was to float logs down the Moon and Musquash Rivers, both of which are riddled with rapids and neither of which has a decent harbour at its mouth. There was only one practical solution to all these problems, and that was a railway to the Muskoka watershed.

Unluckily, several factors delayed its coming. The Northern Railway of Canada, which had tracks running from Toronto to Allandale and Collingwood by 1854, and to Barrie by 1861, was the most obvious candidate to build into Muskoka. But for years this line, after nearly going bankrupt in 1858, was in no mood for any visionary expansionist schemes. Only the threat of being scooped by the Midland Railway—which by the 1870s was extending its tentacles northwest from Lindsay toward Beaverton and Orillia—plus the promise of cash subsidies from various quarters, finally induced the Northern to act. By 1872 it had extended its tracks to Orillia and Atherley—just in time to forestall the Midland!—and by 1873 the line reached Washago. One of the results, incidentally, was the supplanting of the local steamboat services on lakes Simcoe and Couchiching, which ceased to be part of the transport-system from Toronto to Muskoka at this time.

Also at this time, everything seemed to be going wrong. The terrain north of Washago is mostly rugged, ridged with granite outcroppings and laced with muskeg patches. With only picks and shovels and horse teams available, as well as black powder for blasting, railway construction was sure to be difficult. Worse still, the collapse of the price of sawn lumber in the United States in 1873 triggered a depression that nearly paralysed business in both Canada and the U.S. for five years; suddenly, cash became very tight. It took the railway a whole year to advance construction another two miles, as far as the Severn River, and there it ground to a halt. It was feared that the line might never go any farther. Yet somehow, more funding was found, so that the Northern Extensions Railway was able to resume work north of

Muskoka River delta was likewise so shallow that she sometimes ran aground while trying to get to Bracebridge. The Joseph River had such strong rapids at the time that no boat could use it without a portage. It took the government three years to start making improvements, but finally, in 1869, after many petitions and much debate, it tendered a contract to build a lock bypassing the Port Carling rapids; the following year a canal was started across the narrow sandy isthmus separating the southern ends of lakes Joseph and Rosseau, which had the effect of equalizing the levels of the two lakes. The lock was not ready until December 1871, and the canal (at Port Sandfield) was not deep enough for a steamer to pass until 1872, but once completed, the boats could navigate uninterruptedly from Gravenhurst to Rosseau (40 miles), or to Port Cockburn, at the head of Lake Joseph (45 miles). Dredging was also under way by that time, and soon stages were connecting with the boats at Bracebridge (running to Falkenburg, Utterson, and Uffington, and later to Port Sydney and Baysville), Windermere (running to Dee Bank, Ullswater, Raymond, and Ufford), Rosseau (running to Magnetawan and Nipissing village twice a week), and Port Cockburn (running to Parry Sound). By then Mr. Cockburn's steamboat line had expanded from one to three vessels, providing a daily service to

147

148

YELLOW BOAT, WATERCOLOUR, ED NOVAK.

the Severn in the spring of 1875. It was slow going, but gradually the rails crept northward, until by September 1875 the first work-train shuffled into Gravenhurst. It was greeted with jubilation. By November the line reached its real destination: Muskoka Bay, where Muskoka Wharf Station was built. For the next 10 years Muskoka Wharf was the end of the line, and for the next 77 years it was the major transshipping point from the trains to the lake steamers and back again. Painful bumpy stage trips over the Muskoka Road became a thing of the past.

The new line proved its value very quickly. Despite the depression, the lumber companies were soon vying with one another to acquire mill sites on Muskoka Bay, as close to the railhead as possible. Soon Gravenhurst was entering its heady "Sawdust City" days, as one of the busiest and proudest lumber towns in Ontario. Before long the lumber companies were opening camps as far away as the modern Algonquin Park, and feeding sawlogs down the rivers every spring, most of them bound for Gravenhurst. On the larger lakes, steam tugs, a few of which were imported on railway flatcars, were employed to boom the logs and tow them in, thus converting the lakes, as well as the rivers, into arteries of transport—with the incidental side effect of creating navigating hazards for the passenger steamers. The lumber trade was to dominate the Muskoka economy until the 1910s, and in north Muskoka later still.

In north Muskoka, meanwhile, history was busy repeating itself, except that events were happening about a decade later than in the south. The basic road network was taking shape, with all the usual problems, by the 1870s, and for years Captain George Hunt was obliged to walk from Huntsville to Utterson three times a week to collect the mail. Here again, people took to the waterways whenever they could to avoid the horrors of stage travel, but this time with a difference: the government, which was less than overjoyed about lavishing continual grants to keep the roads passable, soon began improving the waterways for navigation by building a lock on the north branch of the Muskoka River a few miles south of Fairy Lake, and installing a control dam at the exit from Mary Lake. It even undertook to raise the bridge across the Vernon River at Huntsville—which was too low to allow a steamer to pass beneath—before a steamboat was ready to enter service! All these improvements were completed by 1876, but it was not until June of 1877 that Captain Alfred Denton of Port Dalhousie was ready to launch the steamer *Northern* at Port Sydney. A small, flat-bottomed sidewheeler, the

Northern was capable of carrying about 200 passengers, and soon she was plying daily to Huntsville, Port Vernon (Hoodstown), and other centres on Fairy and Vernon lakes. From the very start, she was a success. Again, as in south Muskoka, communities on the waterways flourished, while inland centres such as Utterson languished—at least until the railway passed through. On Lake of Bays, meanwhile, Captain Joseph Huckins, backed by the merchants of Baysville, imported the small steamer *Dean*, formerly A. P. Cockburn's *Waubamik*, from Bracebridge, and was soon serving all the tiny settlements around the big lake, connecting with a triweekly stage. At that time there was still no road of any description connecting Dorset and Baysville.

The above-named transport patterns remained unchanged until 1885–86, when the Northern Railway decided to push its tracks onward from Gravenhurst to Callander to connect with the CPR. The result, once again, was to shift the corridors of commerce to new routes, and to reassert the basic primacy of land travel in Canada. Because the railway essentially paralleled the route of the Muskoka Road, it brought prosperity to the communities along this road—notably Bracebridge, Utterson, Huntsville, and Novar. Wherever it crossed a major river, as at Bracebridge, Huntsville, Burks Falls, and South River, or tapped a prominent lake, as at Sundridge and Callander, it usually stimulated the rise of another lumber town, especially since the lumber companies were happy to be spared the time and expense of feeding logs all the way to Georgian Bay. On the other hand, villages that were bypassed by the railway lost most of their trade and either declined—like those on the Nipissing Road—or died out completely; Hoodstown, at the terminus of navigation on northwestern Lake Vernon, is a good case in point, despite its excellent waterpower. The village of Rosseau, which was no longer on the main route to Lake Nipissing, also suffered, along with other ports on the Muskoka lakes, but these were soon to be saved by the tourist trade. The same was true of the steamboat lines, which were now reduced to the role of feeders to the railway. They, too, were left with only the limited local trade, until the rise of the resorts allowed them to retrieve their losses.

The steamer services on the Huntsville lakes and Lake of Bays had little to do with one another until 1888. In that year the government finally got around to deepening the swampy creek linking Fairy and Peninsula lakes. This allowed Captain Denton's steamboats to extend their routes east to Grassmere and the Portage—in other words, to within a mile of Lake of Bays. Here, an enterprising settler named George F. Marsh, who built a sawmill at Marsh's Falls, on the Oxtongue River near Dwight, also managed to gain control of all the shipping by 1886. Soon afterward, intensive competition sprang up between Denton and

Marsh for control of navigation throughout all of the north Muskoka lakes, as each deliberately put steamers into service on the other's routes. On any waterway, local boat services tend to develop into a monopoly, and north Muskoka was no exception. By 1894 Captain Marsh succeeded in buying out his rival and went on to develop the Huntsville and Lake of Bays Navigation Company, which received its charter in 1902.

During the same period, keen rivalry also developed between the towns of Bracebridge and Huntsville, both of which wanted to control the Lake of Bays market. This required effective transport routes to Lake of Bays. Bracebridge interests favoured a local railway spur, to be called the Trading Lake Railway, which was to run from Muskoka Falls to Baysville, thus avoiding having to build an expensive bridge over the Muskoka River. Huntsville in turn favoured navigation and proposed a canal across the Portage to link Lake of Bays with Peninsula Lake. This idea would have made more sense if Lake of Bays were not about 100 feet higher than Peninsula Lake, but as it happened, neither of these schemes ever came to fruition. The problem of access to Lake of Bays was finally solved by Captain Marsh, who, just before his death in 1904, managed to build a tiny railway across the hilly one-mile divide between Lake of Bays and Peninsula Lake, thus granting the palm of victory to Huntsville. By 1905 the Portage Railway—said to have been the shortest commercial railway in the world and referred to as the Little Train—was in full operation, hauling tourists and tanbark across the divide and connecting with the lake steamers at either end.

By this time the Muskoka tourist trade was getting into high gear, thanks largely to the extensive advertising campaigns of A. P. Cockburn and the Northern Railway, and its successor, the Grand Trunk, all of whom kept assuring novelty-seeking American sportsmen that the highlands of Ontario (Muskoka) were the ideal place to hunt and fish and get back to nature. At first the only accommodations expressly designed for tourists were the short-lived but trend-setting Rosseau House, built by William Pratt at Rosseau in 1870, and the Summit House at Port Cockburn, which opened in 1872. But during the 1880s, as the depression lifted and more tourists kept arriving—usually by steamboat—many local settlers around the lakes, sensing the new trend, began enlarging their homes into summer boardinghouses, which in turn often blossomed into resort hotels; about 15 of these sprang up around the Muskoka lakes during the 1880s, with many more to follow in the 1990s. In north Muskoka, the tourist industry didn't really get started until 1902, when Charles Waterhouse of Aspdin opened Deerhurst Inn on Peninsula Lake. But here again, success led to imitation, and within a decade there were dozens of tourist resorts around the Huntsville lakes and Lake of Bays.

The results were impressive. Boat liveries at Gravenhurst, Port Carling, Rosseau, Port Cockburn, and other places were soon turning out punts, canoes, and rowboats by the dozen. Soon some of them, notably Bert Minett and the Ditchburn brothers, were also building steam—later motor—launches. Some wealthy cottagers, not content with these, began importing elegant steam yachts as well, and building huge boathouses to house them. Most of the yachts were built by such firms as the Polson Iron Works and the Bertram Works, both in Toronto, and the Davis Dry Dock Co. in Kingston. Characteristically, they were patterned after American designs, which aimed at speed rather than spaciousness. Most were around 60 to 70 feet long, with white hulls, varnished decks and cabins, and polished brass trim. All required a captain and engineer to run them and keep them immaculate. By the 1910s, however, the steam yacht began to give way to the motor launch.

This period was also the golden age of rail travel in Canada. By about 1905 the Grand Trunk Railway was sometimes obliged to schedule five express trains a day from Toronto Union Station to Muskoka Wharf during the summer months, with direct connections to Buffalo, Detroit, Cleveland, and Chicago. The Toronto-Muskoka portion of the trip was soon reduced from five to three hours as local stops were cut out and more powerful locomotives introduced. Many passengers and their families took the sleeper to Muskoka Wharf, so as to board the morning steamer bright and early. In 1902 the Muskoka Express was extending it runs to Huntsville, and later Burks Falls, while in 1896 the plain little shed at Muskoka Wharf was replaced with a larger, more suitable structure with flaring eaves and Tudor-style architecture. So busy did this famous landmark become that sometimes the train crews barely had time to unload passengers and their baggage before the next train rolled in. Unpaid porters, or red caps, were always on hand to help move luggage and chattels; they had to survive on tips from the tourists.

The steamboat lines, meanwhile, did their part by building larger, faster, and handsomer ships, some of which were proudly touted as "palace steamers." They undoubtedly deserved that title, for ships like the *Sagamo* and the *Cherokee* featured steel hulls, twin propellers, triple-expansion engines, sewage tanks, electric lights, elegant lounges, broad staircases, and oak-panelled, glassed-in dining rooms where elegant meals were served. Soon all the boats were burning coal rather than wood, which cut out many a tiresome stop for fuel, and keeping to very tight schedules. By 1908, when the *Cherokee* entered service, the Muskoka Lakes Navigation Company—originally the Cockburn line—had nine passenger ships in operation, collectively capable of carrying 2400 people. Every morning the lake steamers departed bright and early from Gravenhurst, Bracebridge,

THE *CHEROKEE* WAS EVERYBODY'S FAVOURITE. HERE SHE IS COMING INTO BALA, CIRCA 1910.

Bala, Torrance, Rosseau, Port Cockburn, and sometimes other ports, stopping briefly at every village, resort, post office, and a few private cottages around the lakes; they also connected with one another at such places as Beaumaris, Windermere, Foot's Bay, and sometimes the open lakes. In north Muskoka, meanwhile, the Huntsville and Lake of Bays Navigation Company had three passenger ships connecting with the trains twice daily at Huntsville station (also stopping at the Huntsville town wharf) and plying to Port Sydney and the Portage to meet the Little Train. Across the divide were two or three more steamers to connect with Dwight, Baysville, Port Cunnington, Glenmount, Birkendale, and Dorset. (After 1920, the main route was always to Bigwin Inn.)

The Grand Trunk Railway had hitherto monopolized the very lucrative Muskoka market, but this situation was abruptly changed in 1905–06, when both of Canada's other transcontinentals, the Canadian Pacific and the Canadian Northern, resolved to build connecting lines from the Sudbury basin to Toronto—which meant through the Muskoka District. Soon both lines were simultaneously building past the west side of the Muskoka lakes: the Canadian Pacific through Barnesdale and Bala, and the Canadian Northern through Torrance, Bala Park Island, Foot's Bay, and Lake Joseph Station. Again, new wharfside stations were opened at Bala Park and Lake Joseph, while Bala proper had two stations: a summer station overlooking the wharf and a year-round depot a few hundred yards up the track. For a time it was rumoured that Bala would become a new railway division point, but the CPR decided that another spot about 10 miles north, beside Stewart Lake, was a better site

for sidings; the result was the railway village of MacTier. In 1906, to avoid the ruinous consequences of a rate war, the three lines agreed on a common tariff to Muskoka.

After 1906 the Muskoka transport scene underwent few important changes for the next quarter-century. Not surprisingly, the boat lines had to retrench and cut back services during the First World War, when men and luxuries became scarce, but they came back into their own during the Roaring Twenties. Some of the railways, now badly overextended, did not fare so well, and by 1917 both the Grand Trunk and the Canadian Northern went bankrupt; they were taken over and consolidated into the government-owned Canadian National Railway system. The Canadian National concentrated its main services at Muskoka Wharf, though trains continued to call at the other transfer points; indeed, Bala Park Station was long noted both as a coaling stop for the steamers and as the drop-off point for the daily mails, since the government, anxious to help the CNR as much as possible, usually assigned the mail contracts to it.

By this time the gas-fuelled motorboat had become a familiar feature on the Muskoka scene every summer. As early as 1915 they numbered nearly 500 on the lower lakes alone, outnumbering steam vessels nearly nine to one. These early gasoline boats—frequently built by such local boat-builders as Henry Ditchburn of Rosseau, William Johnston of Port Carling, and Hubert Minett of Minett village—were usually about 18 to 30 feet long and built of cedar, cypress, or pine around an oak or elm frame, and powered by slow-moving, baulky engines burning unprocessed fuel. During the 1920s, however, engine technology made rapid strides, and with them came mahogany hulls featuring forward drive, planing hulls, and sometimes V-shaped bottoms. The name of the game was, of course,

151

ABOVE, HERE'S WHAT PORT CARLING LOOKED LIKE AROUND 1890. IN THIS NORTH-FACING VIEW, THE SWING BRIDGE NEAR THE LOCK IS OPEN. BEHIND IT STANDS THE INTERLAKEN HOTEL, LATER KNOWN AS PORT CARLING HOUSE. TOP, THE OPPOSITE VIEW TAKEN IN THE LATE 1950'S.

speed, and some of the long sleek launches built by such local firms as Minett-Shields, Duke Boats, and the Ditchburn Boat Works became almost legendary; even today, several dozen of these boats survive. Speedboat racing became almost a mania on the lakes during the 1920s and 1930s; in one of these, *Little Miss Canada VI*, a hydroplane boat built by Greavette Boat Ltd. of Gravenhurst, hit speeds of 78 miles an hour. The demand for lengthy 45-foot cruisers suddenly collapsed when the Great Depression struck in 1930, soon taking the Ditchburn company with it; but other firms carried on building smaller models until the 1950s and later. Less-afluent folk meanwhile had to get by with disappearing-propeller boats, or DPs, which made their debut in Port Carling around 1915, or with skiffs and rowboats powered by the ubiquitous outboard motor.

Along with the motorboat came that other omnipresent byproduct of the internal-combustion engine: the motorcar. Automobiles were already numerous enough to be causing traffic problems in the cities, but seemingly there were relatively few of them to be seen in Muskoka during the early 1920s; the first car to be seen in Rosseau is said to have been delivered on board the *Sagamo*! However, in 1927 the Ferguson Highway, an upgraded version of the Muskoka Road, was opened as far as northern Ontario, and vehicular traffic rapidly increased. Responding to this trend, communities such as Gravenhurst and Huntsville erected welcoming arches at their southern entrances. But the Ferguson Highway was still just a gravel road, in many

152

sections only one lane wide, and if two motorcars happened to meet, one was frequently obliged to back up half a mile or so to a place where passing was possible. Driving at night was particularly hazardous, and as late as 1929 a trip to Toronto in a Model-T was likely to take a whole day, with the added attractions of bumps, ruts, wandering horses and cattle, and the occasional hay wagon. Not to mention the risk of a flat tire or an engine breakdown.

But the automobile was soon to remake the world in its own image, bringing with it noise, traffic lights, gas stations, and of course paved roads. Radiating out from the cities, the first asphalted highways reached Gravenhurst in 1930, and steadily began encircling the lakes with their tentacles, until by 1938 most of the larger communities were served by them. Along with automobiles, trucks proliferated, and soon took over most of the hauling business, which greatly added to the wear and tear of the roads themselves. In the process, the old transport services by rail and steamship were slowly strangled, as both tourists and local people took advantage of the new individual mobility. Adding to the discomfiture of the railways—which was

being taxed to help pay for the new roads—the Gray Coach Line began sending its buses up through Muskoka by 1931. The depression merely accelerated these trends, since governments often favoured road construction as a form of unemployment relief. The Muskoka Navigation Company, reeling from diminishing revenues, tried to fight back by establishing its own bus line, with one, later two, motor coaches connecting with the steamers at Port Carling and providing local services to such places as Bala, Foot's Bay, Milford Bay, Bracebridge, and later Gravenhurst. The bus service, which ran from 1934 until 1951, never made much money, but at least it forestalled other operators from doing the same thing.

Yet another dimension was added to the Muskoka transport scene during those years: air travel. In response to petitions from the Town of Gravenhurst and partly to relieve unemployment, the Department of National Defence started building a small airport midway between Gravenhurst and Bracebridge in 1933. Intended as an emergency landing field at a time when air services were rapidly increasing, the airport was completed by June 1936, though

THERE SHOULD BE ENOUGH NOSTALGIA IN THIS PHOTO TO PLEASE EVERYBODY. THE *SAGAMO* DOCKED AT BEAUMARIS WITH THE *ISLANDER* GOING BY IN THE BACKGROUND.

planes were coming in as early as September 1935. Muskoka Airport, as the new facility was officially named in 1938, never attracted much commercial traffic, but it served well as a training base during the Second World War—first for the RCAF and then for the Royal Norwegian Air Force, which moved its base of "little Norway" from Toronto Island Airport to Muskoka in 1943. Hundreds of pilots practised there, and once they were even visited by King Haakon of Norway himself. Once, during the winter of 1940, two training planes collided and went through the ice off Browning Island in Lake Muskoka, taking their crews with them; the planes were never raised. It is also said that the pilots used to simulate dive-bombing attacks on the steamer *Sagamo* while she was conducting her daily 100 Mile Cruise from Gravenhurst, until the manager of the Navigation Company raised complaints and the stunts were stopped.

In other respects, the war had the effect of retarding or even reversing the earlier transport trends in Muskoka. Suddenly new cars and motorboats were almost unobtainable. Gasoline and other commodities were severely rationed, and the roads received only minimum maintenance. Entertainment was limited, too, except for radios and cinemas, and overseas travel became dangerous. One result was that people, who now had jobs, suddenly rediscovered the surviving resort hotels, and the trains and steamers still available to get them there. Before long the lake steamers were sailing again with crowded decks, while the railways had to scrounge to find every piece of rolling stock they could to handle the rush. Obsolete wooden railway

coaches destined for the scrapyards were pressed back into service, and were commonly coupled into the centre portions of trains to cushion them in the event of an accident. The rail services, though, were less than ideal for vacationers, in that the trains were obliged to stop at every way-station; express trains were forbidden in wartime.

The end of the war, and the flood of prosperity that followed, led to a rush of new road-building, as if to make up for lost time, while people indulged their new-found affluence by using wartime savings to buy automobiles and motorboats. Motels and marinas flourished, while the railways declined; the CNR cancelled one tourist train after another, until 1952, when it practically abandoned Muskoka Wharf. The station was demolished in 1959. The CPR continued to run trains into Bala as late as the 1960s, mainly for the benefit of Toronto folk who wanted to dance at Dunn's Pavilion, but this service also petered out. Today, the only surviving railway stations in Muskoka are those at Huntsville, MacTier, and Gravenhurst. The reason Gravenhurst survives is that local citizens persuaded the authorities to turn it into an intermodal transport depot, serving both trains and buses. Just recently, though, the federal government has seen fit to slash Via Rail's service between Washago and North Bay, leaving only the ONR's *Northlander* to serve Huntsville and Gravenhurst. (The Via Transcontinental still runs through Torrance and Foot's Bay, but doesn't stop anywhere in Muskoka.) It may be that passenger trains to Muskoka will soon be just a memory.

The other victim of "progress" has been, of course, the lake steamers. The majestic big passenger ships that were practically the district's trademark for 92 years began to seem like antiquated anomalies in a postwar era, clamouring for the convenience of individual mobility and obsessed with a mania for noise and speed. Like their old allies, the

154

trains, the excursion steamers resumed their genteel decline after 1945, as stop after stop was eliminated and ship after ship was retired from service. The old *Algonquin* sounded her whistle for the last time at Huntsville in 1952, while the *Sagamo* completed her last cruise six years later. In time a new breed of passenger vessel—the squat, safe, commodious, efficient, unromantic steel bus-boat, powered by a noisy diesel engine—emerged to replace the lake steamers and to keep the recreation-cruise tradition alive on the Muskoka lakes. The first of these was the *Miss Muskoka*, launched in 1962: her running-mate, the *Lady Muskoka*, still plies the lakes from Bracebridge to this day.

At present, the Muskoka District is well served by several first-class highways, including part of the Trans-Canada, which now links Foot's Bay with Port Severn. During the 1970s Highway 11, always the main artery to and from Toronto, was upgraded to turnpike status, complete with by-passes around all the major towns. Though millions of cars use these roads every year, the result in part has been to funnel motorists through Muskoka rather than into it, and consequently many tourists end up driving right through without ever seeing the best of what the area has to offer. One cannot see much of the lakes from the roads!

Air traffic has always remained peripheral: although Muskoka Airport averaged over 30,000 plane movements a year, almost all of these are private or charter flights, and no regular commercial service has ever lasted long.

The lakes, meanwhile, belong to the motorboat in summer, and the snowmobile in winter. Lately the opening of cross-country trails, often utilizing old logging roads and abandoned railway lines, has allowed snowmobiles to range all over the district—with far-ranging side effects! The boating scene has also changed, as cedar-strip Peterborough skiffs and mahogany inboards have gradually given way to fibreglass "tupperware" inboard-outboards or aluminum punts—which are almost maintenance-free though hardly in the same class. But sailboats are still seen on the Muskoka lakes, and the occasional canoe, though canoes are more common on the smaller lakes, which are less buffeted by winds and speedboats. Happily, too, an encouraging number of elegant big Minett and Ditchburn motor launches, and even a few DPs, are still lovingly preserved and maintained by their owners, who are never prouder than on those special days when they can display them at the annual antique-boat show. The flawless condition of these splendid craft, with their glittering chrome fittings and shiny polished mahogany in which one can almost see one's reflection, never fails to draw gasps of admiration from the visitors. Now and then one also sees the occasional little steamboat, fussily puffing and wheezing at its dock or quietly puttering about with a graceful dignity of its own.

No story on transportation in Muskoka would be complete without mention of the minor miracle accomplished here in 1981. On June 27 a genuine passenger steamship was reborn, when the Royal Mail Ship *Segwun* emerged from her 22-year retirement with an 11-year $1.2 million refit to resume her former duties as an excursion steamer. Despite occasional teething troubles, red tape, and the confident predictions of experts who insisted that it was impossible to operate a nineteenth-century ship under twentieth-century conditions profitably, the *Segwun* has both sailed into solvency and proved her worth to the Ontario tourist industry. Now one of the world's oldest steamships, she has starred in several movies and become Muskoka's foremost tourist attraction. Not for nothing is she now the Queen of the Muskoka Lakes. Her place in the hearts of cottagers, residents, and visitors alike seems firmly entrenched.

Today, transportation to, from, and within Muskoka has come a long way from the lurching stages and leaky scows of more than a century ago. The rugged scenic lakelands have been settled and partly tamed, but they are no less enchanting, and their attractions are now accessible to everyone. ▷

JOHN DeVISSER

12

A REPUTATION TO CHERISH

100 Years of Boating

BY PAUL GOCKEL

APASSAGE IN THE 1937 *Muskoka Lakes Association Yearbook* declared: "The Muskoka Lakes can truly boast of having not only the greatest number but also the finest motor boats in fresh waters in the world, and ninety-nine per cent of them are built in Muskoka."

These words of almost 60 years ago may sound like quaint hyperbole. But they are not. The elegant launches of the 1920s and 1930s, with their gleaming hulls of mahogany and cedar, represented a pinnacle of craftsmanship that was unequalled anywhere else and one that we in Muskoka are most fortunate to have had. The vintage-boating trend begun in the 1980s is a celebration and an appreciation of those golden years of boat-building.

But over the past 100 years, Muskoka lakes have seen vast numbers and varieties of boats come and go, and things weren't always shining mahogany and chrome. Before and after the period of legendary launch construction, most boats that plied our waters were not immediately recognizable as Muskoka-made craft. Indeed, a century ago, many were not built here, and those that were lacked the elegance of later ones. To fully appreciate Muskoka's boating heritage, we need to examine what happened before and after the golden years.

Boating in Muskoka began as a necessity. The magnificent lakes, rivers, and shorelines beckoned all who gazed upon them, settler and tourist alike. With no roads through the dense forest and rock, the waterways became the roads, and boats the vehicles.

The first watercraft built locally by white men were rowboats. The Johnston brothers experimented with dugout type boats at their Wild Goose Lodge near Brackenrig Bay, but commercial development of the lapstrake, or clinker-built, skiff was probably the beginning of the domestic boat-building industry. Skiffs were soon being made by the Johnstons in Port Carling, Windermere, and Port Sandfield; the Ditchburns at Port Carling, Rosseau, and Gravenhurst;

the Wrenshalls at Port Carling; and numerous other lesser-known builders around the lakes.

With the opening of hotels in Rosseau, Port Cockburn, Port Carling, and Port Sandfield in the 1870s and 1880s, canoes, sailboats, and rowboats kept water-loving vacationers happily occupied. Long summer days could be spent lollygagging about in the various crafts or, for the more adventurous, lengthy tours of the lakes could be undertaken. With the advent of the steamers, less athletically inclined hotel guests could travel almost anywhere the three big lakes stretched. And so, the lakes helped the innkeepers, who helped the tourists, who helped the boat-builders, and so on.

In this symbiotic circle however, we must throw a tangent. The property owner. By the 1890s, concurrent with the burgeoning hotel trade, came people who had bought land and built their own summer homes. They tended to be wealthy, educated, and above all independent of spirit. Vacationing at a resort certainly had appeal, but they wanted a place to call their own with complete privacy and isolation. They, too, of course, had boating needs. A private dock saw anything from a fleet of canoes to a few skiffs to a steam yacht, or often all of the above! Many of their boats were brought in from elsewhere. Sailboats from John Matheson in Toronto and Morse in Hamilton; canoes from Peterborough, and Dean and Bastien; skiffs from Carley in Barrie, and steamboats from Polson and Davis in Toronto and Kingston respectively. A number of these "foreign" early boats can still be seen around the lakes.

For the wealthy, according to Richard Tatley, author of *The Steamboat Era in the Muskokas*, the private steam yacht was the ultimate prestige item. They were something to see. Their enormous size, silent movement through the water, luxurious fittings, and lush appointments of carpets, upholstery, and curtains stirred envy in all who saw them.

Most of the steam yachts in Muskoka were owned by Americans, but the earliest and best known of them all belonged to Hamilton clothing magnate Senator William Sanford. *The Naiad* was built in 1890 by the Polson Iron Works of Toronto, and its first tour of duty was on Lake Ontario as the flagship of the Hamilton Yacht Club. The

THE *FLYING EBONY* WAS ORIGINALLY HAROLD GREENING'S *RAINBOW X*. BUILT BY MORSE OF HAMILTON IN 1943, IT IS NOW OWNED BY THE CARR-HARRIS FAMILY.

yacht's vast array of teak, mahogany, bird's-eye maple, and other species of wood scoured from various parts of the empire, made it an elegant, if rather ostentatious, display of Sanford's wealth. Perhaps he wanted to be seen as the Canadian counterpart of J. P. Morgan, for the 68-foot black-hulled *Naiad* closely resembled Morgan's *Corsair* in colour, shape, design, and appointments, except that the *Corsair* was 304 feet. The *Naiad* was brought to the Muskoka lakes in 1892.

Not only were the steam-yacht engines sophisticated propulsion devices and silent graceful symphonies of motion, they were also works of art. The lagging around an engine's cylinders, which provided insulation against extremes of temperature, was of nickel or polished teak, truly a sight to behold. Polished steel frame members, connecting rods, and valve gear with nickel-plated or brass accessories were also all exposed for the viewers' contemplation and enjoyment—or bewilderment.

The *Naiad* was a wonderful example of these steam yachts' endurance. Though she wintered in a boathouse on Sans Souci Island, she spent her summer days in the wind, rain, and sun. And through all this exposure, she lasted nearly 50 years, remaining on the Muskoka lakes until 1940.

Another steam yacht that really got around during its 30 years was Sir Wilfred Hepton's, and later Dr. T. S. Winslow's, *Willoudee*. Built in 1904 by Davis Dry Dock

SENATOR SANFORD'S *NAIAD* SET THE TONE FOR THE MUSKOKA LAKES. SHE WAS A GREAT ADVERTISEMENT FOR THE FIRM THAT BUILT HER, THE POLSON IRON WORKS OF TORONTO.

Co. of Kingston, she spent her first six years at Loon Island and the remaining years at St. Helens, both on Lake Joe. Legend has it that Winslow paid $10,000 for the *Willoudee* and that Sanford paid a similar amount for the *Naiad*—that comes to nearly $250,000 by today's standards. Dr. Winslow, who was at various times commodore and later president of the MLA, used the *Willoudee* until his death in 1936.

The *Willoudee* began her annual excursions soon after the ice went out, and because of this, a young life was saved. One day in May 1914, as the *Willoudee* was steaming toward the station at Barnesdale on Lake Joseph, the captain, Tom Thorne, discovered an overturned 14-foot Aykroyd dinghy. Clinging to the hull was Jean Jennings, a little girl of nine, who'd taken the dinghy out on her own. The *Willoudee* rushed to her rescue, plucked the shivering Jean from the icy spring waters, warmed her in the *Willoudee*'s boiler room, and towed her dinghy back to Owaisa Island. That was the beginning of a decades-long friendship between the Winslows and the Jennings.

F. C. Gratwick, commodore of the MLA from 1913 to 1921, kept his steam yacht, *Pukwana*, near Craigie Lea.

Like most of these yachts, it lasted into the 1930s, when the boiler seemed to have lived its life. It is further reported that the careers of *Pukwana* and the Forman family's *Iagara* ended when someone remarked on the undulating motion these boats took while bending over the waves. This snakelike behaviour was the final straw. *Pukwana* disappeared into the woods near Craigie Lea never to be seen again, while *Iagara* suffered the supreme ignominy: she became a hot-dog stand near Walker's Point. The *Iagara* was then known as the Ark, and when her useful days as a hot-dog stand were over, she was replaced by the New Ark, which is the name of the establishment today. However, her steering wheel and 34-inch propeller still exist, treasured by her heirs.

By 1940 the steam yacht's days were over. No new ones appeared after 1914. The *Willoudee* had been converted to gasoline in 1934 with the installation of a six-cylinder Sterling Petrol engine, but was destroyed in the St. Helen's fire of 1938. Although beautiful and dependable, steam yachts were expensive, and by then, the greatest yacht designer of them all, Revenue Canada—or the IRS, as the case might be—deemed that such grand sums be given to them and not spent on luxury yachts. Thus ended an incredibly glorious boating tradition on the Muskoka lakes. But other things were happening.

"Fearless for unknown shores on waves of ecstasy to sail," wrote Walt Whitman. His words could be the motto of all Muskoka's sailors. Their enthusiasm has perhaps been most evident in the annual regattas.

The MLA has probably always concentrated more on sailing than any other form of water activity—witness the lengthy rules concerning it in vintage MLA directories. By 1912, the MLA had three classes for sailing vessels alone: the dinghy class, for boats 14 to 16 feet; the yacht class, for boats longer than 16 feet; and the cat boat, for boats 18 feet and longer. All vessels had to be measured by the official measurer, Herb Ditchburn. It's interesting to note that from 1914 to 1934 Gallaghers and Crerars of Loon Island continually won the 16-foot dinghy race in their gaff-rigged boat *Marion*. It's further interesting to note that *Marion* still plies the waters of Lake Joseph at Loon Island. She is believed to have been built by Morse in Hamilton in 1912.

Few of the sailboats used in the early regattas on the Muskoka lakes were built here. Although John Matheson started his career in sailing and building sailboats, he built few once he arrived in Port Carling. Most sailboats were built by Morse, Aykroyd Brothers, Tom Taylor, and others far flung from Muskoka's shores, although Ditchburn's 1908 catalogue lists sailboats of 14, 16, and 18 feet. The same holds true for canoes. While the catalogue lists numerous canoes, it is now believed that Ditchburn never built cedar-strip canoes; rather, the company purchased

unfinished hulls from the master builders in Peterborough. But the paltry number of Muskoka-made boats wasn't to be the situation much longer.

Enter the gasoline engine. It seemed at first more trouble than it was worth. A great, thundering lump of cast iron that developed one horsepower for every thousand pounds of engine weight, it was remarkably undependable and required an inordinate amount of technical expertise to keep it running. Furthermore, dreadfully dangerous gasoline had to be carried on board the same boat where women and children were expected to ride. Gasoline? Deliver me from.

The complaints concerning early gasoline marine propulsion were legion and doubtless justified. Mr. Gratwick's Ditchburn *Wonalancet* was always in the shop for engine repairs. He is quoted as being "sick of it." Crerar's unknown-make gasoline launch, *Snark*, was always being towed to Port Carling—usually behind a sailboat!—so someone could get it running for them. The Johnsons of Elsinore Island in Lake Joseph were so afraid of their gasoline boat that they bought the tiny island next to Elsinore for the sole purpose of isolating themselves from any danger from fire.

A 1902 ad in the MLA directory for the Gasoline Engine

WOW! WHAT A SPECTACULAR BOAT SHOW. THIS WAS EVERYDAY LIFE ON LAKE JOSEPH (FOOT'S BAY) ABOUT 1920. THE STEAMER IS WINSLOW'S *WILLOUDEE*.

WENDY WINSLOW

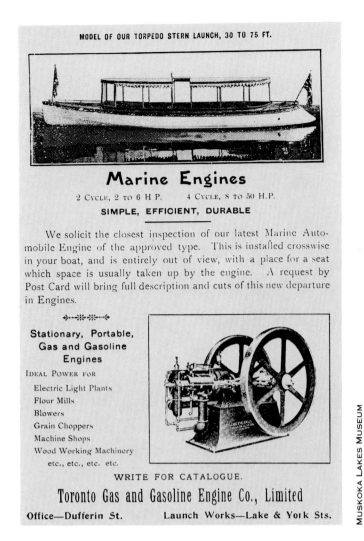

MUSKOKA LAKES MUSEUM

ONE OF THE MANY BOAT-BUILDING ARTIFACTS TO BE FOUND AT THE MUSKOKA LAKES MUSEUM. LEFT, AD FROM THE 1906 MLA YEARBOOK.

Company, however, called their products "Perfect Engines"— no mention made concerning the quality of the boat. A 1905 ad for Auto Boats claimed their engine would "run as long as the gasoline lasts." With such positive statements, we can only assume that early gasoline engines must have been a disaster!

Even Ditchburn, in its 1908 catalogue, had this to say about gasoline power:

For ten actual years we have wrestled with the gasoline engine . . . and think that we have had . . . all the troubles that could be handed to a man with a gasoline engine. If there are any that we did not have, our customers had them, and did not hesitate to tell us about them. Every one of these troubles was an experience. A man does not lie out on the lake all one long dark night in an open boat without doing some deep and serious thinking as to the "why" of it all, and planning a way to prevent a similar experience.

With all these strikes against them it's amazing that gasoline-powered vessels ever got any foothold at all. But benefits could be seen when they were compared to existing alternatives. Rowing was tiring, tedious, and slow, not to mention governed by the weather. For who wants to row from Keewaydin Island to Port Carling in the pouring rain? Or paddle a canoe in the blistering heat or sail on a

160

windless day? Yes, there were steamboats, but the cost of purchasing and operating one was beyond the reach of most. Besides, they, too, had their mechanical foibles. The difference between gas and steam was one of familiarity. Machinery had to be lubricated and maintained, and time was required to load fuel and build steam pressure—and you had to watch that you didn't set your boathouse on fire in the process.

But oh, the advantages of gasoline engines (when they worked)! No start-up or cool-down time was required and they were lighter and cheaper than steam. No cruising about the lakes with a woodlot on board. Gasoline was more dangerous than wood or coal, but it could be more easily transferred and stored. Gasoline was also more efficient. A half ton of coal was needed to power a 30-foot launch 100 miles at seven knots, but the same could be accomplished with only 10 gallons of gasoline. And so, aware of the obvious advantages of gasoline, the pioneers worked diligently to iron out the kinks. The automotive industry helped greatly.

Their work paid off. By 1915, the number of gasoline-powered boats on the Muskoka lakes had reached 329. These early gasoline launches looked like small steamboats

ANTIQUE BOATS, MUSKOKA BAY, SOFT PASTEL, DAN WERSTUK.

without the smokestack. When gasoline engines were found to power boats at higher speeds with lighter machinery, hull designs were changed accordingly. Graceful fantail hulls disappeared in favour of flat-bottom stern, transom launches. Fantail sterns were fine for steam, for they enabled an enormous slow-turning propeller to be swung under a fine-lined hull. But with higher hull speeds, the fantail, which was all cantilevered weight, couldn't support itself on its own stern wave, and so squatted hopelessly at gas engine speeds. By 1912, fantails had gone the way of the dinosaur.

The Johnstons of Port Carling, credited with the first boat production in Muskoka, were also the first to build powerboats here. In 1904 the builder produced the *Dreadnaught* and the *Fearnaught*, which were 27-foot launches equipped with two- or three-cylinder Ferro engines. They were finished in the traditional manner with painted bottom, white topsides, and varnished decks and interior.

The relative success of these models drew the attention of the elusive J. R. C. Hodgson of Calypso Point in Lake Joseph. He made successive orders for launches, and these half dozen or so gasoline-powered crafts established W. J. Johnston as a prominent boat-builder by 1910.

Herb Ditchburn played it safe. Out of a possible 13 different hull shapes, styles, and sizes offered in the 1908 Ditchburn catalogue, six of them were gasoline-powered, the balance being sail-, oar-, or paddle-powered. But from their 16-foot skiff to their 30-foot cabin cruiser, no engine manufacturer was mentioned or recommended.

Bert Minett was one of the early Muskoka boat-builders whose skill and subsequent reputation transcended most other North American builders. The earliest Minett boat still known to exist is the Pioneer. Typical of early gas boats, it has a canoe stern, white topsides, and varnished deck with peripheral interior seating.

With all the boat-builders in the area making not only gasoline-powered boats now, but faster and faster ones at that, the MLA kept pace by including powerboat racing in their annual regattas. The 1912 yearbook revealed that powerboat races had two categories: the open, in which any powerboat could participate; and the motorboat under 15 miles an hour. One of J. R. C. Hodgson's Hummingbirds won the open-class race at the 1911 regatta.

On July 6, 1913, a Tango, built for the Formans by Minett, appeared at Cliff Island, the first of many Tangos at Cliff. Mrs. Forman's journal entry called it a "fine motor boat." Given the limits of her nautical verbosity, the Tango was no doubt quite exceptional.

As the war years approached, Muskoka's summer population steadily increased. Local boat-builders were kept busy building everything from rowboats to speedy motor launches when they weren't busy repairing some of the now aging craft.

DITCHBURN'S MUSKOKA WHARF BOAT LIVERY.

During the First World War the MLA published rules concerning the safe operation of motorboats. These were little more than the standard "rules of the road," but with more and more people piloting their own boats, and many not needing the services of a professional driver as steamboats often did, the risk of marine disasters increased. These rules became stiffer during the 1920s, aimed at owners of "gas and steamboats who cause upset to the operators of canoes, rowboats and small launches."

One area that cannot be overlooked is the role played by professional boat crews. The need for captains and engineers, especially for the steam yachts, not only provided excellent summer employment to many well-trained year round residents, but also gave a relaxing carefree ride to the boat owners. Rupert Duke and Thomas Thorne spent 25 years in the employ of Mrs. Winslow, seeing to the safe operation, both mechanically and nautically, of her *Willoudee*. Sam Croucher was the engineer on Forman's *Iagara*, and if for any reason he couldn't be there, his brother, Alf, stepped in. They performed the same service for Mr. Gratwick on his steamer *Pukwana*. Over the years, the Gratwicks also employed Charlie Campbell, Don Reid, Harry Liesley, and Harry Bailey. J. Y. Murdock of Foot's Bay hired Wesley and Stan Wright of Redwood to drive his two launches, *Wimur I* and *Wimur II*. So necessary were these skilled men to the boat owners that when a pilot died and another capable one could not be procured, the boats were usually sold.

Motorboat-hull designs were still generally of the displacement type, that is, most of the wetted surface remained below the water line. After the First World War, some of the hull designs of the locally built boats began to change; the seeds of speed had been sewn and the role of the naval architect was to gain more prominence in pleasure-boat production than ever before.

The early 1920s saw a great expansion in quantity and quality of boats produced in Muskoka. Ditchburn's production was now principally in Gravenhurst, and the plant was enormous. Bert Minett had long since moved from the shores of Lake Rosseau to a large brick building in Bracebridge. The Disappearing Propeller Boat Co., which built only one standardized product, had become well established in a three-storey building in Port Carling and employed nearly the entire town, claiming to be the largest manufacturer of boats in Canada. Matheson, too, had a Port Carling shop, but he kept his production low. Bastien, the only foreign builder, kept liveries at both Port Carling and Royal Muskoka. The choices of boats available to the summer visitor was boundless.

The days of the white-sided cedar, cypress, or yellow pine launches were gone. Nearly every boat built here during the 1920s was an item of superb craftsmanship, with lavish attention given to detail. As the end products were varnished, not painted, mistakes could not be concealed. Why this skyrocketing of craftsmanship occurred in this place at that time is open to speculation. We had the lakes, trees, and water, and people would

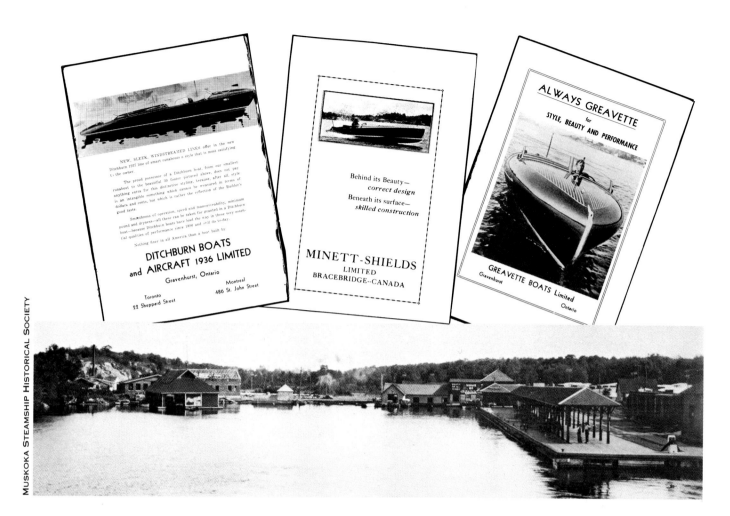

TOP, BOAT MANUFACTURERS FOUND THE MLA
YEARBOOK A GOOD PLACE TO ADVERTISE. BOTTOM,
THE MUSKOKA WHARF WITH DITCHBURN'S FACTORY.

have bought anything that floated and ran anyway, wouldn't they? Perhaps not.

The Roaring Twenties did not really roar until the decade was nearly over. In fact the early postwar years, albeit peaceful, were fraught with depression and uncertainty. Unemployment abounded. As always, however, the wealthy remained wealthy, and the Muskoka lakes still had its share of them during the summer months.

As a result, boat-building firms had to produce better and better boats to keep their well-heeled customers interested. Mahogany was used more than ever before, and in more places and shapes than ever before. This luxurious but hard-to-bend wood was used extensively in topside planking in place of cedar, in decking in place of oak, and in floors in place of pine or spruce – not just ordinary floors furthermore, but lattice-work floors that made the viewer dizzy! Mahogany was steamed and rigorously bent for cockpit coaming, fitting so well to the shape of the cockpit itself that no trim was necessary to hide the joint, something that had not previously been attempted by builders on a regular basis.

The list continues. White cedar bottoms were riveted to elm or oak ribs, not merely connected with clout nails. The job with clout nails rarely requires more than one man and work proceeds quickly, whereas riveting is a two-man job; it's also tedious and noisy, but strong and lasting. Covering boards on decks had a minimum of three hooks in their joints; they were also re-sawn so the port side matched the starboard in shape as well as in grain. And then there were those long endless decks of mahogany. All were blind-fastened so that not a screw, plug, nail, or bit of putty showed anywhere. A plug in a deck plank today means either the covering boards or the deck have been replaced by a less than meticulous workman.

A last-ditch attempt was made to save the hide of even the little DP (dis-pro, or disappearing propeller) boat. About half a dozen all-mahogany models were built, and they, too, had steam-bent mahogany coaming, gunwales, seats, and floorboards.

All of this workmanship might go unappreciated—until it is compared with similar boats from elsewhere. Most of the instant eye-appealing features may be the same, but close scrutiny of foreign boats reveals how few of the truly elegant details are there. One of the maxims of Ditchburn's was that it didn't matter how long it took to complete a task just provided it was completed properly.

Many of Muskoka's boats of the 1920s were like the more expensive cars of the 1930s. You didn't simply

163

CARRYING ON THE TRADITION, A DISPLAY OF "DIPPYS"
AT THE 1981 MLA ANTIQUE BOAT SHOW. ABOVE, THE
DITCHBURN *SOPHIA*.

164

pick one from the lot and drive off. Orders were placed a year in advance for everything from a 21-foot launch to a 50-foot cruiser.

Remember that great, thundering lump of cast iron—the early gasoline engine? Most of these have slipped into oblivion now, but at one time Packard, Lycoming, Liberty, Sterling, Scripps, Kermath, Red Wing, Hall-Scott, and Van

Blerk engines were all used by Muskoka's large boat-builders. These American-built engines came in sizes from four to 12 cylinders, noisily powering the elegant craft across the lakes.

One of the most notorious launches was Harold Greening's *Rainbow VII*. Built by Ditchburn in 1928, it took 15 people across Lake Ontario at 60 miles an hour. Try that in your Pachanga! It had two 517-horsepower Liberty V-12 engines. Liberty engines had been developed in 1917 by the combined efforts of Packard and Hall-Scott for aircraft use. The same boat and pilot went on to win the Lipton Cup later that year in Detroit. Thanks to Greening, and his ability to afford the enormous consumption of gas and oil, the twenties really roared!

Not everyone appreciated the roar, however. Complaints about noise from powerboats were brought to the attention of board members at more than one MLA annual meeting. Sound familiar? The difference between then and now is that then, the noise-makers were pioneers in engine performance; now we're just noisy.

In 1927 Ditchburn, which was making a number of beautiful boats, took out its first ad in the MLA directory; the family launch, as well as the winning speedboat, was touted. Minett-Shields' first ad didn't appear until 1931, and it used a photograph of J. Y. Murdock's *Wimur II* operating at speed.

It's interesting to compare the products of these two pillars of the boat-building industry in Muskoka. The year 1927 seems to have been a banner one in boat production for both Ditchburn and Minett-Shields. Most of Ditch-burn's output stuck to tradition. A family launch built in 1927 didn't look too different from one built in 1921—the same flat windshields, plumb stems, high freeboard, centre drive, displacement hull, and soft chines. But many 1927

DUKE MARINE, WATERCOLOUR, ED NOVAK.

Minett-Shields family launches, with their combination displacement/planing hulls, low freeboard, hard chines, forward drive, raked windshields, and spoon bows, looked as though they were speeding when they were tied to the dock! There were exceptions of course, such as Ditchburn's Viking model with its stepped hull, but in the late 1920s Minett-Shields seems to have been the more stylishly progressive builder. They were adopting many of the designs from John L. Hacker, a designer of runabouts from Detroit. At the same time, however, Ditchburn employed Bert Hawker, a true naval architect.

The competition between the two firms was legendary, and much has been written about these paragons of launch-building. Justifiably, I believe, for many of the boats built then are still afloat today, which speaks volumes of the quality of workmanship that went into them. It also speaks of the care they've received over the years, for wooden boats need assiduous, you might say loving, maintenance.

It must be remembered that these two firms didn't reinvent boat-building. Theirs is a conservative industry. Only so much can be done with cedar, mahogany, rivets, and

varnish, but Ditchburn and Minett-Shields managed to take those resources and combine and refine them to such a state that their magnificent vessels are still coveted the world over.

These two firms always tend to overshadow the other builders in the area. For instance, the Disappearing Propeller Boat Co., whose home was Port Carling. What story on boating in Muskoka could be complete without mention of the DP, the "poor man's launch," the Model T of the waterways? Cheap, numerous, and belittled as they were, they were a presence on the lakes for nearly 40 years, experiencing a revival during the 1980s. Their legendary cantankerous performance—due mostly to owners' mechanical ineptitude, sometimes fuel or ignition difficulties, but seldom engine malfunction and never hull problems—may be the very feature that brought them into the hearts and memories of old and young alike. During the 1960s and 1970s, when I was scrounging through old marinas (weren't old marinas great?) in the hopes of finding the DP motherlode, many was the time I heard to my dismay, "Oh, we took all that ol' junk out in a ol' hull, chopped a hole in the

165

bottom of it and let 'er sink." I gave brief consideration to underwater salvage—until I learned that the treasures had been consigned to depths of 200 feet!

Many was the trick played on the navigation company steamers and their crews by early DP owners. Two senior MLA members have related to me their youthful tomfoolery. Their favourite trick was to cross in front of a steamer and then one of them, with sauve legerdemain—or in this case legerdepied—would shut off the DP's ignition with his toe. Clanging bells and blowing whistles, accompanied by colourful swearing, would come from the big steamers as they tried desperately to keep from making two DPs out of one. Not very yachtsmanlike of our DP pilots! And not a stunt likely to have been pulled had they been piloting a Minett.

Nevertheless, when a DP boat was behaving in its usual recalcitrant manner, the person most likely to help get it started, gratis, was an engineer from one of the big steamers. He was always ready to help Mrs. Cottager make her Silent Dis-Pro a little less silent.

Cantankerous as the machinery could be and mischievous as a few of the operators could be, the DP boats were still a lovely sight to behold. It's difficult to look at them today without some historical perspective, but their grace of sheer plumb stems, beautifully laminated foredecks and splashboards, gleaming copper water-jackets, brass carburetors, and polished bow lights might have been appealing.

HERE'S THE WALLACE FAMILY PICNIC ON LAKE JOSEPH IN 1929. IN THE BACKGROUND IS THE LAUNCH _VIOLA_.

They could also have been considered the world's greatest anachronism; all that brass was passé by the 1920s.

Yet the Disappearing Propeller Boat Co. was the only boat-manufacturing concern in all of Muskoka to have every piece of hardware manufactured especially for them. Now that was elegant! It was also the only firm to use brass fastenings below the waterline. Not even Ditchburn or Minett-Shields did that. Remember these things the next time the subject of the poor man's floating Model T is discussed.

After the first demise of the DP-building concern in 1924 (the company went through two), the Port Carling Boat Works was founded. Their first ad in the MLA yearbook doesn't appear until 1931, however, seven years after the company was formed. Their Johnston Special, a model designed by W. J. Johnston to compete directly with the dis-pro, was a failure, probably because little double-ended boats were hopelessly obsolete by the late 1920s. Their next attempt was a launch that clearly resembled the 21-foot Ditchburn. Although lapstrake in construction, it was reportedly less expensive than its competitor's model. They eventually developed their Sea Bird line of boats with their alliterative motto "Safe, Swift, Serviceable." During the 1930s, the Port Carling Boat Works produced more

FACTORY AND WAREHOUSE OF THE DISAPPEARING
PROPELLER BOAT CO., PORT CARLING, AS THEY APPEARED
FROM 1921 TO 1929. BOATS WERE MOVED FROM THE
FACTORY TO THE WAREHOUSE BY OVERHEAD RAIL.
RIGHT, A 1939 SEA BIRD AD IN THE MLA YEARBOOK.

inboard powerboats than anyone else in Canada. It's interesting to note that by the mid-1930s, those who were
becoming fed up with their DPs were trading them in for
Sea Birds. These newer boats were the next step in an
affordable alternative.

The longest-surviving boat-builder in Muskoka is Duke
in Port Carling. Founded in 1924 by C. J. Duke and Ernie
Greavette, their launch-building business kept up with the
demands of their customers in quality and quantity and
moved along with the times. In 1968 they produced their
last new launch and have since been involved with the
repair, maintenance, and restoration of the other long-gone
boat-builders' products. It wasn't until the 1960s that Duke
bought advertising space in the MLA yearbook.

The earliest Duke launches resembled those of their
competitors. Flared forward sections, curved decks at the
dashboard and plumb aluminum stems made for a dashing
appearance. Many similar launches, with only slight modifi-
cations, appeared before the arrival of the economical and
popular Playmate. Built from 1935 to 1956, the Playmate

went through only one major style change in 1938, which
moved the driver forward. They built custom as well as
standard launches.

W. J. Johnston, after the closing of the Disappearing
Propeller Co., and after his falling-out with the Port Carling
Boat Works, opened up his own shop at the site of the former DP factory. He and the late Bert Riddiford spent one
winter removing the top two floors of the old building, and
the lumber went to build Bert Riddiford's house on the
Indian River. In those days good used building materials
didn't end up as landfill.

After the folding of the DP, Johnston built probably
fewer boats in Port Carling than anyone else, but they were
"honest boats." He specialized in mid-priced carvel and lapstrake launches. This was typical of Port Carling boat-
builders. The town had a good number of boat-building
concerns, but they tended to avoid the exotic and produced
full lines of the affordable.

Tom and Ernie Greavette had both worked for Ditchburn since the early part of the century. Ernie even had
a stint with the Disappearing Propeller Co. and was
known as the fastest planker in the plant; he also helped
organize Duke Boats in 1924. The brothers then formed
their own company in Gravenhurst, Greavette Boats, and
bought space in the MLA yearbook for the first time in
1931. The ad stressed that their four models could be

167

procured instantly and that their value far exceeded that of other builders.

These four models were mass-produced, sawn-frame types. Such volume building seems to have been little trouble for them, but unfortunately they didn't get the requisite volume sales. After numerous ups and down in production and design they finally settled on custom work with a few low-production models, the best known of which was the Streamliner. Designed by John Hacker and Douglas van Patten, it was available in lengths from 18 to 34 feet. Known affectionately for years as "cigar boats," Greavette Streamliners were a surefire way to capture the attention of young women in the 1940s!

Each boat-building concern eventually found its own niche in the market. By the 1930s, anyone could purchase almost anything his heart desired in Muskoka, and all the major builders carried ads in the MLA yearbook.

The Great Depression seemed somewhat buffered in Muskoka. The boat-builders were occupied, though not to the degree they'd been in the 1920s. Some were struggling to survive, and a few employees took to building on their own at night to augment their incomes.

And through it all, the MLA carried on pretty much as usual. It continued to hold its annual regatta; the Crerars' *Marion* still won the 16-foot-class race. The yearbooks were filled with more topics relating to boating safety,

ABOVE, BOW LIGHT DETAIL ON THE MINETT-BUILT "SEAHORSE." LEFT, BOB PURVES, THE ORGANIZER OF THE FIRST MLA ANTIQUE BOAT SHOW AND THE DECAL DESIGNED FOR ENTRANTS IN 1971. RIGHT, ANTIQUE AND CLASSIC BOAT SHOW, 1987, HELD AT PORT CARLING.

Corinthian yachting—competitive yachting done solely for pleasure, no financial rewards—and a particularly interesting topic to many entitled "Help Yourself to Service." Author Captain Stanley Usher, a member of the Society of Automotive Engineers, advised becoming familiar with your machine and its instruction manual first before tinkering—and if it works, don't fix it! Good reading for amateur mechanics today.

The 1936 yearbook ran an ad for Buchanan Engines of Orillia, which by then was the sole supplier for area builders; the heyday of the great, roaring, American-built engines was over. Buchanan built rugged, serviceable marine engines and accessories that for many years served as replacement engines for ones installed during the 1920s. Many of them are still in use today, which attests to their excellent workmanship.

In 1936 the MLA suffered the tragic loss of its first American president. Dr. Thomas Scudder Winslow died under mysterious circumstances on a New York operating table on May 28. He and his family, whose cottage was on

St. Helen's Island, had always taken an avid interest in the MLA and were enthusiastic participants in sailing, swimming, tennis, golf, and canoeing. They also enjoyed and took meticulous care of their 75-foot steam yacht *Willoudee*, their two smaller launches—both named *Willow*—and numerous rowboats.

By the late 1930s the winds of change were blowing. With our country on the brink of war, such leisure pursuits as boating were far from people's minds. The 1938 MLA yearbook was the last one in which Ditchburn ran an ad and, according to Gray and Duke, was also their last year of production. The firm had been having difficulty for nearly seven years and finally closed their doors for good. Minett-Shields' death was more prolonged—it built a few boats for the war—but by the mid-1940s they, too, had shut down.

Port Carling's builders kept chugging along during and after the war. Sea Bird continued to crank out its many lines of relatively low-priced boats, as well as the odd custom launch. Duke kept pace with a variety of styles and sizes and, of course, their ever-popular Playmate. Greavette was still producing Streamliners, dis-pros, and the odd runabout and rowboat.

The MLA's annual motorboat races, which had begun around 1912, ended with the beginning of the Second World War. That dealt another blow to the competitive spirit of the local boat-builders. Without the races and no further call for the classic-style launches of the 1920s and 1930s, the only boats being built were relatively small craft. But boating remained popular throughout the 1950s and 1960s. And the big beautiful launches certainly didn't disappear; they continued to take cottagers to and from their islands, or simply cruise around the lakes.

By 1960 W. J. Johnston had retired, and the Port Carling Boat Works had been sold to one of its employees. Only Greavette and Duke were still building, but business was augmented by their skilful rebuilding of older launches. Even with the influx of fibreglass boats—craft made far from Muskoka shores once more—some people, motivated by sentiment, prestige, an appreciation of aesthetics, or all three, were interested in preserving their old made-in-Muskoka family launches.

However, these boats, despite modern engines, had all sorts of problems—leaky bottoms, blistered varnish, and filthy bilges. To a plastic-boat afficionado they were just ugly old brown boats and hopelessly out of fashion. But luckily

a few people thought for themselves, and were determined to preserve what they had. Some actually went out during the 1950s and bought Minett-Shields and Ditchburn boats. What strange looks they must have received!

In 1971 the first antique boat show took place at the Muskoka Lakes Golf and Country Club. It was organized by the late Bob Purves, and the invitation to display was open, informal, and impromptu, calling for every sort of boat built before 1940. Anything that could make it there that day probably did. The show was fun. There was no judging, and lots of people all with a common interest. And that was the beginning.

By the late 1970s and early 1980s, people were scrounging through everything from abandoned boathouses to swamps to find anything that could be identified as once having been a boat. Many of these were in a delightful state of disaster. Duke and Greavette were deluged with work. More restoration shops opened to meet the demand. The antique-boat world went crazy and some of the prices followed suit. The shows now had judges. People were even having boats restored that were only 30 years old!

But the Muskoka-built boats of the 1920s and 1930s still

THE *MINNIE ESTELLE*, AN EARLY GASOLINE-POWERED LAUNCH OF UNKNOWN MANUFACTURE, BONA VISTA, KEEWADIN ISLAND.

represent the pinnacle of boat-building. The MLA continues to hold its biannual antique-boat shows. Many of the boats on display have been in the families for years. Some owners have searched high and low to find every possible piece of authentic hardware, including engines, so that their boats can remain truly antique—not just modern replicas. And a whole new generation of craftsmen has sprung from the ashes of plastic decadence. It's no easy task duplicating the skills necessary to restore a Muskoka boat properly, especially when the original craftsmen are no longer around to lend a helping hand. But the efforts are valiant. The trick for the judges is to decide which wood is old and which wood has been replaced. The trick for the craftsmen is to blend them as invisibly as possible.

And now, as the Muskoka Lakes Association celebrates its centennial, residents and cottagers can still boast that their lakes are graced by some of the finest-made boats in the world. Muskoka-made. A 100-year tradition. ▷

ACKNOWLEDGMENTS

I wish to thank the following people for their kind assistance: Charles Amey, Robert D. Blair, Paul Dodington, the late Aud Duke, Dev and Ted Gratwick, William Gray, Rob Haggar, Jerry Hamlin, William Jennings, Josephine Nobbe, the late Bert Riddiford, Will Ruch, Bruce Rudolph, Richard Tatley, Harriet Winslow Wheeler, Wendy Winslow Lofting, and James Woodruff.

– P. G.

THE *WANDA III*, ONCE OWNED BY THE EATON FAMILY, WILL RETURN TO THE WATERS OF MUSKOKA IN THE SUMMER OF 1994, THANKS TO THE MUSKOKA HERITAGE FOUNDATION. WITH IT WILL COME THE REMEMBRANCES OF THE ELEGANCE AND CHARM OF THE POSTWAR ERA OF 1921.

MRS. ALLEN FRASER

MLA
A CENTURY OF CONCERNS

The History of the Muskoka Lakes Association

BY JUDY ROSS

IN THE 1890s TORONTO and Hamilton were in the midst of an economic boom. At the top of their social hierarchies were families who had the ways, means, and insight to buy summer property in the scenic lake-studded land to the north. Georgian Bay, with its 30,000 Islands, was the choice of some; others were claiming land in the Kawarthas. But the greatest number headed to Muskoka—in particular lakes Rosseau, Joseph, and Muskoka—by then considered the most fashionable of all summer watering holes.

MLA FOUNDERS

On a cold winter night in February 1894 a prominent group of citizens from Toronto and Hamilton gathered in downtown Toronto at the King Street headquarters of the Toronto Athletic Club. They had come to share their concerns about Muskoka, an area they all loved. Most of them had first discovered the sparkling lakeland on fishing and hunting trips and, quickly smitten, bought property and built cottages so their families could enjoy summers on the lake.

The February 19 meeting resulted in the forming of the Muskoka Lakes Association. Its goals were threefold: to protect and promote the interests of the residents; to preserve the healthful sanitary condition and scenic beauty of the area; and to encourage aquatic and other sports.

The MLA founders were a noteworthy group. The first honorary president was Hon. John Beverley Robinson, former lieutenant-governor of Ontario, who summered at Governor's Island on Lake Joseph. The first president was Rev. E. Michael Bland, an Anglican minister at Christ Church Cathedral in Hamilton. Like others in the group who were impatient with the workings of the Muskoka Navigation Company, Bland and another MLA founder, W. B. McMurrich, bought their own steam launch in 1888, believed to be the first private steamer on Lake Joseph. Many more were to follow.

MANY FAMILY COTTAGES HAVE BECOME THE HOME OF ALMOST A CENTURY OF MUSKOKA LAKES ASSOCIATION YEARBOOKS.

Several founders, including Bland, had first come to Muskoka as guests of J. Herbert Mason, who had a cottage on Chief's Island in Lake Joseph. (Mason was affiliated with the Muskoka Club, a group of the earliest cottagers in Muskoka, whose loosely organized club predated the Muskoka Lakes Association by some 30 years.) Bland's first cottage was at the headquarters of the Muskoka Club on Yoho Island in Lake Joseph. Like many of the founding members of the MLA, the minister was not a young man. He later moved from Yoho to Reef Island where he remained until the death of his wife in 1907, at which point he sold his island cottage and moved to Bermuda.

Another founding member was lawyer W. B. McMurrich, who had been mayor of Toronto in 1881 and 1882. He was an elder in the Presbyterian church where John Campbell, a founder of the Muskoka Club, was minister, and it was this connection that first brought him to Muskoka. The growing division between the locals and the "tourists," as early cottagers were called, is seen in this excerpt from an article in the Gravenhurst Banner in 1902:

Some people say that Professor John Campbell, W. B. McMurrich, K.C., and a few other enterprising Ontario boys paddled around the lakes many years ago and came to the conclusion that nature intended that region for a grand national playground.

In 1877, 17 years before the Muskoka Lakes Association was founded, its predecessor, the Muskoka Club, folded, and John Campbell purchased all the club's island assets in Lake Joseph. In turn, W. B. McMurrich bought several islands from Campbell. Islands were passed around like baseball cards in those days. McMurrich chose Bungamena Island to build his spectacular cottage, Harmony Hall, in 1883. Its illustrious guest list included, it is rumoured, Teddy Roosevelt.

The lavish lifestyle at elegant resorts and cottages attracted a glittery crowd to the shores of Muskoka lakes, and the society pages of Toronto newspapers were filled with the antics of Muskoka cottagers and hotel guests. Faith Fenton, a columnist for the *Toronto Weekly Empire*, was a regular visitor at Sans Souci, the luxurious Lake Rosseau home of Senator W. E. Sanford of Hamilton whose parties were legendary and whose guest list could have filled the *Who's Who of Canada*.

Many came also for their health. They believed in the restorative powers of the fresh pine-scented air, which offered relief from hay fever. The MLA founders were no doubt swayed by such publications as the 1888 Ministry of Agriculture booklet, which extolled the virtues of Muskoka:

Of places of desirable summer resort there are now many in Canada to which the wearied and overworked professional man or devotee of commerce may hasten to reinvigorate the system by the restorative influences of a change of scene and air. Few of these resorts possess greater attractions than do the lakes and woodlands of the Muskoka District in the bracing atmosphere of which almost every essential will be found for the recuperation of invalidism, for the "setting-up" of the annually increasing army of "run-downs" or for the delight and entertainment of those who may have the good fortune to be more or less robust.

This belief in Muskoka's health-giving attributes was supported by the medical profession, some of whom were on the MLA executive. Dr. E. Herbert Adams, an eminent Toronto doctor interested in climatology, was a member of the MLA as well as the Citizens Committee of Toronto. The committee published a guidebook in 1894 entitled *Toronto and Adjacent Summer Resorts*, which promoted Muskoka's beneficial climate. Adams was also one of the doctors responsible for choosing Gravenhurst as the location for a tuberculosis sanatorium.

Another founding member of the MLA was one of the first cottagers on Lake Rosseau. Prof. Alfred Baker bought Ishkaugua Island in 1875 at the mouth of the Indian River. A mathematics professor at the University of Toronto, Baker was highly regarded and his skill as an after-dinner speaker was thought to be unmatched. In 1895 he was appointed MLA vice-commodore, adding to his long list of affiliations, which included the Queens Own Rifles, British Empire League, and the Canadian Military Institute. In the 1910 edition of *Who's Who in Canada* his recreations are listed as walking, rowing, and sailing *Shu-shu-ya* on Lake Rosseau.

Reuben Millichamp, who was introduced to the joys of Muskoka by J. Herbert Mason—brother-in-law of Muskoka Club founder John Campbell—was also among the group who attended that February meeting. An enterprising businessman, Millichamp was a director of several companies, including the Siche Gas Company, which manufactured some of the gas-driven water pumps in early Muskoka

174

TWO MLA FOUNDERS: TOP, THE REVEREND E. MICHAEL BLAND, THE FIRST PRESIDENT; BOTTOM, JOHN BEVERLEY ROBINSON, THE FIRST HONORARY PRESIDENT.

cottages. He was also a founder of Havergal College in Toronto. His cottage was near Windermere and he was one of the original vice-commodores of the MLA, but his name disappears from the yearbooks after the turn of the century.

The association began publishing a yearbook in 1894 and has continued to do so without interruption until the present day. The membership listings indicate the distances that people travelled in those days to reach their beloved Muskoka cottages. A large contingent of Americans from the Pittsburgh area were early cottagers at Beaumaris, and many of their descendants still occupy the large summer homes built on "Millionaire's Row" at the turn of the century. The MLA yearbook of 1895 also lists members from New York, Ohio, Virginia, and Tennessee, and even as far afield as Texas and Louisiana.

Many of the MLA founders were elderly—men who had already retired from academic or ecclesiastical professions and were therefore able to spend the entire summer in Muskoka. As a result, minutes of their meetings reveal that much time was spent discussing appropriate condolence messages to be sent to the families of members who had died during the previous year. But the first vice-president was Walter Read, only 37; in 1895 he succeeded Rev. E. Michael Bland as president. Read was a lawyer of United Empire Loyalist stock and, like many of the others, an alumnus of University College in Toronto. His cottage was at Port Sandfield.

Like Rev. Bland, a number of founding members were from Hamilton. One was F. W. Fearman of Fearman's Hams and Bacon, whose family owned half of Gibraltar Island on Lake Muskoka. Another was Col. J. R. Moodie of a Hamilton knitwear company that made women's and children's underwear. Moodie bought Point Failthe—gaelic for "a thousand welcomes"—on Lake Rosseau in 1904. Ever after known as Moodie's Point, it was noted for having the only boathouse in Muskoka with its own lighthouse.

The majority of MLA founding members had cottages on lakes Rosseau and Joseph, but a small contingent with property on Lake Muskoka also played an important role. Frank D. Manchee, Hugh Neilson, Newman Fairhead, and H. Gummer had already formed a Lake Muskoka association, but when they learned of the fledgling MLA formed in Toronto on a winter's night, they all joined as the representatives from Lake Muskoka.

By the time the Muskoka Lakes Association published their second yearbook in 1895, the membership had grown to 360. A most auspicious beginning.

RIGHT, THREE REGATTA REVELLERS ENJOY THE 1907 REGATTA AT PORT SANDFIELD. SINCE ITS INCEPTION IN 1894, ONE OF THE MAIN EVENTS OF THE SUMMER HAS BEEN THE ANNUAL MLA REGATTA. IN THE EARLY YEARS ITS LOCATION MOVED AMONG THE THREE LAKES.

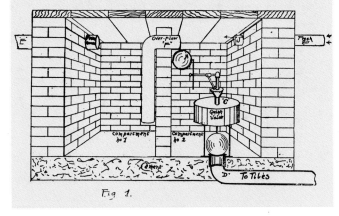

14

say 100 gallons, there should be 200 4-inch tiles laid, as the tiles should all be filled to distribute equally the liquid.

Fresh air should be brought into the tank by an in-take pipe, as indicated in the cut, while any gases which might accumulate in the tank are constantly carried away to be discharged by the housepipe above the roof. In practice, however, the gases are nearly all held in solution and carried away with the discharged water.

The economy of the system is easily estimated by anyone who knows the cost of cement and tiles; while the automatic flush valve is more convenient and cheaper than a siphon, and can be more readily set in order than the latter. Either, however, if in working order, will serve the purpose equally well. It is desirable, and with large buildings necessary, to have a porous soil so that filtration will go on rapidly, and a proper selection of the location of the tank and filter-bed should be made.

A PAGE FROM THE 1912 YEARBOOK AND AN
ILLUSTRATION OF A CIRCA 1911 BATHING COSTUME
(FROM *IN STYLE* BY CAROLINE ROUTH) GIVE US A PEEK
AT THE BEGINNING OF THIS CENTURY. FAR RIGHT, TOP,
TILTING HAS BEEN A REGATTA EVENT FOR ALMOST 100
YEARS; FAR RIGHT, BOTTOM, EVEN IN 1907, THE TURN
OUT FOR THE REGATTA WAS IMPRESSIVE.

THE FIRST 25 YEARS (1894–1919)

A primary concern at the inaugural meeting of the MLA was the inefficiency of the railway and navigation companies. In those days cottagers were dependent on trains and steamboats to get to their summer properties. They deplored the haphazard timetables and what they considered disgustingly high freight rates charged by the steamers—25 to 50 cents for a canoe! And so, a transportation committee was established to deal with the seemingly endless problems with trains and steamboats. Regular meetings were held between MLA executives and navigation-company officials, one of whom was J. S. Playfair, also an executive member of the MLA. Years of rancour seem to be summed up in this letter written by J. Hardy, the president of the MLA in 1910, to the members of the association:

We have been unable to prevail upon the railway companies to extend weekend tickets from Friday morning until the following Monday. The Canadian Northern Railway Co. has seen fit this year to place in service a train leaving Toronto at 1:30 on Saturday afternoon during the months of July and August for the benefit of those living on the lakes but so far the navigation company has not seen its way to provide boat connections with this train.

Also of utmost importance at the inaugural meeting was fishing and hunting. As nearly all the founders did one or both, they wanted their new association to play a role in setting up programs to stock the lakes and instal fish hatcheries. Fishing in Muskoka was important enough to make the front page of the Toronto *Globe* on August 7, 1905. The report read:

Big fish are still the talk in the river at Port Carling. A pickerel 30 inches long with a girth of 15 inches was caught, but it took a gasoline launch, a steam boat and a canoe to land it. Then, when landed no single family would attempt to eat such a monster. It was therefore cut into steaks and sold to various parties.

In 1903 a sanitation committee was formed, headed by J. Herbert Mason. Two pages in that year's directory outlined methods for disposal of house waste, including advice on how to separate waste and begin a compost heap. Also included in the directory was a detailed drawing of a septic system that would "deal automatically with sewage wastes" and could be easily installed by the homeowner. (These primitive septic systems later became the bane of the environmental committees!)

Much of the concern about sanitation and sewage in these early years had more to do with health and the fear of epidemic outbreaks than with the future of the environment.

This is because a publicized health hazard would have ruined the Muskoka tourist business, which was based on the virtues of clean air and water.

For years the MLA was aware that sewage from the steamboats was going directly into the lakes. In 1911 the chief health officer of Ontario, Dr. J. W. S. McCullough, attended the annual MLA meeting and provided the impetus for change. The Muskoka Navigation Company soon spent $4000 "in fitting up their boats to comply with the law."

The matter of steamboat sewage came up again, however, in 1915 when it was learned that on some boats "live steam was blown into the tanks and then the matter was discharged into the lakes in deep water." At the annual meeting the head of the sanitation committee reported this unpleasant situation, adding that he personally "did not wish to drink sewage—raw or cooked!" At this point the entire room collapsed in laughter.

The much-touted clean, health-giving Muskoka air back in the early 1900s was not, in fact, all that clean. With dozens of steamboats plying the lakes and stoking their furnaces with soft coal, the air was often filled with black soot. This was particularly distressing for the summer tourists who always dressed in their starched white cottons when they went to meet the steamers. The problem of sooty air was frequently raised at MLA meetings but never really resolved.

Another issue that kept MLA members busy was the annual regatta. In those days everyone spent weeks training and practising their rowing and paddling skills, and the MLA regatta committee spent the entire year preparing for the event. Traditionally an "at home" dance was held in the evening. In 1895 the yearbook report suggests the dance was less than successful:

If the dancing was not an entire success, owing to the inability of some participants to keep their heads "above board," the fault certainly must have lain with the trippers of the "light fantastic toe," and not with the indefatigable members of the subcommittee on arrangements . . .

The regattas continued to be held during the war years until 1918, when the MLA executive decided to cancel until the war ended. MLA president J. Hardy did not agree with this decision, and in a letter to H. Prowse of the Beaumaris Hotel where the regatta was to be held, he expressed his regret, adding that personally he was "of the opinion that all sports should go on as usual, and we should not let the Germans think they have been the means of stopping the ordinary course of events." By the following year, of course, the war had ended, and a special victory regatta was held at Windermere.

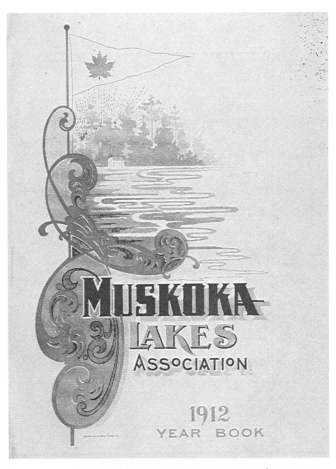

THE COVER OF THE 1912 YEARBOOK. BELOW, A PAIR OF REGATTA MEDALS FROM THE ROARING TWENTIES.

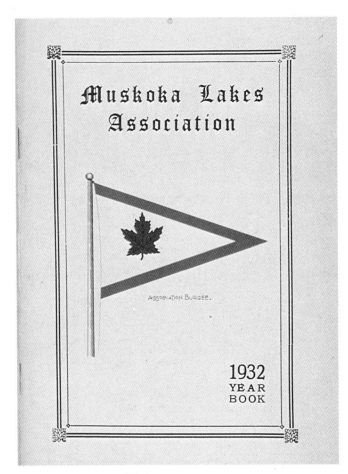

IN THE 1930S, THE MLA YEARBOOK COVER LOOKED LIKE THIS, AND JANSEN WAS SELLING A ONE-PIECE BATHING SUIT DESIGNED TO SHOW OFF A BEAUTIFULLY TANNED BACK (FROM *IN STYLE* BY CAROLINE ROUTH). TOP RIGHT, POWERBOATS RACING IN MUSKOKA—"AND HE WINS BY A *BOW*".

THE SECOND 25 YEARS (1919–1944)

The 1920s were a buoyant time for many, and especially for Muskoka's summer visitors. In 1920 the Muskoka Lakes Golf and Country Club opened, thanks to the efforts of a group of MLA members who had purchased the 150-acre Massey-Treble farm. The club became the permanent home of the annual MLA regatta. In 1923 it was decided to hold a children's regatta on the weekend following the regular regatta, and so the festivities now stretched over two weekends.

During this time Harry Greening became a legendary figure in powerboat racing with his famous Ditchburn-built Rainbow racing boats. He had a cottage at Beaumaris, used the lake as a testing ground, and made regular appearances at the MLA regattas in the 1930s. Powerboat racing continued in Muskoka until the beginning of the Second World War, when the MLA decided to cancel the races "for the duration." They were never resumed.

Environmental concerns during this 25-year period focused on an insidious insect larva discovered in 1927. Called a looper, it attacked and killed the hemlock trees. A special MLA committee met with the Department of Forestry and arranged to load a seaplane with the insecticide calcium arsenate and spray the area. The plane, however, was damaged en route, and torrential rains during the month of June prohibited the program. The following summer the spraying did take place, loading the environment with the poisonous chemical.

The year 1937 brought a terrible revelation. At the MLA annual meeting, Dr. J. H. Elliott of the sanitation committee reported that ragweed was "spreading northward along our railroads and highways." For years Muskoka had been advertising itself as a place mercifully free of the dreaded weed. But despite attempts by the Department of Agriculture to get rid of the weed, the reputation of Muskoka as a hayfever sufferers' haven never recovered.

Cherokee at M.L.A. Regatta,

181

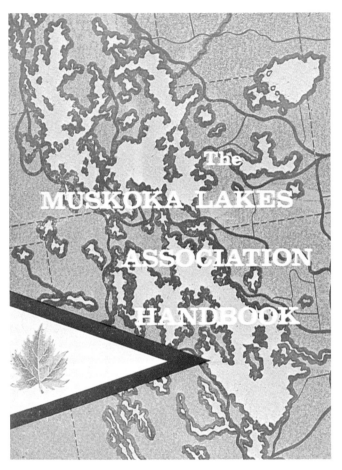

THE 1957 HANDBOOK WAS PUBLISHED IN THE INTEREST OF "LOVERS OF THE LAKES" BY THE MUSKOKA LAKES ASSOCIATION. IT PROBABLY INCLUDED THE WEARER OF THIS SWIMSUIT BELOW (FROM *IN STYLE* BY CAROLINE ROUTH) AND ALL THE PARTICIPANTS TO THE RIGHT.

THE THIRD 25 YEARS (1944–1969)

In the early 1940s milk pasteurization became an issue that affected the local farmers in Muskoka. For years they had been selling milk straight from the cow to the summer tourists, but now a new law required that all milk must be pasteurized. The MLA sanitation committee set out to enforce the law, causing some bad feeling between the locals and the summer people.

Noise pollution was being discussed by the late 1940s because of the increasing numbers of motorboats on the lakes. And at the 1948 annual meeting, several members also complained about noisy airplanes flying at low altitudes.

By the 1950s, even though most cottagers were blithely dumping empty tins and bottles into the lake, they became alarmed when garbage began washing up on the shore. It was known that the steamboat Sagamo was still dumping garbage overboard, and members of the sanitation committee were dispatched to deal with the boat operators.

For the regatta committee the postwar years were spent trying to revive interest in the canoeing and rowing events that had been so popular before motorboats replaced paddles and oars. Unwilling to let the annual tradition die out, the committee worked hard to keep the regatta a popular summer tradition by devising new skill-testing events.

The 1960s were the first time that the MLA began to study pollution in the lakes. In 1963 John Neal, the chief biologist for the Ontario Water Resources Commission, addressed the annual meeting and introduced the members to new concerns and a new vocabulary—phosphates, algae, and nutrient enrichment. In 1965 a special meeting on water pollution was held on the Victoria Day weekend at the Port Carling town hall. It drew a large crowd, who came to hear how the detergent industry planned to handle the problem of phosphates, the culprit in the overproduction of algae.

As a new era of environmental awareness was being ushered in, some old actions of the MLA came back to haunt them. In particular, in 1951 the association had organized spraying with DDT to rid the area of forest tent caterpillars; in 1966 the Department of Lands and Forests wrote to the MLA to say that DDT may have caused irreparable damage to birds and fish in the area, if not humans themselves.

183

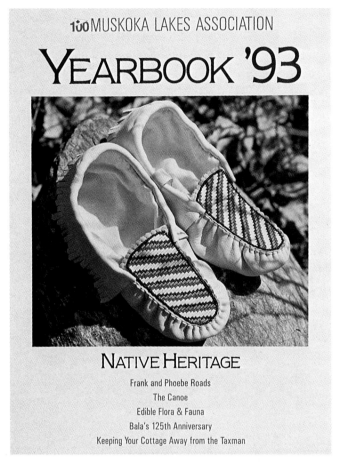

100 MUSKOKA LAKES ASSOCIATION

YEARBOOK '93

NATIVE HERITAGE

Frank and Phoebe Roads

The Canoe

Edible Flora & Fauna

Bala's 125th Anniversary

Keeping Your Cottage Away from the Taxman

AND SO A CENTURY HAS PASSED. MUCH OF MUSKOKA REMAINS THE SAME WITH A COUPLE OF EXCEPTIONS: THE YEARBOOK IS BIGGER AND BATHING SUITS ARE SMALLER. (1973 BIKINI FROM *IN SYLE* BY CAROLINE ROUTH) TOP RIGHT, CLOCKWISE: OUT IN THE LEAD IN A ROWBOAT RACE, THE FIRST MLA ANTIQUE BOAT SHOW, 1971, AND NEARING THE FINISH LINE IN A CANOE RACE.

THE LAST 25 YEARS (1969–1994)

The problem of nutrient enrichment in the lakes appeared to be escalating by 1960. Members were becoming more vocal, accusing the sanitation committee of operating in a "namby-pamby way, lacking in positive action." This wasn't an entirely fair accusation, since the MLA had, in fact, convinced the Ontario Water Resources Commission to institute an $80,000 study of the Muskoka lakes.

In 1971 students canvassed the lakes, giving out boxes of soap flakes to be used instead of detergents, and water sampling that year showed an appreciable reduction in all areas.

Acid rain became a major issue in the 1980s. The MLA played a significant role in raising funds for the Coalition on Acid Rain, which was formed in 1980 to unite varying interest groups and call for the reduction of emissions of sulphur dioxide and other gases that cause acid precipitation on both sides of the border. After many years of battle, laws regarding acid rain have been passed both in Canada and the U.S. It appears our lakes now have a good chance of recovery.

In 1977 the MLA yearbook was given an entirely new look. Until this point it had been a small book consisting of membership listings, annual meeting reports, and advertisements. But under the direction of magazine publisher Jeff Shearer, the 1977 yearbook became the large editorial-filled magazine it is today.

The 1980s represented a boom time in Muskoka real estate, but the decade was also a time of concern for the number and speed of boats entering the lakes, and the overdevelopment of shorelines. By now the MLA had committees dealing with land use, recreational safety, taxation, environmental protection, and winter activities, among others. The association sponsored a successful ad campaign in the local papers to promote safe boating, and negotiations continue at the federal legislative level regarding new rules.

And so, as the MLA heads into its second century with more than 3000 family members representing over 14,000 individuals from all parts of the globe, it will continue the battle to keep Muskoka beautiful. ▷

185

OFFICERS

Since formation of the Muskoka Lakes Association in 1894

HONORARY PRESIDENTS
1894 – Hon. J. B. Robinson
1895 – Rev. E. M. Bland
1896–97 – Walter Read
1898–99 – W. R. McMurrich
1900–01 – George Bell
1902 – F. J. Phillips
1903–05 – W. L Standish
1906–10 – J. H. Mason
1911–29 – F. W. Winter
1922 – J. Hardy
1923–24 – Lt. Col J. R Moodie
1931–55 – G. E. Milburn
1929–32 – N. H. Conley
1933–42 – A. J. Hardy
1936–42 – George W. McLaughlin
1943–1948 – Arthur Poyntz
1949–68 – C. E. McLaughlin
1952–72 – J. W. Alexander
1974– J. Bryan Vaughan, CM
1974– John W. Millar
1980– Phyllis L. Parker

PRESIDENTS
1894 – Rev. E.M. Bland
1895 – Walter Read
1896–97 – W.B. McMurrich
1888–89 – Professor Alfred Baker
1899 – George Bell
1900–01 – F.J. Philips
1902 – H. Gummer
1903–21 – J. Hardy
1922–23 – Lt. Col. J.R. Moodie
1924–28 – N.H. Conley
1929–30 – G.E. Milburn
1931–32 – A.J. Hardy
1933–35 – George W. McLaughlin
1936 – Dr. Thomas S. Winslow
1937–44 – J.H. Brogan
1945–47 – C.E. McLaughlin
1948–49 – R.L. Clause
1950–51 – J.W. Alexander
1952–53 – W.S. Pardoe

1954–55 – J. W. Millar
1956–58 – J. Lorne Davidson
1958–61 – Ralph Mills
1962–63 – J. Bryan Vaughan
1963–64 – Walter A. Bean
1965–66 – Frank H. Fisher
1966–70 – Alan P. Clark
1971–72 – Dr. Robert H. Wesley
1972–73 – John R. Campbell
1973–75 – Richard J. Boxer
1975–76 – Fred M. Gaby
1977–78 – Phyllis Parker
1978–80 – Peter Cragg
1980–82 – William H. Leak
1982–84 – Jeffrey W. Shearer
1984–86 – Michael Vaughan
1986–88 – Robert G. V. Purves
1988–90 – William F. Clark
1990–92 – John D. Patterson
1992– Joan M. Booth

COMMODORES
1894 – A. Y. Scott
1895 – W. B. Mcmurrich
1896 – E. H. Adams
1897 – A. H. O'Brien
1898 – George Bell
1899 – Professor Alfred Baker
1900 – Hugh Neilson
1901 – Professor Alfred Baker
1902 – J. Herbert Mason
1903–04 – S. F. McKinnon
1905 – Rubin Miller
1906–07 – Sir Wilfred Hepton
1910 – Colonel J. R. Moodie
1911–12 – P. D. Crerar
1913–21 – F. C. Gratwick
1922 – F. A. Turner
1923–27 – G. E. Milburn
1928–30 – W. L. Clause
1931–32 – Dr. T. S. Winslow
1933 – Ewart McLaughlin
1934–36 – Reg. N. Boxer
1937–38 – R. L. Clause
1939–41 – D. R. McLaughlin
1942–43 – E. F. Hauserman
1944–46 – Dr. W. L. Whittemore
1947–52 – Lt.-Col. J. E. Frowde Seagram
1953–59 – Carl A. Pollock
1960–64 – Lt.-Col. D. E. Catto
1965–75 – Robert W. Purves
1975–80 – R. Barry Graham
1980–82 – Donald B. Grant
1982–84 – Robert G. V. Purves
1984–86 – William H. Leak
1986–88 – Norman M. Seagram
1988–90 – James M. Woodruff
1900–92 – Peter P. Armstrong
1992– James R. Balfour

HON. COMMODORES
1975–80 – Robert W. Purves
1990– Robert G. V. Purves

SECRETARY–TREASURERS
1894 – E. H. Adams
1895 – A. H. O'Brien
1896–1911 – J. D. McMurrich
1912–22 – Hugh Neilson
1923–44 – Walter R. Winter
1950–55 – Edward H. Humphreys
1956–63 – J. Alex Greig
1964–66 – Hon. Mr. Justice J. W. Brooke
1966–69 – Dr. Robert H. Wesley
1970–72 – Fraser M. Fell (Sec.)
1970–72 – John M. Hall (Treas.)
1972–78 – F. W. D. Campbell
1978–80 – Robert G. V. Purves
1980–84 – Robert G. V. Purves (Treas.)
1980–82 – William E. Patterson (Sec.)
1982–90 – Desmond M. O'Rorke (Sec.)
1984–85 – James I. McKinney (Treas.)
1985–88 – John K. Heineck (Treas.)
1988–92 – John P. Hilborn (Treas.)
1990 – James B. Christie
1992 – Wilmer Crawford (Treas.)

HONORARY MEMBERS
(with date of resolution)
Mr. Thomas G. Elgie (1894)
Rev. Canon Bland (1896)
W. B. McMurrich (1899)
Dr. J. W. S. McCullough
Sir Robert L. Borden
Lady Borden
Hon. C. C. Ballantyne (1920)
Mr. Hugh Neilson (1922)
Sir Thomas White (1929)
Mr. J. H. Forbes (1937)
Dr. Robert E. Joyce (1957)
John W. Millar (1971)
Hon. John B. Aird (1981)
Hon. Stan Darling (1992)

BIBLIOGRAPHY

A Legacy Almost Lost. Kilworthy Historical Committee, May 1992.

Aberdeen, Lady Ishbel. *The Canadian Journal of Lady Aberdeen 1893–1898*. Toronto: 1960.

Adam, Graeme Mercer. *Muskoka Illustrated. With Descriptive Narrative of this Picturesque Region*. Toronto: Wm. Bryce, 1888.

Adams, Ezra Herbert. *Toronto and Adjacent Summer Resorts ... Souvenir and Guide Book*. Toronto: Federick Smily, 1894.

Ahlbrandt, Patricia Walbridge. *Beaumaris*. Erin, Ontario: The Boston Mills Press, 1989.

Anderson, Allen and Ralph Beaumont. *Postcard Memories of Muskoka*. Cheltenham, Ontario: The Boston Mills Press, 1978.

Avery, Sidney G. *Reflections: Muskoka and Lake of Bays of Yesteryear*. Bracebridge, Ontario: Herald-Gazette Press, 1974.

Bala United Church: 100th Anniversary, 1880–1980. Bala, Ontario: The Church, 1980.

Bala United Church, Dedication Services: May 12 to May 15, 1935. Bala, Ontario: The Church, 1935.

Barry, James. *Georgian Bay ... The Sixth Great Lake*. Toronto: Clark Irwin, 1968.

Barry, Larry, editor. *Memories of Burks Falls and District, 1835-1978*. Burks Falls, Ontario: 1978.

Beahen, William. *Development of the Severn River and Big Chute Lock Station*. Ottawa: National Historic Parks and Sites Branch, Parks Canada, Environment Canada, 1980.

Bell, Robert. *Field Notes*. Ontario: Department of Lands and Forests, 1848.

Bennett, Ruth G. *Adventures as a Muskoka Maid: An Autobiography*. Gravenhurst, Ontario: R. G. Bennett, 1979.

Bice, Ralph. *SemiCentennial–Town of Kearney–Incorporated 1908–District of Parry Sound, Ont.* 1958.

Blackwood, Algernon. *Episodes Before Thirty*. London: 1950.

Boyer, Barbaranne. *Muskoka's Grand Hotels*. Erin, Ontario: The Boston Mills Press, 1987.

Boyer, Ethel Victoria. *Memories of Bracebridge: A Pictorial History of Some of the Homes of Early Business-Men in the Bracebridge Community at the Turn of the Century and Before*. Bracebridge, Ontario: Herald-Gazette Press, 1975.

Boyer, George W. *Early Days in Muskoka: A Story About the Settlement of Communities in the Free Grant Lands and of Pioneer Life in Muskoka*. Bracebridge, Ontario: Herald-Gazette Press, 1970.

Boyer, Patricia. *The March of Days: [As Viewed from Muskoka]*. Bracebridge, Ontario: Muskoka Graphics, 1980. My Bob ... and Muskoka's. 1972. A pamphlet about Bob Boyer, 1913–   .

Boyer, Patricia et al. *Looking at our Century: Random Recollections of Bracebridge in Centennial Year, 1975*. Bracebridge, Ontario: Herald-Gazette Press, 1975.

Boyer, Robert J. *Early Exploration and Surveying of Muskoka District, Ontario, Canada*. Bracebridge, Ontario: Herald-Gazette Press, 1979. *A Good Town Grew Here: the Story of Bracebridge, Ontario, from 1860 to Municipal Incorporation, 1875, and from 1875 to 1914*. Bracebridge, Ontario: Herald-Gazette Press, 1975. *Pictorial History of Woodchester Villa, Bracebridge Ontario*. Bracebridge, Ontario: Muskoka Graphics, 1982.

Boyle, Joyce. *Muskoka Holiday*. Toronto: Macmillan, 1959. For children.

Brashear, John. *A Man Who Loved the Stars*. Pittsburgh: University of Pittsburgh Press, 1924.

Brown, Ron. *Ghost Towns of Ontario, Vol. 1*. Toronto: Cannonbooks, 1978. *Ghost Towns of Ontario, Vol. 2: Northern Ontario & Cottage Country, Toronto*. 1983.

Brunton, Sam. *A Miscellany of Notes and Sketches on the History of Parry Sound Compiled and Edited by Sam Brunton for the Parry Sound Historical Society*. Parry Sound, Ontario: Parry Sound Public Library, 1969.

Buffalo and the Highlands of Ontario: Niagara Falls, Muskoka Lakes, Lake of Bays. Montreal: Desbarats Printing Company.

By Wagon and Water. Dwight, Ontario: Haystack Bay Women's Institute, 1980.

Callan, Kevin. *Cottage Country Canoe Routes*. Erin, Ontario: The Boston Mills Press, 1993.

Canada. Atmospheric Environment Service. *Muskoka*. Ottawa: Environment Canada, Atmospheric Service, 1984.

Canada. Department of Agriculture. *Muskoka and Lake Nipissing Districts*. Ottawa: 1880. "Information for intending settlers."

Carmichael, Hugh. G. *Who's Where on the Muskoka Lakes*. Bracebridge, Ontario: Muskoka Publishing Company, 1976.

Carroll, Jacqueline. *Muskoka's Boathouses*. Erin, Ontario: The Boston Mills Press, 1990.

Census of Canada, 1871. Schedule 6, Return of Industrial Establishments, deals with water-mill statistics in Muskoka.

Cockburn, Alexander Peter. *To the Shareholders of the Muskoka and Georgian Bay Navigation Company*. 1902.

Conway, Abbott. *The Tanning Industry in Muskoka*. 1974.

Conwell, James. *Muskoka and her People*. Compiled by Martin Morrison. Toronto: Historical Publishers Association, 1933.

Cookson, Joe. *Tattle Tales of Muskoka*. Bracebridge, Ontario: Herald-Gazette Press, 1976. Includes information on river log drives and early resorts. *Roots in Muskoka*. Bracebridge, Ontario: Herald-Gazette Press, 1978. A sequel to *Tattle Tales of Muskoka*.

Coombe, Geraldine. *Muskoka Past and Present*. Toronto: McGraw-Hill Ryerson Ltd., 1976. Full of pictures and stories of even the smallest villages in Muskoka, such as Barkway.

Cope, Leila. *A History of the Village of Port Carling*. Bracebridge, Ontario: Herald-Gazette Press, 1956.

County of Simcoe: Municipal Council. *Minutes*. June, 1865.

Courtney, Clarence C. *The Story of Ka-wig-a-Mog Lodge*. Pittsburgh, 1922.

Cullen, Thomas S. *Memories of Camp Ojibway*. 1952.

Cumberland, Barlow. *The Northern Lakes of Canada: The Niagara River & Toronto, the Lakes of Muskoka, Lake Nipissing, Georgian Bay, Great Manitoulin Channel, Mackinac, Sault Ste. Marie, Lake Superior; a Guide to the Best Spots for Waterside Resorts, Hotels, Camping Outfits, Fishing and Shooting, Distances and Routes of Travel ...* Toronto: Hunter, Rose & Company, 1886.

Dale, Joseph. *Canadian Land Grants in 1874*. London: 1875.

De la Fosse, Frederick M. *Early Days in Muskoka*. Ontario History, Volume XXXIII, 1939.

Dean, William George. *Toronto into Muskoka; A Geographic Traverse*. Toronto: 1966.

Demaine, Marjorie, editor. *Chronicles of Stisted Township*. Bracebridge, Ontario: Herald-Gazette Press, 1976. *Stories of Early Muskoka Days–Memoirs of W. H. Demaine*. Bracebridge, Ontario: Herald-Gazette Press, 1971.

Denis, Leo G. *Electric Generation and Distribution in Canada*. Ottawa: Commission of Conservation, 1918. Includes information about hydroelectric stations on the Muskoka River.

Denison, John. *Micklethwaite's Muskoka*. Erin, Ontario: The Boston Mills Press, 1993. A lavish collection of the photographs of Frank Micklethwaite, a well-known turn-of-the-century Toronto photographer who lovingly recorded his Muskoka summers.

Dennis, Lloyd A. *Marching Orders: A Memoir*. Markham, Ontario: Fitzhenry & Whiteside, 1988.

Denniss, Gary. *A Brief History of the Schools in Muskoka*. Bracebridge, Ontario: 1972. *Free Methodist Hill, a Centennial History: Bracebridge Free Methodist Church, 1879-1979*. Bracebridge, Ontario: Herald-Gazette Press, 1979.

Devitt, Ed. *"Echoes of the Past": Resounding in the Present: A Brief Illustrated General History of a Central Region in Southern Ontario Formed by Two Muskoka and Ten Haliburton Townships*. 198-?

Dickson, James. *Camping in the Muskoka Region*. Toronto: C.B. Robinson, 1886. *Camping in the Muskoka Region: a Story of Algonquin Park*. A reprint with a foreward by Leslie M. Frost. Toronto: Ontario Department of Lands & Forests, 1960.

District Municipality of Muskoka: Proposed Economic Development Strategey. Muskoka, Ontario: District Municipality of Muskoka, Office of the Chief Administrative Officer, 1983.

District of Muskoka. *Land Patent Books*.

District of Parry Sound. *Land Patent Books*.

Dodington, Paul, et al. *The Greatest Little Motor Boat Afloat, the Legendary Disappearing Propeller Boat*. Erin, Ontario: The Boston Mills Press, 1983.

Douglas, R. J. W., editor. *Geology and Economic Minerals of Canada*. Ottawa: Geological Survey of Canada, 1976. Contains information on the glaciation of Muskoka.

Dufferin and Ava, Hariot Georgina Hamilton-Temple-Blackwood, Marchioness of. *My Canadian Journal, 1872-8; Extracts from my Letters Home, Written while Lord Dufferin was Governor-General*. New York, 1891.

Duke, A. H. and W. M. Gray. *The Boatbuilders of Muskoka*. Erin, Ontario: The Boston Mills Press, 1985.

DuVernet, Sylvia. *Beams from the Beacon; Poems of Georgian Bay*. Illustrated by Barker Fairley. Bracebridge, Ontario: Herald-Gazette Press, 1974. *An Indian Odyssey: Tribulations, Trials and Triumphs of the Gibson Band of the Mohawk Tribe of the Iroquois Confederacy*. Muskoka Publications, 1986. *L.M. Montgomery & the Mystique of Muskoka*. Islington, Ontario: DuVernet, 1988. *The Muskoka Assembly of the Canadian Chautauqua Institution: Points of View and Personalities*. Bracebridge, Ontario: Muskoka Graphics, 1985. *Muskoka Mosaic*. Bracebridge, Ontario: Muskoka Graphics, 1984. Poems. *Muskoka Poetry*. Bracebrdige, Ontario: Herald-Gazette Press, 1973. *Muskoka Seasons: Poems*. Bracebridge, Ontario: Muskoka Publications, 1987. *The Muskoka Tree: Poems of Pride for Norman Bethune*. Bracebrige, Ontario: Herald-Gazette Press, 1976. *Pai-Chiu-En: Poems the Chinese People Told Me about Norman Bethune*. Bracebridge, Ontario: Harold-Gazette Press, 1978.

Eaton, Flora McCrea. *Memory's Wall, The Autobiography of Flora McCrea Eaton*. Toronto: Clarke, Irwin & Company Limited, 1956.

Edbauer, John, editor. *The New Guide and Key to Niagara Falls, Toronto, Muskoka Lake*. Buffalo: John Edbauer Publisher, 1926.

Elgin House, Muskoka, Ontario, Canada. Toronto: Rous & Mann, 192? A collection of pictures.

Farmers' and Business Directory, for the Counties of Bruce, Grey, and Simcoe. Ingersoll, Ontario: Union Publishing Company, ca. 1896.

Feasey, Velma. *Footprints in Muskoka*. Coldwater, Ontario: Little Print Shop, 1982. About geneology.

Findlay, Mary Lynn. *Lures and Legends of Lake of Bays*. Bracebridge, Ontario: Herald-Gazette Press, 1973.

Finlay, Tom. *The Muskoka Book of Lists*. Toronto: Venture Press, 1982.

Fraser, L.R. *History of Muskoka: A Complete History of the Pioneer Days, Navigation, Lumbering, Farming....* Bracebridge, Ontario: Thomas, 1946.

Fryer, Mary B. *Emily Stowe, Doctor and Suffragist*. Toronto: Dundurn Press Limited, 1990.

Garrett, Jessie Featherstonhaugh. *My Happy Years at Lake of Bays*. Ontario: The author, 1988.

Gerow, Carole and John Bayfield. *Penetanguishene ... This Was Yesterday*. Midland Printers, 1982.

Gibson, David L. *Chronicles of Keewaydin Island: Muskoka Lake with the Seven Sisters Islands, 1880-1910*. Port Carling, Ontario: D. L. Gibson, 1986.

Godfrey, Henry Herbert. *Patriotic Canadian Songs and Melodies*. Toronto: Canadian American Music Company, 1890.

Grant, George Monro, editor. *Picturesque Spots of the North: Historical and Descriptive Sketches of the Scenery and Life in the Vicinity of Georgian Bay, the Muskoka Lakes, the Upper Lakes, in Central and Eastern Ontario, and in the Niagara District*. Chicago: Alexander Belford & Company, 1899.

Gravenhurst: An Album of Memories and Mysteries. The Gravenhurst Book Committee Review, 1993.

Gray, William M. *Lake Joseph 1860-1910: An Illustrated Notebook*. Toronto: W. M. Gray, 1991.

Grigg, Muriel Jean Rogers. *Magnetic Muskoka*. Gravenhurst, Ontario: Baxter Press, 1971.

Guide to Muskoka Lakes, Upper Maganetawan & Inside Channel of the Georgian Bay. The famous fishing, hunting & pleasure resorts of Ontario. Gravenhurst: Muskoka & Nipissing Navigation Company, 1888.

Hamilton, William Edwin. *Guide Book & Atlas of Muskoka and Parry Sound Districts*. Toronto: H. R. Page, 1879. Contains descriptions and history, including locations of water mills on maps. Muskoka Sketch. Dresden, Ontario: 1884.

Hathaway, Ann [pseudonym for Mrs. Fannie Cox]. *Muskoka Memories: Sketches from Real Life*. Toronto: William Briggs, 1904.

Hedley, Thomas. *Notes of a Hunting Trip with the Dwight-Winman Club in the Muskoka District, Canada*. Toronto: Trout & Todd, 1884.

Heritage Muskoka: Notes on the History of Muskoka District as Presented by Guest Speakers.... Parry Sound, Ontario: Algonquin Regional Library System, 1976.

Hewitt, D. F. *Geology and Mineral Deposits of the Parry Sound-Huntsville Area*. Toronto: Ontario Department of Mines, 1967. (Geological Report 52. Covers the western portion of the Muskoka watershed.)

Higginson, T. B. *A Sportsman's Paradise: Historical Notes on the Burk's Falls District, 1835-1890, and the Village of Burks Falls [sic], 1890-1965*. Burks Falls, Ontario: 1965.

Highlands of Ontario: Muskoka Lakes/Grand Trunk Railway System and Muskoka Navigation Co. Grand Trunk Railway System, 1903.

Hitchman, Elaine. *Second Homes and their Conversion to Principle Residences: A Case Study in the District Municipality of Muskoka*. Toronto: York University M.A. Thesis, 1976.

Hosking, Carol. *Clevelands House: Summer Memories*. Erin, Ontario: The Boston Mills Press, 1988.

Hunt, Maureen. *William Proudfoot, 1851-1925: Muskoka Master Builder*. Huntsville, Ontario: M. Hunt, 1984.

Hunter, Andrew Frederick. *A History of Simcoe County*. (Two Volumes, 1909). Revised edition Barrie: 1948.

Huntsville, Ontario: A Guide to the Historical & Architectural Heritage of Downtown Huntsville. Huntsville, Ontario: Research Committee of the Muskoka Pioneer Village.

Hutcheson, George F. *Head and Tales: Memoirs of George F. Hutcheson*. Bracebridge, Ontario: Herald-Gazette Press, 1972.

Irwin, W.H. *Gazetteer and Directory of the County of Simcoe, Including the District of Muskoka and the Townships of Mono and Mulmur for 1872-3*. Elmvale, Ontario: East Georgian Bay Historical Foundation, 1985.

Jackes, Lyman Bruce. *Indian Legends of Muskoka and the North Country*. Toronto: Canadian Historical Press, 1953.

James MacLaren Company. *Report to the District Municipality of Muskoka on the Initial Assumption, Operation and Financing of—Sewage Treatment Works, Trunk Sewers and Watercourses*. Toronto, 1971.

Jestin, Mrs. G.R. *The Early History of Torrence*. Bracebridge, Ontario: 1938.

Jocque, Violet. *Pioneers and Latecomers*. Minett, Ontario: 1979.

Johnson, George H. *Port Sydney Past*. Erin, Ontario: The Boston Mills Press, 1980.

King, Mrs. Harriet Barbara. *Letters from Muskoka by an Emigrant Lady (1871-1875)*. London: R. Bentley & Son, 1878.

Kinton, Ada Florence. *Vignettes of Muskoka: With Pen, Brush and Pencil*. Huntsville, Ontario: Forester, 190?

Kirkwood, Alexander, and J.J. Murphy, editors. *The Undeveloped Lands in Northern and Western Ontario*. Toronto: Hunter, Rose and Company, 1878.

Lake of Bays, Highlands of Ontario. Montreal: Grand Trunk Railway System, 1915.

The Lake Shore Line of the Muskokas: Short Line Between Toronto, Muskoka Lakes and Parry Sound. Toronto: Canadian Northern Ontario Railway, 1907.

Lavallee, Omer. *Narrow Gauge Railways of Canada*. Montreal, 1972.

Lehto, Frank Ilmari. *Physiographic Change in Muskoka*. Toronto: University of Toronto B.A. Thesis, 1966.

Lille Norge Avison. Toronto: Royal Norwegian Air Force Training Centre, 1945. About Camp "Little Norway," Muskoka.

Lockhart, Wilfred Cornett. *Norway Point Church: the First Seventy-Five Years, 1908-1983*. Toronto: Hogarth Printing Company, 1983.

Long, Gary. *This River the Muskoka*. Erin, Ontario: The Boston Mills Press, 1989.

Mac, Captain [McAdam, J. T.]. *The Muskoka Lakes and Georgian Bay*. Ottawa: Grip Printing and Publishing Company, 1884.

MacArthur, Frankie. *The Story of Washago*. Washago, Ontario: 1975.

MacKay, Niall. *By Steam Boat and Steam Train, The Story of the Huntsville and Lake of Bays Railway and*

Navigation Companies. Erin, Ontario: The Boston Mills Press, 1982.

MacKay, Roderick and William Reynolds. *Algonquin*. Erin, Ontario: The Boston Mills Press, 1993.

MacKenzie, Norman Hall. *The Economic and Social Development of Muskoka, 1855–1888*. Published 1943.

MacLaren Plansearch (consultant). *Muskoka River System—Water Management Improvement Study, Recommendations (1984)*. (Prepared for Environment Canada and Ontario Ministry of Natural Resources.)

Mansel, William C. *Muskoka Daze*. Cobalt, Ontario: Highway Book Shop, 1976. Anecdotes.

Mason, D. H. C. *Muskoka: The First Islanders and After*. Bracebridge, Ontario: 1957.

Mason, Helen. *Horsing Around Toronto and Beyond*. Vancouver/Toronto: Whitecap Books, ca. 1993.

McClellan, Scott. *Straw Hat and Grease Paint: 50 Years of Theatre in the Summer Colony*. Bracebridge, Ontario: Muskoka Publications, 1984.

McEachern, Ruth, Kerry Greenaway and Susan McKay. *Dorset*. Bracebridge, Ontario: Herald-Gazette Press, 1976.

McLean, Fleetwood K.: *Early Parry Sound Ontario History*, Volume LVI, 1964.

McMurray, Thomas. *The Free Grant Lands of Canada, from Practical Experience of Bush Farming in the Free Grant Districts of Muskoka and Parry Sound*. Bracebridge, Ontario: 1871.

McTaggart, Douglas. *Bigwin Inn*. Erin, Ontario: The Boston Mills Press, 1992.

Meek, Seth Eugene. *Notes on a Collection of Fishes and Amphibians from Muskoka and Gull Lakes*. Chicago, 1899.

Mills, Alex. *A Cottager's Guide to the Birds of Muskoka and Parry Sound*. Barrie, Ontario: Alex Mills, 1981.

Montgomery, L.M. *The Blue Castle*. Toronto: McClelland and Stewart Limited, 1926.

Muldrew Lakes Cottagers' Club. *The History of Muldrew Lake; a Record of By-Gone Days in and around the Lake....* Toronto, 1953.

Municipal Electric Commission Centennial Histories (1967) for Bracebridge, Gravenhurst, Huntsville, and Orillia.

Murray, Florence B. *Muskoka and Haliburton 1615–1875: A Collection of Documents*. Toronto: University of Toronto Press, 1963. This book contains an extensive bibliography that includes manuscripts in private and public collections, newspapers, government reports, statutes, books, and many other items. The topics cover Muskoka's local history, geological formation, social development, description, and accounts from personal reminiscence.

Muskoka. Canada: Canadian National-Grand Trunk Railways, 1921.

Muskoka (Ontario: District Municipality). *Interesting Facts about the District Municipality of Muskoka*. 1974.

Muskoka (Ontario: District Municipality). Planning and Development Committee. *Official Plan for the Muskoka Planning Area; Working Draft*. Bracebridge, Ontario: District Municipality of Muskoka, 1975.

The Muskoka Lakes: *A Place of Health and Pleasure, the Sportsman's Paradise*. Grand Rapids, Michigan: James Bayne.

Muskoka Lakes Association. *Year Book ...Containing Constitution, By-laws, Officers, Members, etc.* Toronto: Oxford Press, 1899.

Muskoka Lakes Navigation and Hotel Company. *Muskoka Lakes*. Gravenhurst, Ontario: Muskoka Lakes and Navigation Company, 1931. Includes summer timetable. *Muskoka Lakes*. Gravenhurst, Ontario: Muskoka Lakes and Navigation Company, 1942. *Muskoka Lakes: A Daily Scenic Cruise*. Gravenhurst, Ontario: Muskoka Lakes Navigation & Hotel Company, 1941. Includes summer timetable.

Muskoka Memories. Toronto: Parkview Press. Poetry.

Muskoka Pioneer Village (Ontario) Research Committee. *Huntsville: An Historical and Scenic Guide to the Lakes of Vernon, Fairy, Peninsula, Mary*. Huntsville, Ontario: Muskoka Pioneer Village Research Committee, 1984.

Muskoka Second Home Study Questionnaire Analysis: A Joint Project of the District Municipality of Muskoka and the Muskoka Lakes Association. Prepared by the District Planning Department. Bracebridge, Ontario: The Department, 1984.

Ontario. Bureau of Mines. *Guide Book*. Toronto: Printed by L. K. Cameron, 1913. Includes Muskoka.

Ontario. Department of Lands and Forests. *Sawmill Licentiate Book, 1924–30*. Lists licensed watermills on the Muskoka River and indicates their capacity.

Ontario. Department of Municipal Affairs. *Muskoka District Local Government Review: Final Report and Recommendations*. Toronto: Queen's Printer, 1969.

Ontario Hydro. *Annual Report, 1908–1964*. Includes information on hydroelectric developments on the Muskoka River. *Statistical Yearbook, 1971–1980*.

Ontario. Laws. *The Municipal Act, 1887, and the Act Respecting the Establishment of Municipal Institutions in the Districts of Algoma, Muskoka, Parry Sound, Nipissing, Thunder Bay, and Rainy River. Together with the Municipal Amendment Act, 1888*. Toronto: Hart, 1888.

Ontario. Ministry of the Environment. *Preliminary Report on the District Municipality of Muskoka Sewage Lagoon Network for Septic Tank and Holding Tank Wastes*. Toronto: Ontario. Ministry of the Environment, 1975.

Ontario. Ministry of the Environment. Abatement East Section. *Cottage Pollution Control Program, Muskoka-Haliburton*. Gravenhurst, Ontario: Ministry of the Environment, 1988.

Ontario. Ministry of Natural Resources. *Leslie M. Frost Natural Resource Centre Fisheries Management Plan 1986–2000*. Toronto: Ontario Ministry of Natural Resources, 1988. *Water Level Regulation in Muskoka*. 1977.

Ontario. Office of the Provincial Secretary. *Annual Statements*. For: Huntsville & Lake of Bays Navigation Company Ltd., Muskoka & Nipissing Navigation Company Ltd., Muskoka & Georgian Bay Navigation Company Ltd., Muskoka Lakes Navigation & Hotel Company Ltd.

A Paradise for Anglers and Hunters: Grand Trunk Railway and Muskoka Navigation Cos. to the Picturesque Muskoka Lakes. 1895.

Paterson, Donald M. *Muskoka District Local Government Review*. Gravenhurst, Ontario: Ontario Department of Municipal Affairs. Local Government Reviews, 1967–69.

Pearce, Robert J. *The Windermere, Ronto and Smallman Sites: Salvage Excavations of Prehistoric Iroquoian Hamlets*. London, Ontario: Museum of Indian Archaeology, 1983.

A Peek Behind the Scenes; or the Days Before Yesterday. Orillia, Ontario: Packet and Times, 1935.

Picturesque Canada: The Country as It Was and Is. Edited by George Monro Grant. Toronto: Belden Brothers, 1882–1884. Issued in 36 parts.

Picturesque Views and Maps of the Muskoka Lakes Canada. Toronto: Rolph, Smith & Company, 1893.

Pioneer Days in Muskoka. Port Sydney, Ontario: 1927?

Pioneer Muskoka: Notes on the History of Muskoka District as Presented by Guest Speakers.... Parry Sound, Ontario: Algonquin Regional Library System, 1975.

Podmore, Percy St. Michael. *Ozunkein: Story of a Muskoka Seneca Girl*. London: Ward Lock, 1904. *A Sporting Paradise, with Stories of Adventure in America and the Backwoods of Muskoka*. London: 1904.

Porter, Cecil, et al. *The Light of Other Days*. Gravenhurst, Ontario: Gravenhurst Historical Committee, 1967.

Preview of a Vacation in Muskoka and Algonquin Park, Canada. Gravenhurst, Ontario: Muskoka Tourist Development Association. Published between 1939 and 1945.

Project Planning Associates (Toronto, Ontario). *Recreation and Community Development on the Canadian Shield Portion of Southern Ontario*. Toronto: 1970. This is a two-volume study commissioned by the Department of Tourism, dealing with concepts for a model recreation community in Muskoka and Bala.

Pryke, Susan. *Explore Muskoka*. Erin, Ontario: The Boston Mills Press, 1987. *Explore Muskoka Lakes*. Erin, Ontario: The Boston Mills Press, 1990.

Rawson, Mabel. *The Story of Port Severn: Yesterday, To-Day and To-Morrow: Western Gateway from the Georgian Bay to the Severn-Trent Rideau Waterway*. Midland, Ontario: Simcoe Press, 1976.

Research Committee of the Muskoka Pioneer Village; Hunt, Maureen, et al. *Pictures from the Past, Huntsville*. Erin: The Boston Mills Press, 1986.

Rice, Harmon Edmund. *A Brief Centennial History of Huntsville, Muskoka, Canada*. Huntsville, Ontario: Forester Press, 1964.

Roberts, Charles G. D. *The Canadian Guide-book: The Tourist's and Sportsman's Guide to Eastern Canada....* New York: D. Appleton, 1891.

Roger, Alexander. *Central Electric Stations in Canada, Part II— Directory*. For May 1, 1928. Water Resources Paper 55. Ottawa: Department of the Interior, 1929. Gives statistics on hydro stations on the Muskoka River.

Rogers, John. *Guidebook & Atlas of Muskoka and Parry Sound Districts*. Second offset edition edited by Ross Cumming. Owen Sound, Ontario: Printed by Richardson, Bond & Wright, 1972. *Muskoka Lakes Blue Book and Chart*. Toronto: 1915. *Muskoka Lakes Blue Book, Directory and Chart 1918*. Port Sandfield, Ontario: 1918.

Roper, Edward. *By Track and Trail*. London: 1891. *Muskoka; the Picturesque Playground of Canada*. Toronto: Hart & Company, 1883.

Rosewarne, Pearce Victor, and Winnifred. *The Family History of Thomas B. Rosewarne of Cornwall, England and Muskoka, Canada, his Ancestors and Descendants, 1716–1968*. Ottawa, 1968.

189

Ross, Judy, and John de Visser. *At the Water's Edge: Muskoka Boathouses*. Erin, Ontario: The Boston Mills Press. *Muskoka*. Erin, Ontario: The Boston Mills Press. Summer Cottages. Erin, Ontario: The Boston Mills Press.

Royal Canadian Legion. Huntsville Branch, No. 232. Old Home Week Committee. *Huntsville and District's Old Home Week, July 10th to July 16th, 1967: Official Centennial Souvenir, 1867–1967, Royal Canadian Legion, Branch 232, Old Home Week Committee*. Huntsville, Ontario: The Committee, 1967.

Royal Muskoka Hotel, Muskoka Lakes. Lake Rosseau, Ontario: The Hotel, 19–.

Royal Muskoka, in the Heart of the Highlands of Ontario, Lake Rosseau, Muskoka Lakes District. Gravenhurst, Ontario: Muskoka Lakes Navigation and Hotel Company, 1905.

Sandys, Edwyn. *A Highland Holiday*. Battle Creek, Michigan: 1897.

Scarfe, W. Lucien, editor. *John A. Brashear, the Autobiography of a Man Who Loved the Stars.* New York, 1924.

Schell, Joyce I. *Through the Narrows of Lake Muskoka*. Bracebridge, Ontario: 1974. *The Years Gone By; A History of Walker's Point and Barlochan-Muskoka, 1870–1970*. With pen and ink illustrations by Kerry Schell. Bracebridge, Ontario: Herald-Gazette Press, 1970.

Scott, David. *Ontario Place Names*. Vancouver/Toronto: Whitecap Books, ca. 1993. Contains some entries on Muskoka towns.

Scott, Harley E. *More Tales of the Muskoka Steamboats*. Bracebridge, Ontario: Muskoka Graphics, 1980. *Steam Yachts of Muskoka*. Bracebridge, Ontario: 1975. *Tales of Muskoka Steamboats; A History of Muskoka*. Bracebridge, Ontario: Herald-Gazette Press, 1969.

Scovell, Beatrice. *The Muskoka Story*. Self-published.

Shaw, R. *Water Quality of Morrison Lake: Town of Gravenhurst, District Municipality of Muskoka*. Toronto: Ontario Ministry of the Environment, 1976.

Shea, Bert. *History of the Sheas and the Paths of Adventure*. Utterson, Ontario: D. Shea, 1974.

Smily's Canadian Summer Resort Guide. Toronto: 1910.

Smith, Ken. Cottage Gardening. Erin, Ontario: The Boston Mills Press.

The Society of Directors of Municipal Recreation of Ontario. *Recreation and Education in Our Expanding Leisure; Proceedings of the Ninth Annual Training Institute, Muskoka Sands Inn, November 11–12, 1965*. Toronto: 1966?

Souvenir Presented to Members of the American Public Health Association: On the Occasion of its Fourteenth Annual Meeting, Held at Toronto, Canada, October, 1886. Toronto: Hunter, Rose and Company, Printers, 1886. Includes extracts from "Muskoka and the Northern Lakes of Canada," (Barlow Cumberland).

Sparrow Lake and Severn River. Toronto: Canadian Northern Ontario Railway, 19–? Pictures.

Stephens, Ray. *The Canadian Entertainers of World War II*. Gravenhurst, Ontario: c.1993.

Stevens, G.R. *The Canadian National Railways*. Toronto: 1960.

Stott, Derek V. *Kawandag ... A Story of Changing Muskoka*. Rosseau, Ontario: Spectracolor Printing, 1981.

Sutton, Frederick W. *Early History of Bala*. Bracebridge, Ontario: 1970.

Tatley, Richard. *The Steamboat Era in the Muskokas, Vol. 1: To the Golden Years*. Erin, Ontario: The Boston Mills Press, 1983. *The Steamboat Era in the Muskokas, Vol. 2: The Golden Years to Present*. Erin, Ontario: The Boston Mills Press, 1984. *The Story of the Segwun: A Short History of the Sole Surviving Passenger Steamship on the Muskoka Lakes.* Bracebridge, Ontario: Muskoka Litho, 1981.

Taylor, Dave. *Ontario's Wildlife*. Erin, Ontario: The Boston Mills Press.

Thomas, Redmond. *Reminiscences (Bracebridge, Muskoka)*. Bracebridge, Ontario: Herald-Gazette Press, 1969.

Tyrrell (J. W.) (Firm). *Clovelly, Lake of Bays, Muskoka*. Hamilton, Ontario: 1914.

The Union Publishing Company's Farmers and Business Directory for the Counties of Durham, Haliburton, Northumberland, Peterboro and Victoria–and Districts of Muskoka, Nipissing, Parry Sound, Algoma, Rainy River and Thunder Bay, for 1899. (Volume XI). Ingersoll, Ontario: 1899.

United Church of Canada. Muskoka Presbytery. Acid Rain Committee. *All Nature Is Groaning: The Report of the Acid Rain Committee, Muskoka Presbytery, The United Church of Canada*. Toronto: Department of Stewardship Services, 1982.

Van Sickle, Melvin Leigh. *The Filling in of Lakeshores with Cottages; Lake Muskoka*. Toronto: 1967.

Vardon, Roger [pseudonym of Frederick De la Fosse]. *English Bloods*. Ottawa: Graphic Press, 1930.

Walker, Frank N. *Four Whistles to Wood-Up: Stories of the Northern Railway of Canada*. Upper Canada Railway Society. Bulletin No. 37. 1953.

Walker, W. W. *By Northern Lakes; Reminiscences of Life in Ontario Mission Fields*. Toronto: 1896.

Water Survey of Canada. *Historical Streamflow Summary, Ontario, to 1986*. Environment Canada, 1987. Includes information about the Muskoka River.

Watson, Dr. B.A. *The Sportsman's Paradise, or the Lake Lands of Canada*. Philadelphia, 1887.

Wells, Kenneth McNeil. *Trailer Boating Where the North Begins*. Toronto: Kingswood House, 1961.

White, James. *Altitudes in the Dominion of Canada*. Ottawa: Commission of Conservation, 1915. Includes information about the Muskoka River.

Wolfe, Roy I. *Recreational Land Use in Ontario*. Toronto: 1954. *The Summer Resorts of Ontario in the Nineteenth Century; Ontario History*. Volume LIV, 1961.

Wyatt, George H. *The Traveller's and Sportsman's Guide to the Principle Cities, Towns & Villages Near the Hunting and Fishing Grounds of the Great Northern Lakes in Canada & Manitoba*. Liverpool: Liverpool Printing and Stationery Company, Limited, 1880.

Your Vacation at Huntsville: Heart of the Lake of Bays District. Huntsville, Ontario: Board of Trade, ca.1930.

Zaryski, William James. *The Location of Marinas as Outlets for Petroleum Products; The Case of Western Muskoka*. Toronto: 1968.

ARTICLES

Ford, Isabel. "Solid Comfort Fishing Club." 1987.

Harshman, G.A. "A History of the Sharon Fishing Club." 1981. "Reminiscences of Fairhaven, 1886–1986."

Leighton, Tony. "Beauty and the Boats." *Equinox*, March/April, 1985.

Marshall, Charles. "Bracebridge." *The Canadian Dominion*, 1870.

McNeice, L. G. "Matthias Falls Power Development on South Branch of Muskoka River." *Electrical News and Engineering*, Vol. 59, No. 10, 1950, 38–41.

Ontario. Ministry of Natural Resources. "Skeleton Lake Meteor Crater Proposal." *Earth Science Inventory Checklist*, 1979.

Peake, Virginia. "A Growing Tradition." *Muskoka Lakes Association Yearbook*, 1987.

"Report of the Commissioner of Public Works." *Ontario Sessional Papers*. Toronto, 1868–1956. Includes information on government locks and dams in Muskoka.

Sharpe, D. R. "Quaternary Geology of the Gravenhurst, Bracebridge, and Huntsville Areas, District Municipality of Muskoka." *Summary of Field Work, 1978, by the Ontario Geological Survey* (M.P. 82), 152–54. Deals with glacial deposits in Lake Algonquin.

Smith, Gail. "Bird's Woollen Mill." *An Introduction to the History of Muskoka*, Section B. Muskoka Board of Education, 1975.

Wadsworth, V. B. "History of Exploratory Surveys Conducted by John Stoughton Dennis, Provincial Land Surveyor in the Muskoka, Parry Sound and Nipissing District, 1860–1865." *Association of Ontario Land Surveyors, Annual Report*, 1926.

Wallace, W. S. "The Early History of Muskoka." *Queen's Quarterly*, Vol. 49, 1942.

Walton, W. W. "Kawigamog." *Pickerel River Tales*. Cobalt, Ontario: 1976.

Wood, Marty. "Lumbering in Muskoka." *Muskoka Sun* (1979).

BROCHURES

Beaumaris Castle. London: Her Majesty's Stationery Office, 1943.

The Bigwin Inn, Lake of Bays, Highlands of Ontario, 1927.

Birch Hollow Collection. Birch Hollow Antiques. Bracebridge, Ontario.

The Canadian Men and Women of the Time, 1898.

Lakes of Muskoka, 1883.

Map Chart: Muskoka Lakes, 1896.

Muskoka and Georgian Bay Navigation Company. Advertisement. Includes a calendar for 1894.

Muskoka Lakes: Highlands of Ontario, 1903, 1906, 1909, 1910, 1916.

Muskoka Lakes Navigation Company: Brochures, 1911–1919, 1922–1925, 1935, 1939–1940, 1944, 1946–1947, 1950, 1953.

The Northern Railway, 1882.

Official Guide: Huntsville & Lake of Bays Navigation Company, Ltd., 1905.

Silver Anniversary: Bigwin Inn, Lake of Bays, Muskoka, Canada, 1944.

INDEX

The Second Annual Meeting was held at the Toronto Athletic Club Toronto on February 26. 1895.

Oweing to the illness of President Bland of Hamilton the Vice President Walter Read. took the chair.

The Vice-President's adress dealt with many important matters in reference to the work of the past year and the future weal of the association

The condolences of the association were extended to the friends of the following deceased members. Dr. Pomeroy of Cleveland Ohio. Mrs Dr. Cheesborough of Toronto and Chas. Madeson.

Commodore A. Y. Scott's report showed that the first Annual Regatta held at Windermere in August last was the most successful regatta ever held in Muskoka.

Dr. E. Herbert Adams then read the report of the secretary-treasurer, for the past year.